Walks of a Lifetime
from Around the World

FALCON®

An imprint of Globe Pequot, the trade division of
The Rowman & Littlefield Publishing Group, Inc.
4501 Forbes Blvd., Ste. 200
Lanham, MD 20706
www.rowman.com

Falcon and FalconGuides are registered trademarks and Make Adventure Your Story is a trademark of
The Rowman & Littlefield Publishing Group, Inc.

Distributed by NATIONAL BOOK NETWORK

British Library Cataloguing in Publication Information available

Library of Congress Cataloging-in-Publication Data

Names: Manning, Robert E., 1946– author. | Manning, Martha, author.
Title: Walks of a lifetime from around the world : extraordinary hikes in
  exceptional places / Robert Manning, Martha Manning.
Description: Essex, Connecticut : Falcon, [2023] | Includes bibliographical
  references. | Summary: "Firsthand descriptions of forty of the world's
  great multiday walks spanning six continents, ranging from inn-to-inn
  walks to backpacking treks. Features color photographs and maps
  throughout"— Provided by publisher.
Identifiers: LCCN 2023010127 (print) | LCCN 2023010128 (ebook) | ISBN
  9781493072378 (paperback) | ISBN 9781493072385 (epub)
Subjects: LCSH: Hiking—Guidebooks. | Trails—Guidebooks. |
  Backpacking—Guidebooks.
Classification: LCC GV199.5 .M364 2023 (print) | LCC GV199.5 (ebook) |
  DDC 796.51—dc23/eng/20230313
LC record available at https://lccn.loc.gov/2023010127
LC ebook record available at https://lccn.loc.gov/2023010128

Printed in India

Walks *of a* Lifetime
from AROUND THE WORLD

EXTRAORDINARY HIKES *in* EXCEPTIONAL PLACES

Robert and Martha Manning

ESSEX, CONNECTICUT

Appalachian National Scenic Trail
in Shenandoah National Park

Hikers ascend and descend the Grand Canyon on the dramatic South Kaibab Trail.

To those who manage and maintain the trails we walk—thanks for all your good work.

Some trails offer delightful camping opportunities; for example, campsites are spaced every 5 to 7 miles along much of the Chesapeake and Ohio (C&O) Canal Towpath.

Now shall I walk

Or shall I ride?

"Ride," Pleasure said;

"Walk," Joy replied.

—*W. H. Davis*

Lost Coast Trail

Ohio and Erie Canal Towpath Trail

Contents

John Muir Trail

Maritime Alps

Czech Greenways

Vermont's aptly named Long Trail is the first long-distance trail in the United States; it crosses a series of country roads, mountain streams, and remnants of historic farms.

Introduction

A number of years ago, we made a prophetic decision to walk the aptly named Long Trail in what was then our home state of Vermont. The first long-distance trail in America, the Long Trail runs 272 miles along the spine of our beloved Green Mountains from Massachusetts to the Canadian border. The trail is crossed by small country roads that allowed us to walk the trail in sections, often a day or two at a time as schedules and weather permitted. The trail took us to places that reminded us of why we were so fortunate to live in Vermont. We looked forward to every opportunity to get back on the trail, and we used the small map in our guidebook to keep track of our progress by coloring the trail segments we'd just completed. It was immensely satisfying to color that last section; we'd finished what we set out to do—a long and sometimes challenging walk the length of our state. We'd enjoyed the adventure of walking one of the world's great long-distance trails and now had a much richer sense of the place where we lived, an appreciation that comes only with the pace and intimacy of walking. But we missed our weekends on the trail and started looking for other long walks.

Since then, walking has been an increasingly important part of our lives. Like many people, we walk every day, but we've tried to be more deliberate about it, walking to work and back, around our neighborhood, to the market, with friends and family. Walking is so simple for most people, but paradoxically it can also be profound: The evolution and mechanics of walking are unique parts of what make us human; walking is infused in human history and culture; walking contributes to our physical, social, and emotional well-being; and walking is a personal and often joyful way to experience, know, and appreciate the world.

Our walking has taken us around the globe to walk the world's great long-distance trails. For the purposes of this book, our definition of a long-distance trail is one that can be walked in a few days to a few weeks, trails that range from about 50 to 500 miles. While the notion of a long-distance trail might sound intimidating, we hope it doesn't; perhaps "multi-day walks" or "walking vacations" are more welcoming terms. You'll notice that we tend to use the word "walk" in this book more often than "hike" because the former may sound less intimidating than the latter. However, we use both words for the sake of interest and variety and to avoid the hopeless task of rigorously parsing the difference between the two words. Our purpose in preparing this book is to emphasize the accessibility of walking in general, and walking the trails we describe in particular. These trails are well marked and managed; many offer commercial services, if wanted, including accommodations and even guides and baggage transfer; and there are an increasing number of companies standing ready to help plan and arrange walking vacations (though we generally prefer to hike independently and to be as self-sufficient as possible). The trails we describe can be walked by ordinary people like us—and you.

The book includes our favorite long walks—forty of them that span six continents. These are walks through the great natural and cultural landscapes of the world, and many of these walks are among the world's most iconic. Walk the classic circuit around the Mont Blanc Massif; walk in the footsteps of medieval pilgrims along the Camino de Santiago; walk among the historic towns that compose Italy's Cinque Terre; walk to Machu Picchu along the Inca Trail; walk among the world's great mountain ranges, including the Sierra Nevada, Rockies, Appalachians, and Alps; walk the great coastlines of North America, Europe, Australia, and New Zealand; walk across the Grand Canyon; walk with the historic stampeders along Alaska's Chilkoot Trail; walk across England; walk above the Arctic Circle on Sweden's famed Kungsleden; walk the world's great cities. And much more. We've made a deliberate effort to offer a diversity of choices in terms of geography, length, landscape, attractions, type of accommodations, presence and type of commercial services, and degree of challenge. We've been purposeful in not including any of world's "super" long-distance trails such as the 2,200-mile Appalachian Trail, as walking these trails is just not feasible for most people (including us). However, several of the trails we feature are parts of these very long-distance trails; for example, the southern 100-mile section of the Long Trail is part of the Appalachian Trail (one of the best parts in our opinion!).

Long-distance walking is good for us and good for the earth. It promotes personal health and well-being and is one of the most sustainable forms of recreation. In our increasingly complex and frantic world, walking is a way to simplify our lives. Walking guru Colin Fletcher wrote that walking is the yin that can complement the more hectic yang of our everyday lives. Walking is also adventurous; despite all the guidebooks, maps, and apps, one can never be quite sure what's around the next bend in the trail, and every day brings new and sometimes unexpected experiences. We sense a growing yearning among many people for more authentic experiences, and walking allows more intimate contact with local places and people. Walking vacations can also help protect local places through their economic impact, especially when using local services such as B&Bs, small inns, and huts/refuges, and eating local foods. But most of all, walking is a joyful celebration of life and the diverse, beautiful, and curious world in which we live.

The rest of the book offers firsthand descriptions of forty of the world's great long-distance trails. We've been privileged to walk all these trails, and this has been an important part of our lives— enjoying the excitement of planning these hikes, learning about other places and people while we're on the trail, and reflecting on the joy these walks have brought us. While we've walked other trails as well, we've chosen these trails as our favorites and to represent the great diversity of long-distance walking. These trails are found on six continents and include eighteen countries and most US states and Washington, DC. All of these trails are extraordinary, and they can be walked by ordinary people. We hope you'll sense and share our enthusiasm for long-distance walking and these trails in particular.

The book includes a map showing the general location of each of the forty trails described in the book, and this is followed by a table that lists the trails in alphabetical order and provides key information about each, including location, length, type of accommodations, availability of baggage transfer, ability to walk the trail in sections, and an assessment of the challenges associated with walking the trail.

With regard to length, be aware that the length of some trails can vary depending on which routing options are chosen. For example, the Tour du Mont Blanc offers several variants that can be chosen—a lower-elevation, shorter route can be taken if the weather is poor. The length of trail we list is the most "standard" route. Moreover, we suggest you read the description of the trails in which you may be interested to see if you'd prefer completing a portion rather than their entirety. For example, we've listed the length of the Kungsleden in the table as 270 miles (its full length), but many people walk only the northern section of the trail because of its special character and beauty, and this reduces the effective length of the trail to about 120 miles; we make these considerations clear in the trail descriptions.

We categorize accommodations as falling into three categories: commercial (e.g., inns, B&Bs), huts/refuges, and backpacking/camping. Commercial accommodations provide private rooms, baths, and often include breakfast and possibly dinner. Huts/refuges are usually basic facilities that include either private or communal sleeping areas, baths (some with showers), and meals or cooking areas. Some trails are backpacking only. You'll notice from the table that many trails offer more than one kind of accommodations.

Baggage transfer refers to the option to send your luggage from accommodation to accommodation by commercial service, which allows walkers to carry only a daypack. Ability to walk the trail in sections refers to the fact that many trails are crossed by roads and other access points, and this allows walking these trails in segments of one to a few days at time over all or part of their distance.

Our rating of the challenges associated with walking each trail is subjective by its very nature, and most long-distance trails are highly variable over much of their length, almost by definition, and the table reflects this. We considered the difficulty of walking (e.g., length, elevation, climbing and descending, trail conditions, wayfinding), but also scrutinized the availability (or lack thereof) of facilities and services and other issues. For example, the full length of the Camino de Santiago is 500 miles, but the walking is often relatively easy and there are lots of commercial accommodations and huts/refuges, so we've noted its degree of challenge as "moderate." Alternatively, the Kalalau Trail is only 22 miles long (round-trip), but it's a backpacking trip with lots of ascents and descents, hot and humid conditions, and some exposure to steep drop-offs; consequently, we note its degree of challenge as "high." As always, the trail descriptions offer more information about all this. We've been deliberate about including a great spectrum of long-distance trails in terms of length, attractions, location, landscape, commercial facilities and services, and challenge.

The bulk of the book is devoted to our firsthand descriptions of each of the forty trails we've selected. The trail descriptions are designed to tell you what you need to know in deciding which trails you'd like to walk. Trail descriptions begin with a brief personal anecdote (which brings a smile to our face when we think about walking the trail), a description of the natural and cultural history of the area the trail traverses, the highlights of walking the trail, a selection of representative photographs we've taken along the way, a generalized trail map, and the logistical issues associated with planning and walking the trail.

Trail descriptions end with a list of additional resources, including websites, detailed guidebooks, maps, and apps, where this information is available. Only apps that have been specially prepared for these trails or are officially endorsed by the trail management entity are included; otherwise, you can find the latest available apps on the internet. The resources we've listed are the best sources available at the time of publication of this book, but this information can change quickly; we encourage you to do an internet search for the most up-to-date information.

Consider trails you might like to walk by looking at the map and table to get a good sense of the range of walking options. Thumbing through the book's photographs might also be useful in deciding which trails to walk; we've taken all these photos while on the trail, and they're representative of the landscapes and attractions you'll encounter. Then read the full descriptions of the trails you find most appealing. Finally, consult the resources we suggest at the end of each trail description for detailed trip planning.

We hope we'll cross paths with you soon.

—Bob and Martha Manning

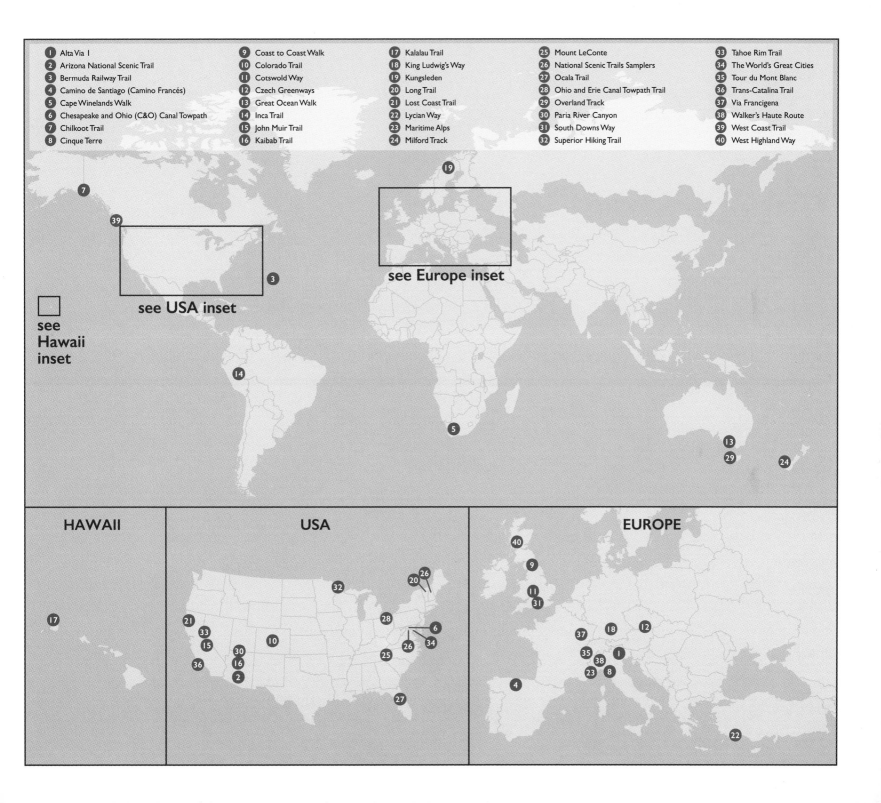

1 Alta Via 1
2 Arizona National Scenic Trail
3 Bermuda Railway Trail
4 Camino de Santiago (Camino Francés)
5 Cape Winelands Walk
6 Chesapeake and Ohio (C&O) Canal Towpath
7 Chilkoot Trail
8 Cinque Terre
9 Coast to Coast Walk
10 Colorado Trail
11 Cotswold Way
12 Czech Greenways
13 Great Ocean Walk
14 Inca Trail
15 John Muir Trail
16 Kaibab Trail
17 Kalalau Trail
18 King Ludwig's Way
19 Kungsleden
20 Long Trail
21 Lost Coast Trail
22 Lycian Way
23 Maritime Alps
24 Milford Track
25 Mount LeConte
26 National Scenic Trails Samplers
27 Ocala Trail
28 Ohio and Erie Canal Towpath Trail
29 Overland Track
30 Paria River Canyon
31 South Downs Way
32 Superior Hiking Trail
33 Tahoe Rim Trail
34 The World's Great Cities
35 Tour du Mont Blanc
36 Trans-Catalina Trail
37 Via Francigena
38 Walker's Haute Route
39 West Coast Trail
40 West Highland Way

see USA inset

see Europe inset

see Hawaii inset

HAWAII

USA

EUROPE

Table of Trails

Walk	Location	Length	Accommodations	Baggage Transfer	Option to Walk in Sections	Degree of Challenge
Alta Via 1	Italy	75 miles	Commercial (e.g., Inns, B&Bs): Some Huts/Refuges: Yes Backpacking/Camping: No	No	Most	Moderate-High
Arizona National Scenic Trail	Arizona, United States	800 miles	Commercial (e.g., Inns, B&Bs): Some Huts/Refuges: Limited Backpacking/Camping: Yes	No	Yes	Moderate-High
Bermuda Railway Trail	Bermuda	18 miles	Commercial (e.g., Inns, B&Bs): Yes Huts/Refuges: No Backpacking/Camping: No	No	Yes	Low-Moderate
Camino de Santiago (Camino Francés)	France and Spain	500 miles	Commercial (e.g., Inns, B&Bs): Most Huts/Refuges: Yes Backpacking/Camping: Limited	Yes	All	Moderate
Cape Winelands Walk	South Africa	60 miles	Commercial (e.g., Inns, B&Bs): Yes Huts/Refuges: No Backpacking/Camping: No	Yes	All	Low-Moderate
Chesapeake and Ohio (C&O) Canal Towpath	Maryland and Washington, DC, United States	185 miles	Commercial (e.g., Inns, B&Bs): Some Huts/Refuges: No Backpacking/Camping: Most	No	All	Low
Chilkoot Trail	Alaska, United States, and British Columbia, Canada	33 miles	Commercial (e.g., Inns, B&Bs): No Huts/Refuges: No Backpacking/Camping: Yes	No	No	High
Cinque Terre	Italy	Variable	Commercial (e.g., Inns, B&Bs): Yes Huts/Refuges: Some Backpacking/Camping: No	No	All	Low-Moderate
Coast to Coast Walk	England	190 miles	Commercial (e.g., Inns, B&Bs): Yes Huts/Refuges: Some Backpacking/Camping: Some	Yes	All	Moderate

Walk	Location	Length	Accommodations	Baggage Transfer	Option to Walk in Sections	Degree of Challenge
Colorado Trail	Colorado, United States	567 miles	Commercial (e.g., Inns, B&Bs): Some Huts/Refuges: No Backpacking/Camping: Yes	No	Some	Moderate-High
Cotswold Way	England	102 miles	Commercial (e.g., Inns, B&Bs): Yes Huts/Refuges: No Backpacking/Camping: Limited	Yes	All	Moderate
Czech Greenways	Austria and Czech Republic	350 miles	Commercial (e.g., Inns, B&Bs): Yes Huts/Refuges: No Backpacking/Camping: No	Yes	All	Moderate
Great Ocean Walk	Australia	68 miles	Commercial (e.g., Inns, B&Bs): Some Huts/Refuges: Some Backpacking/Camping: Yes	Yes	Yes	Low-Moderate
Inca Trail	Peru	30 miles	Commercial (e.g., Inns, B&Bs): No Huts/Refuges: No Backpacking/Camping: Yes	Porters	No	Moderate-High
John Muir Trail	California, United States	211 miles	Commercial (e.g., Inns, B&Bs): Few Huts/Refuges: No Backpacking/Camping: Yes	No	Some	High
Kaibab Trail	Arizona, United States	21 miles	Commercial (e.g., Inns, B&Bs): Limited Huts/Refuges: No Backpacking/Camping: Yes	No	Some	High
Kalalau Trail	Hawaii, United States	22 miles (round-trip)	Commercial (e.g., Inns, B&Bs): No Huts/Refuges: No Backpacking/Camping: Yes	No	No	High
King Ludwig's Way	Germany	75 miles	Commercial (e.g., Inns, B&Bs): Yes Huts/Refuges: No Backpacking/Camping: Some	Yes	All	Low-Moderate
Kungsleden	Sweden	270 miles	Commercial (e.g., Inns, B&Bs): Some Huts/Refuges: Yes Backpacking/Camping: Yes	No	Some	Moderate-High
Long Trail	Vermont, United States	272 miles	Commercial (e.g., Inns, B&Bs): Some Huts/Refuges: Three-sided shelters Backpacking/Camping: Yes	No	Yes	Moderate-High
Lost Coast Trail	California, United States	60 miles	Commercial (e.g., Inns, B&Bs): Some Huts/Refuges: No Backpacking/Camping: Yes	No	Some	Moderate

Walk	Location	Length	Accommodations	Baggage Transfer	Option to Walk in Sections	Degree of Challenge
Lycian Way	Turkey	330 miles	Commercial (e.g., Inns, B&Bs): Some Huts/Refuges: Some Backpacking/Camping: Yes	No	Some	Moderate-High
Maritime Alps	France	65 miles	Commercial (e.g., Inns, B&Bs): Yes Huts/Refuges: Some Backpacking/Camping: Limited	Yes	Most	Moderate
Milford Track	New Zealand	33 miles	Commercial (e.g., Inns, B&Bs): Yes Huts/Refuges: Yes Backpacking/Camping: No	No	No	Low-Moderate
Mount LeConte	North Carolina and Tennessee, United States	Variable	Commercial (e.g., Inns, B&Bs): Yes Huts/Refuges: No Backpacking/Camping: Yes	No	No	Moderate
National Scenic Trails Samplers	United States	Variable	Commercial (e.g., Inns, B&Bs): Some Huts/Refuges: Some Backpacking/Camping: Some	No	Some	Variable
Ocala Trail	Florida, United States	72 miles	Commercial (e.g., Inns, B&Bs): Some Huts/Refuges: No Backpacking/Camping: Yes	No	Yes	Low
Ohio and Erie Canal Towpath Trail	Ohio, United States	90+ miles	Commercial (e.g., Inns, B&Bs): Yes Huts/Refuges: No Backpacking/Camping: Some	No	All	Low
Overland Track	Australia	51+ miles	Commercial (e.g., Inns, B&Bs): No Huts/Refuges: Yes Backpacking/Camping: Some	No	No	Moderate
Paria River Canyon	Utah and Arizona, United States	38 miles	Commercial (e.g., Inns, B&Bs): No Huts/Refuges: No Backpacking/Camping: Yes	No	Some	Moderate
South Downs Way	England	100 miles	Commercial (e.g., Inns, B&Bs): Yes Huts/Refuges: Some Backpacking/Camping: Limited	Yes	All	Low-Moderate
Superior Hiking Trail	Minnesota, United States	312 miles	Commercial (e.g., Inns, B&Bs): Some Huts/Refuges: No Backpacking/Camping: Most	Some	Most	Moderate-High

Walk	Location	Length	Accommodations	Baggage Transfer	Option to Walk in Sections	Degree of Challenge
Tahoe Rim Trail	California and Nevada, United States	165 miles	Commercial (e.g., Inns, B&Bs): Most Huts/Refuges: No Backpacking/Camping: Yes	No	All	Moderate–High
The World's Great Cities (e.g., Washington, DC)	Variable (e.g., Washington, DC)	Variable	Commercial (e.g., Inns, B&Bs): Yes Huts/Refuges: Some Backpacking/Camping: No	No	Yes	Low
Tour du Mont Blanc	France, Italy, and Switzerland	105 miles	Commercial (e.g., Inns, B&Bs): Most Huts/Refuges: Yes Backpacking/Camping: Limited	Most	Most	Moderate–High
Trans-Catalina Trail	California, United States	38+ miles	Commercial (e.g., Inns, B&Bs): Some Huts/Refuges: No Backpacking/Camping: Yes	Some	Some	Moderate–High
Via Francigena	England, France, Switzerland, and Italy	1,180 miles	Commercial (e.g., Inns, B&Bs): Yes Huts/Refuges: Some Backpacking/Camping: No	Some	Yes	Moderate
Walker's Haute Route	France and Switzerland	132 miles	Commercial (e.g., Inns, B&Bs): Most Huts/Refuges: Yes Backpacking/Camping: Limited	Some	Most	High
West Coast Trail	British Columbia, Canada	47 miles	Commercial (e.g., Inns, B&Bs): No Huts/Refuges: No Backpacking/Camping: Yes	No	Limited	High
West Highland Way	Scotland	96 miles	Commercial (e.g., Inns, B&Bs): Yes Huts/Refuges: Some Backpacking/Camping: Some	Yes	All	Moderate

The Alta Via 1 runs 75 miles through the dramatic Dolomite Mountains of northern Italy.

Alta Via 1

Our second day on the Alta Via 1 was challenging, and we were grousing a little. We'd walked up and over Forcella del Lago (a nearly 8,000-foot pass) that day, down a steep descent, and were now climbing again, this time to Rifugio Lagazuoi, perhaps the most dramatically sited refuge in all of the Dolomites and our destination for the night. We were cold and tired and looking forward to a hot shower, a warm meal, and a comfortable bed. But as we climbed to the refuge, we passed the obvious remains of the prolonged and brutal mountain warfare between the Austrians and Italians in World War I—trenches, tunnels, lookouts, barbed wire, discarded mess tins, and bomb damage. These soldiers endured unimaginable hardship and had no down jackets, lightweight backpacks, and breathable rainwear. Thinking of the life of soldiers during this awful war put things in perspective, and we didn't feel sorry for ourselves any longer—we continued on to our refuge without another complaint.

———— ≋ ————

The Dolomites are a wonderland of jagged mountain peaks and deep green valleys in the eastern Alps, mostly in northern Italy. This mountain range includes eighteen peaks rising to more than 9,000 feet, and its stunning and dramatic beauty earned its designation as a UNESCO World Heritage Site. The mountains are composed of limestone formed at the bottom of an ancient sea; these seabeds were later pushed up by tectonic forces and finally molded into their present form by glaciation and erosion. This limestone is what gives them their distinctive and appealing whitish or light gray color, and the abundance of the mineral, dolomite, is what gives the mountains their name.

The Dolomites are laced with trails, many of which had their beginnings as ancient mule tracks and old military roads. The Alta Via 1 (Alta Via means "high route," and the trail is sometimes called the Dolomite High Route 1) was the first of what are now several long-distance routes through the mountains—and many walkers think it's the most beautiful. Running for about 75 miles (depending on what variants are selected) between Lago di Braies in the north (an attractive alpine lake

LOCATION
Italy

LENGTH
75 miles

ACCOMMODATIONS
Commercial (e.g., Inns, B&Bs): Some
Huts/Refuges: Yes
Backpacking/Camping: No

BAGGAGE TRANSFER
No

OPTION TO WALK IN SECTIONS
Most

DEGREE OF CHALLENGE
Moderate–High

The Dolomites are composed
principally of limestone, which gives
the mountains their distinctive and
pleasing whitish or light gray color.

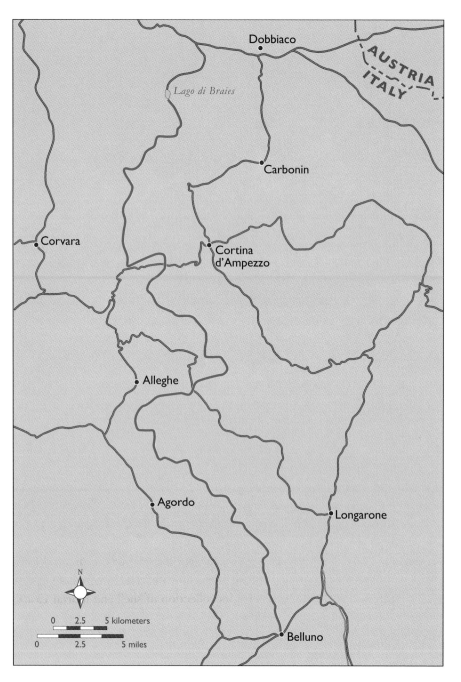

surrounded by peaks and pine forests near the Austrian border) to the small historic city of Belluno in the south, the AV1 weaves its way through many of the most famous peaks in the Dolomites. Known for their prominent role in the development of rock and ice climbing (you'll see intrepid climbers in several locations near the trail), the Dolomites are popular today for skiing in winter and walking in summer.

Rugged spires and pinnacles mark the mountain peaks, while the trail undulates between scenic high mountain passes and rich alpine meadows filled with wildflowers, with deep forests and blue-green lakes in between. Look carefully for marine fossils in the rocks, which signal the mountains' origins. Wildlife includes chamois and ibex (both species of wild mountain goats), deer, marmots (with their piercingly sharp whistles), and golden eagles.

(ABOVE) The Alta Via 1 undulates between scenic high mountain passes and rich alpine meadows.

(BELOW) This dramatic peak is part of Cinque Torri, five rock towers that continue to support the region's historic climbing culture.

A distinguishing feature of the Alta Via 1, like many trails in the Alps, is its *via ferrata* ("iron way" in Italian) sections—pitches that are steep and/or exposed and for which a series of metal rungs, ladders, cables, or chains have been fixed. A few short sections scattered along the Alta Via 1 will give you a taste of what it's like to use a *via ferrata*, but a long and challenging *via ferrata* section in the Schiara area just north of Belluno deserves serious consideration; this section can easily be avoided (as we did) by using a variant of the main trail.

We've conveniently romanticized away most of the harder parts of the walk and have fond memories of many places and events: our walk along the base of the impressive "wall of walls," a 5-mile-long series of vertical rock walls that are used for advanced rock climbing; our night at Rifugio Lagazuoi, at 9,000 feet, the highest point along the trail with mountains in all directions, where we felt we were literally on top of the world; the unusually clear mountain air; our futile attempts to appreciate *grappa*, the local spirit; the evening alpenglow that turned the mountains pink; Cinque Torri, five rock towers that continue to support a culture of mountaineering; the chorus of bells worn by countless cows and goats; the 3,000-foot tunnel (called Galleria Lagazuoi) constructed by the Italian army mountaineers to secretly move troops; the international group of walkers we met along the way.

This is an especially fascinating adventure for history buffs, as the stark evidence of World War I battles is written in the rocks; after all, how many walks feature foxholes and tunnels? One refuge was as much museum as lodging with its collection of shell and mortar casings spilling out onto the large porch. Culturally, the northern portion of the trail seemed very Germanic (because of its historical association with Austria), and German was spoken more often than Italian; this brought home to us the fluidity of European borders over the past several hundred years.

(LEFT) Walkers on the Alta Via 1 find many remnants of brutal mountain warfare during World War I; note the gun placements and fortifications at the base of the peaks.

(RIGHT) Hikers along the Alta Via 1 are supported by a historic system of comfortable huts that offer lodging, meals, and the company of like-minded walkers.

Access to the southern end of the trail is relatively easy by train to Belluno. Reaching Lago di Braies is more difficult, as it is at the end of a long mountain road—we used a taxi service from Belluno, but it was expensive. The trail is reasonably well marked by red and white painted stripes, and the symbol of the trail (the number "1" inside a triangle) is found at regular intervals; wayfinding is generally not difficult, though we had to pay close attention to our guidebook in several places. The trail is in good shape, though we were happy to have our hiking poles on some downhill stretches and where there was snow and ice on the trail (we walked in September, just as most of the trail's refuges were closing for the year). The trail is served by a series of welcoming refuges (*rifugios* in Italian) at higher elevations and small hotels at periodic road crossings. The trail is usually walked in eight to ten days; daily stages are not long, but the full route includes nearly 22,000 feet of elevation gain. There are a few ski lifts that can be used to moderate the route, and some walking companies offer "best of" packages, allowing customers to walk only selected sections of the trail. Camping is forbidden, but the prevalence of so many refuges means one can still walk the Alta Via 1 without spending a lot on lodging. The walking season is generally from mid-June to mid-September, and reservations at accommodations are recommended in July and August. Like most mountain trails (and maybe even more so here), you must be prepared for all kinds of weather, even in summer. English is not spoken along the trail as universally as in urban areas of Europe, and it may be wise to take German and Italian phrase books if only to avoid dinner surprises.

The Dolomites are among the classic mountain ranges of the world and should be on the résumé of all serious walkers. Walking the Alta Via 1 is an excellent way to appreciate these mountains—long enough to fully immerse walkers in these distinctive peaks and passes, and routed to take full advantage of the rich history of this region of the world. Like many of Europe's long-distance trails, the Alta Via 1 includes lots of variants—trail options to hike higher or lower elevations, shorter or longer routes. The Alta Via 1 is often discussed with the Tour du Mont Blanc and Walker's Haute Route (described in later chapters) as the three classic long-distance hikes in the European Alps.

Resources

Website
Refuges: www.rifugios.net

Guidebooks
Gillian Price, *Alta Via 1—Trekking in the Dolomites* (5th edition), 2022
Andrew McCluggage, *Trekking the Dolomites AV1*, 2020

The Italian flag flies proudly at Refugio Lagazuoi, perhaps the most dramatically sited refuge in all the Dolomites.

The 800-mile Arizona National Scenic Trail (AZT) passes through two national parks, Grand Canyon and Saguaro; the latter features the nation's richest stands of giant saguaro cactuses, otherworldly plants resembling human figures.

Arizona National Scenic Trail

After living much of our adult lives in beautiful, peaceful Vermont, we decided to move to Arizona to be closer to all the parks, public lands, and trails in the Southwest and the greater western United States. And it's sure working for us. One of the most enticing trails we've been walking is the Arizona National Scenic Trail; as the name suggests, it's part of the US National Trails System. And it's a long one—800 miles—so we've been pecking away at it, hiking it in sections in conjunction with our travels around this big, surprisingly diverse state, and we've been delighted. We've now walked a substantial portion of the trail and wanted to include it in this book. But as you'll see in this chapter, the sections we've hiked encompass much of Arizona's natural and cultural diversity. Consider walking the AZT as a thru-hike or in sections, and we think you'll be delighted, too.

———— ≈ ————

The flagships of America's remarkable National Trails System are the eleven National Scenic Trails, long-distance pathways that traverse much of the best of America. These are well-marked and maintained routes that highlight much of the nation's history and natural history. (See the chapter on National Scenic Trails Samplers for more about this system of trails.) Former Secretary of the Interior Stewart Udall wrote, "A national trail is a gateway into nature's secret beauties, a portal to the past, a way into solitude and community. It is also an inroad to our national character. Our trails are both irresistible and indispensable." One of the hallmarks of these trails is their democratic character; these are national trails, designed for everyone. But that means it's up to all of us—especially those of us who hike them—to care for them as well. These trails wouldn't exist without the extensive network of volunteers who have helped establish and maintain them.

The Arizona National Scenic Trail (locals call it the AZT) is an exemplar of this community spirit. In the 1970s, Dale Shewalter, a fifth-grade schoolteacher in Flagstaff, Arizona, first envisioned a trail that ran the length of the state, from the Mexican border to Utah, a distance of about 800 miles. Shewalter personally scouted and walked a route for the trail and spent much of the next two

LOCATION
Arizona, United States

LENGTH
800 miles

ACCOMMODATIONS
Commercial (e.g., Inns, B&Bs): Some
Huts/Refuges: Limited
Backpacking/Camping: Yes

BAGGAGE TRANSFER
No

OPTION TO WALK IN SECTIONS
Yes

DEGREE OF CHALLENGE
Moderate–High

Just south of Flagstaff, the AZT reveals layers of geology that are found in the Grand Canyon well to the north.

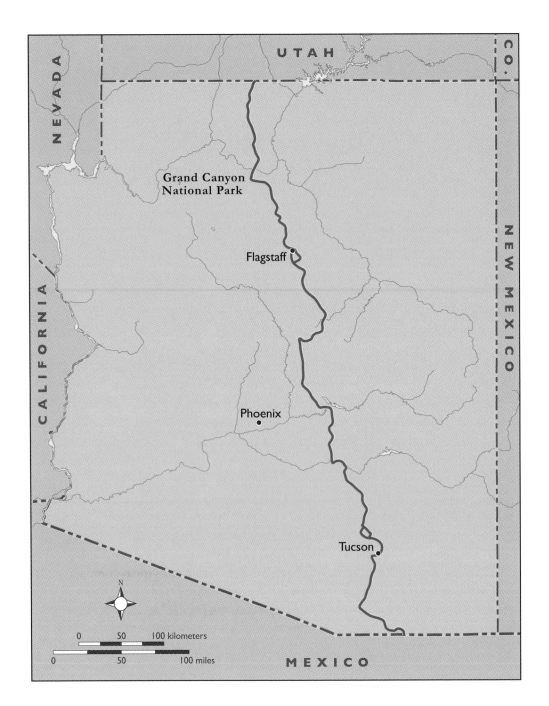

decades advancing his vision, earning him wide recognition as the "Father of the Arizona Trail." The Arizona Trail Association (ATA), a nonprofit, membership organization established in 1994, protects and maintains the trail. Establishment and management of the trail is one of the largest volunteer efforts in Arizona history, identifying and connecting existing trails, building new trails where necessary, maintaining all these miles of trails, and bringing trail users and government agencies into a statewide trail community. Much of this effort is funded by dues from ATA members. Given the

The most famous section of the AZT follows the Kaibab Trail through the Grand Canyon, the world-famous hike through nearly 2 billion years of geologic history.

length of the trail, this all constitutes a heroic effort. The trail was designated a National Scenic Trail in 2009 and completed in 2011.

For those who don't live in Arizona, there's often an assumption that the state is mostly desert, but this is profoundly incorrect, as all AZT hikers are keenly aware. The state is the sixth largest in the country and the geography varies considerably. For example, elevations range from a low of 72 feet above sea level along the Colorado River to the 12,633-foot summit of Mount Humphries. Yes, a substantial portion of the state is part of the extensive and strikingly beautiful Sonoran Desert, but the state also includes several mountain ranges, extensive grasslands, great swaths of ponderosa pine forests, perennial and seasonal streams, and innumerable canyons, including, of course, the Grand Canyon.

The ATA's guidebook, *Your Complete Guide to the Arizona National Scenic Trail*, divides the trail into forty-three "passages" that vary in length from 8 to 31 miles. Starting in the south, the trail begins in Coronado National Memorial (a unit of the National Park System) at the Mexican border. Traveling north, hikers climb through the Huachuca and Santa Rita Mountains and walk through the historic town of Patagonia. Near Tucson, the trail passes through dramatic Saguaro National Park and the stark Santa Catalina Mountains. Well east and then north of the Phoenix metropolitan area, the trail passes through the Superstition Mountains, around Roosevelt Lake, and climbs 3,000 feet through the Mazatzal Mountains to the vast escarpment called the Mogollon Rim and the lush-seeming Coconino Plateau. Hikers have the option of passing around the small city of Flagstaff to the east or west and then through the high country of the San Francisco Peaks. Hikers walk several days to the Grand Canyon, which is traversed on the South Kaibab and North Kaibab Trails, one of the world's great hikes (described in a later chapter in this book). The trail ends with several days of relatively easy hiking across the Kaibab Plateau through forests and meadows to reach the Utah border. Nearly all the trail is on public lands, most of it in national forests, some in national parks and lands administered by the federal Bureau of Land Management, and some managed by the State of Arizona.

In keeping with the range of elevations in the state, the AZT is especially diverse biologically. In fact, the concept of "life zones" was coined by naturalist C. Hart Merriam, cofounder of the National Geographic Society, based on his fieldwork in Arizona; here he found a large range of elevations and associated vegetation, noting that as elevation increases, precipitation also increases, but temperature decreases, and these relationships result in a great variety of plants and animals. Notable plants include a mixture of cactuses (including the iconic saguaros and more than twenty species of cholla), yucca, and agaves at lower elevations, and ponderosa pine and pinyon/juniper forests and aspens at higher elevations. Animals include mule deer, mountain lions, wolves, bighorn sheep, coyotes, javelinas, and elk, along with a great variety of reptiles and endemic and migratory birds,

At higher elevations, the AZT offers several days of walking among the region's stately ponderosa pine forests.

especially in riparian areas. Hikers on some of the AZT's passages will experience more than one life zone over a one- or two-day period. "Sky Islands" are a distinctive feature of some sections of the AZT, especially in the southern region of the trail. These high, isolated mountains rise more than 6,000 feet above the surrounding desert floor, and these two drastically different environments support equally dissimilar plants and animals; by analogy, the mountains are "islands" in desert "seas."

Arizona and the AZT are also culturally diverse and rich, affected by Native Americans, Spanish explorers, and European Americans (including miners and cowboys), and this diversity is reflected in place names, language, food, mythology, and other human cultural expressions. Though the trail doesn't cross any lands currently owned by sovereign tribal nations, Native American ancestors regularly created and traveled along trails that are now part of the network of roads and trails used by contemporary Americans, including portions of the AZT. Moreover, it's not uncommon to see artifacts of these civilizations (e.g., petroglyphs, pottery sherds, remains of dwellings) along the AZT and surrounding areas; such artifacts should not be removed and must be treated with respect. Ranches, mineral exploration relics, and water tanks are evidence of historic periods of American and Spanish occupation.

The southern end of the AZT begins in Coronado National Memorial, a unit of the National Park System, located directly on the nation's long border with Mexico.

Given the length of the AZT, many hikers should consider walking short sections of the trail. Several of these sections have well-deserved reputations as especially appealing. Of course, traversing the Grand Canyon on a two- to three-day hike (this is Passage 38 and is 21.4 miles) is the "glamour" section; after all, Arizona is the "Grand Canyon State," as proclaimed on license plates. (We describe this hike in a later chapter.) The AZT crosses one other national park—Saguaro National Park—as part of Passage 9; however, this is another especially challenging hike of 21.6 miles with more than 6,000 feet of elevation gain. Consider starting at the southern end of the Passage at Hope Camp (which requires a 3-mile hike to reach), traveling north as far as you wish, then turning around and retracing your steps. You'll be hiking through the richest stands of giant saguaro cactuses on earth; these otherworldly plants resemble human figures. Their white blooms (usually in June) are the Arizona state flower.

Other especially diverse segments of the AZT include the southern end of the trail where it begins in Coronado National Memorial (commemorating Francisco Vasquez de Coronado's expedition into the American Southwest in 1540 in search of the mythical Seven Cities of Cibola) at the Arizona-Mexico border. Here, you'll start directly on the border marked by a monument, some low barbed-wire fencing, and an isolated section or two of the controversial large steel border wall. Take a long look to the south at the sweeping grasslands of the San Rafael Valley that cover this part of Mexico. Walk north on the AZT for about 2 miles to reach a major trailhead at Montezuma Pass that's served by a park road. The trail wanders through lovely grasslands, desert vegetation, and evergreen oak woodlands, and offers a short spur trail to the top of Coronado Peak (where the concept of the AZT was envisioned). Note that this is an out-and-back hike that must start at Montezuma Pass (since the AZT is the only access to the border), proceed to the Mexican border, and then return to the pass.

Complementing the starkly arid character of the southern end of the trail are the high-elevation forests of the AZT as it winds through the San Francisco Peaks just north of Flagstaff. Begin your hike at Aspen Corner Trailhead on the Snowbowl Road and follow a long contour that traverses rich forests of pines, firs, and aspens punctuated by lush meadows, wildflowers, and long views over the high plains to the north and the San Francisco Peaks to the south. Walk as far as you wish and then return to the trailhead. Try to time this hike with fall foliage, when aspens light up the landscape and the mountain peaks are dusted with snow.

Like all long-distance trails, hiking the AZT requires careful planning, maybe more than any other national scenic trail. In the words of former ATA executive director Dave Hicks, "fail to plan—plan to fail." Low-elevation sections can be dangerously hot, and high-elevation areas can hold snow and ice well into the summer. Some passages (e.g., Grand Canyon) are heavily used, while many others are solitary. But the limiting factor along the entire trail is water. Take more than enough, and read your guidebook carefully to determine where the next water supply can be expected. Experienced AZT hikers don't think much in terms of "miles per hour," but more in "liters per mile." The ATA has developed strong relationships with thirty-two "Gateway Communities" along or near the trail; these hiker-friendly towns have facilities and services that cater to hikers and are found every 50 miles or so. No permits are needed along the trail except for camping at Saguaro and Grand Canyon National Parks, and AZT thru-hikers are eligible for these permits on a preferred basis. The AZT is signed, but detailed maps and GPS are highly recommended for wayfinding over this lengthy and often lonely trail; use the detailed AZT trail guide noted below for directions, and search the ATA website for local contacts and trail conditions.

Don't let the length of the Arizona National Scenic Trail discourage you. Remember, it's divided into segments, and so far we haven't found a segment that hasn't surpassed expectations—and the 800-mile length offers so many opportunities!

Resources

Website
Arizona Trail Association: https://aztrail.org

Guidebook
Mathew Nelson and the Arizona Trail Association, *Your Complete Guide to the Arizona National Scenic Trail*, 2014

App
Arizona Trail by FarOut (recommended by the Arizona Trail Association)

Just north of Flagstaff at over 7,000 feet, the AZT passes through large stands of aspens that light up the landscape with their fall foliage.

The Bermuda Railway Trail allows walkers to explore the island's dramatic coastline.

Bermuda Railway Trail

You can never be quite sure what you're getting when you rent a property online. But in Bermuda, we hit the jackpot. We made arrangements to rent a guesthouse advertised as "adjacent to the Bermuda Railway Trail," and it turned out that our hosts were avid walkers and helped make sure our hike was successful. The guesthouse was just 150 yards from the trail, newly renovated, appealing, and well stocked, and the owners provided us with more-detailed maps than we'd been able to find, advised us on how the island's public transportation system worked, and even offered us rides when needed. It was like having instant best friends when we arrived in Bermuda, just another example of the "trail magic" that seems to happen so often in the hiking community.

The large archipelago of Bermuda consists of nearly 200 islands located in the Atlantic Ocean, 650 miles off the coast of the American Southeast. Bridges connect eight islands to form what most visitors assume is one landmass, generally called Bermuda. The archipelago totals about 21 square miles and includes 64 miles of tantalizing coastline, and Bermuda is home to more than 70,000 residents who enjoy a subtropical climate with mild winters and warm, humid summers. The islands are a British territory, but the population is a diverse mixture of Native Americans, Spanish Caribbeans, English, Irish, Scots, and Portuguese; the British cultural overlay is obvious and charming.

Perhaps the most unusual thing about Bermuda is its unexpected railroad history. To maintain the island's scenic and peaceful character, automobiles were banned beginning in 1908, and the area's transportation system consisted primarily of boats and horse-drawn carts and carriages (and walking, of course!). But as the population and economy prospered in the early part of the twentieth century, the need arose for a more efficient form of public transportation, and construction of a 22-mile railroad system spanning the main islands began. After long delays, the railroad opened in 1931 and provided passenger and freight service; locals endearingly called it the "Old Rattle and Shake." Automobiles were finally allowed on the island shortly after World War II, dooming the railway, which

LOCATION
Bermuda

LENGTH
18 miles

ACCOMMODATIONS
Commercial (e.g., Inns, B&Bs):
Yes
Huts/Refuges: No
Backpacking/Camping: No

BAGGAGE TRANSFER
No

OPTION TO WALK IN SECTIONS
Yes

DEGREE OF CHALLENGE
Low-Moderate

closed in 1948. Fortuitously, the government of Bermuda purchased the railroad shortly thereafter, and conversion into the present-day 18-mile "rail trail" began in 1964. Both residents and visitors now enjoy the trail, and it was designated a national park in 1986.

The Railway Trail offers an unusual way to enjoy and appreciate the lovely group of islands that compose Bermuda, including their natural and cultural history, and its leafy path offers an active

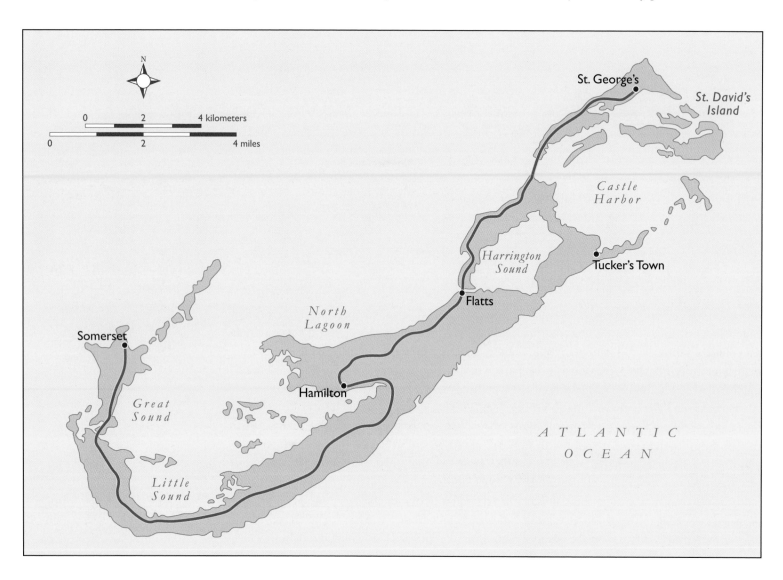

contrast to more passive beachgoing. Some of the trail is accessible by bicycle, but all of it can be walked. It connects many of the area's alluring coves and inlets as it passes panoramic landscapes and seascapes and winds through Bermuda's flower-covered hills; bridges and trestles and deep cuts through limestone bedrock remind walkers of the route's origins.

The trail follows the island's generally east–west orientation. The eastern end of the trail features the most historic portion of the islands and was a favorite of ours. Founded in 1612, the town of St. George's is thought to be the oldest continuously inhabited municipality of English origin in the Western Hemisphere and is a UNESCO World Heritage Site. The well-preserved town offers (literally) colorful examples of Bermudian architecture spanning the past four centuries. Take time to wander through the narrow streets and visit the area's historic fortifications and artillery. The Railway Trail makes its way west out of the St. George's section with striking views of the Atlantic Ocean to the north and Mullet Bay to the south.

Leaving St. George's behind, the trail travels the north shore of Hamilton Parish, passing the Sea Breeze Cricket Oval (the season runs from April through September) and along beautiful coastal pathways. The public beach at Shelly Bay is popular for swimming and picnics. Just west, find the interesting Railway Museum; the Bermuda Aquarium, Museum, and Zoo are located a short walk off the trail. Farther west you'll find panoramic views of the North Channel, Bermuda's primary shipping lane, where you might see cruise and container ships arriving and departing the island. A new section of the trail (farther west still) skirts the town of Hamilton, the capital of Bermuda, and offers access to several visitor attractions, including

The Bermuda Railway Trail winds its way for 18 miles through the island's flower-covered hills.

(ABOVE) The eastern end of the trail features the town of St. George's, founded in 1612 and now a World Heritage Site.

(ABOVE RIGHT) Deep cuts through the island's native limestone remind walkers of the trail's heritage as a railroad.

Bermuda's National Sports Center, the Arboretum, and the Bermuda Botanical Gardens (the latter highly recommended).

Continuing to the west, the trail passes through the 450-foot Rural Hill Tunnel and among quiet residential neighborhoods. Be sure to notice how each home collects water from its roof and stores it in tanks beside or below the buildings; rainwater collection is the primary source of fresh water for island households. Near here, the trail offers two highly recommended diversions, one to Gibbs Hill Lighthouse and the other to Horseshoe Bay Beach. The lighthouse is a bit of a climb but offers the very best views of the island and is well worth the effort. We also recommend walking and lounging on the dramatic shoreline of the bay, often touted as one of the world's great beaches. Approaching the west end of the trail, you'll pass the entrance of the former US Naval Annex, a busy facility in World War II, and Somerset Bridge, thought to be the shortest drawbridge in the world, its opening only wide enough for sailboat masts. The westernmost section of the trail offers beautiful views out over the ocean, swimming beaches, Scaur Hill Fort, and striking views of the Great Sound. At the trail's western terminus, you can walk into Somerset Village to catch a bus or ferry or continue on to the Royal Naval Dockyard, where you can learn about Bermuda's naval history and enjoy shops, galleries, and restaurants.

In addition to the trail markings, the Bermuda Railway Trail is punctuated with signage telling the interesting history of the railroad and the island. Streets cross the trail in many locations; these crossings make for good starting and ending points for those interested in walking trail segments, as public transportation (primarily buses and taxis) can be used to reach these intersections. Of course, where the trail crosses or travels along public streets, take appropriate caution. Most of the trail is

Some of the finest views of Bermuda's lovely harbor are found along the Bermuda Railway Trail.

the old railroad bed, so it's generally flat; the trail surface is paved in places but generally is dirt or gravel. Island weather in the summer is often hot and humid, so drink lots of water. Be cautious of crime just as you would in any populated area; don't walk alone and don't carry or wear valuables.

The Bermuda Railway Trail offers an unusual opportunity to explore a historic and lovely isolated Atlantic Ocean island archipelago on foot. Take a break from the bustling portions of the island and enjoy spectacular ocean and coastal views, isolated beaches with their distinctive pink sand and turquoise water, lush vegetation and colorful flowers, the rich history of the area, and the diverse cultures that call this island home. Our walk took us three days.

Resources

Website
Bermuda Railway Pages: www.bermudarailway.net

Guidebook and Map
Bermuda Railway Trail Map and Guide—available at tourist information sites on the island

Gibbs Hill Lighthouse is a short walk off the trail and offers great views of the island from its lookout.

Pilgrims approach Astorga, one of the many historic, beautiful, and religiously significant towns along the 500-mile Camino de Santiago.

Camino de Santiago (Camino Francés)

"*Buen camino*." We'd exchanged this greeting with other pilgrims (*perigrinos* in Spanish) hundreds of times over the course of our walk on the Camino. It's an all-purpose phrase that can mean "hello," "goodbye," or many other things, but most of all it means "I hope you find what you're searching for." Of course, many people walk the Camino for spiritual reasons, but others walk during one of life's transitions and are searching for meaning and direction in their lives. Others walk for adventure, to immerse themselves in a new landscape or culture, to appreciate the deep history of the walk, to meet like-minded walkers from around the world, or for many other reasons. *Buen camino* seemed to have special resonance this morning, the last day of our walk, the day we reached Santiago de Compostela. We'd stayed the previous night in Lavacolla, where pilgrims traditionally washed and prepared for their entry into the Cathedral of St. James the next day. It was a short walk into Santiago, where we joined with hundreds of others for the traditional noon mass devoted to arriving pilgrims, and we recognized many of the walkers we'd met along the way. Exchanging the traditional *buen camino* greeting was especially meaningful this morning, as we'd surely found what we were looking for (and more!).

The Camino de Santiago (more specifically, the Camino Francés) is a pilgrimage route running west for about 500 miles, starting in France but traveling mostly across northern Spain, to the city of Santiago de Compostela. This pilgrimage was popular in medieval times, and pilgrims have been walking this route for over a thousand years. But where does the trail begin? Originally, pilgrims started from their homes in Europe and eventually joined one of the several routes leading to Santiago, many of them eventually feeding into what is now simply called the Camino (or to be precise, the Camino Francés, as it was the main feeder route from France). In modern times, the traditional starting point is the village of Saint-Jean-Pied-de-Port on the French side of the Pyrenees Mountains, though one

LOCATION
France and Spain

LENGTH
500 miles

ACCOMMODATIONS
Commercial (e.g., Inns, B&Bs): Most
Huts/Refuges: Yes
Backpacking/Camping: Limited

BAGGAGE TRANSFER
Yes

OPTION TO WALK IN SECTIONS
All

DEGREE OF CHALLENGE
Moderate

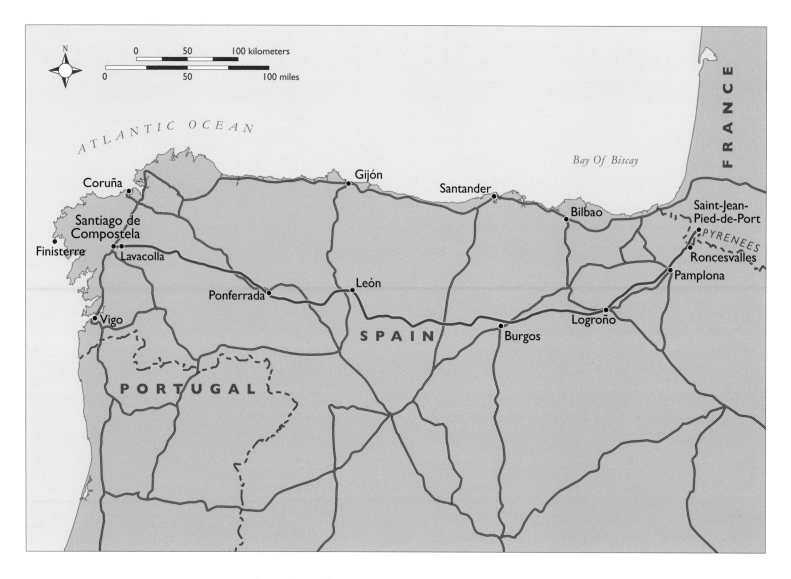

can begin the walk at any point along the route. The Catholic Church requires walking at least the final 100 kilometers (62 miles) to Santiago for walkers to receive a *Compostela*, certification of having completed the pilgrimage.

Camino de Santiago means "the road of Saint Iago" or, more commonly, "the Way of St. James." St. James was one of the Twelve Apostles and is the patron saint of Spain. While the story of St.

James is murky after all these years, it's believed that his remains were found in Spain and laid to rest in Santiago, where they've been venerated since 841 CE. A large and impressive cathedral was built to honor his memory, and Christians have made their way to Santiago to pay their respects ever since. A half million or more pilgrims made the journey each year in medieval times, but use dropped off substantially until quite recently; now, as many as a few hundred thousand people walk a significant portion of the trail each year, substantially more during holy years when St. James Day (July 25) falls on a Sunday. Santiago is considered the third most important site in Christendom (after Rome and Jerusalem), and the Camino is far and away the most popular Christian pilgrimage.

The walk is long but not difficult. Climbing over the Pyrenees Mountains and wandering across the north of Spain from town to town, the route is remarkably rich in history and culture. Guidebooks list over 1,800 buildings of great historical, architectural, spiritual, and artistic interest, and the old town of Santiago is a World Heritage Site. (In fact, the whole route has been designated a World Heritage Site!) Some buildings along the trail date from the ninth century. Most of the communities along the route—some large like Pamplona, Logrono, Burgos, León, and Santiago, but most small—grew up around the trail and were designed to serve the needs of pilgrims. All towns have at least one church and one or more *hospitales* originally intended to house and care for pilgrims. Many of these are still in use as lodgings (most are akin to huts/refuges) and are generally called *albergues*, providing simple and inexpensive lodgings for pilgrims.

The *Codex Calixtinus* is a further manifestation of the Camino's history. This twelfth-century illuminated manuscript celebrates the life of St. James and includes "A Guide for the Traveler," offering route-finding information for the Camino and identifying places to stay as well as places to

(ABOVE) Galicia is the last and perhaps loveliest region of Spain through which the Camino passes; its hilly and green character is distinctive and is a favorite of many walkers.

(ABOVE RIGHT) The historic monastery at Samos now serves as an *albergue*, welcoming pilgrims with simple accommodations; note the scallop shell ornamentation in the fence.

(ABOVE) The Pilgrim's Mass is celebrated each day at noon at St. James Cathedral in Santiago, a highlight for all pilgrims.

(ABIVE RIGHT) Local shops along the Camino sell remembrances of this historic pilgrimage; most pilgrims wear a scallop shell while walking, a symbol of the trail.

avoid. Considered the world's first guidebook, the *Codex* helped popularize the pilgrimage to Santiago de Compostella.

Using a surprisingly moderate route, the walk begins by crossing the Pyrenees, one of the world's great mountain ranges. The trail then traverses the rolling hills of the Basque Country, with its distinctive architecture, language, and "lively" politics. In less than a week's time pilgrims reach Pamplona, widely known for the heritage associated with the "running of the bulls."

Next up is the Meseta, a long, high plateau that runs for roughly 125 miles between Burgos and Astorga; this northern section of central Spain is primarily agricultural and was once known as "Rome's bread basket." Some pilgrims skip this region because it can be hot in summer and cold in winter, and they believe it to be monotonous, but we found the expansive landscapes and big sky to be spectacular, offering time for reflection during some of our favorite walking days. Near the end of this section is León, one of the more beautiful cities we've visited with its cathedral (known as The House of Light), a palace built by Antonio Gaudi (Spain's most famous architect), medieval walls, and tourist-friendly old town.

After Astorga, walkers enter El Bierzo, a hilly region famous for its mines long before Romans added the area to their empire. Our favorite stop was the town of Ponferrada with its Knights

Templar castle dating from the days when Christian knights emerged to fight the Moors and protect pilgrims. There are many significant buildings and ruins in the El Bierzo region.

Located in the westernmost section of the Iberian Peninsula, lush and hilly Galicia is the final definitive section of the Camino and a favorite section of most walkers. It has its own language (related to Portuguese), small-scale agriculture, many *horreos* (small elevated granaries), and a distinctive Celtic heritage, including use of bagpipes in traditional music.

It's difficult to select highlights of our five weeks on the trail because there were so many, but we fondly remember the crosses everywhere fashioned by pilgrims out of stones and tree branches; the storks nesting in the church steeples; the varied route that includes quiet country lanes, paths across farm fields and vineyards and through cool forests and along streams, and ancient Roman roads; the regional foods (e.g., local cheeses and honey, *caldo galego* and *tarta de Santiago*); and inexpensive and delightful wine. History and spirituality permeate the trail, and it's quite moving to know you're walking where millions of others have walked before.

Of course all walkers are excited to reach Santiago, and it doesn't disappoint. It's a relatively large city (about 100,000 residents), but has a small, walled old town that caters heavily to visitors and especially pilgrims. The Cathedral of St. James, begun in 1075, is especially impressive and meaningful. The old town also has a 500-year-old university, impressive statues and fountains, stately public buildings, more than enough sidewalk cafes, and many well-deserved shops and carts serving local *helado* (ice cream). It's traditional to attend the Pilgrims Mass upon arrival, even for those who were not on a religious quest. We were fortunate to experience the grandest finale to our walk (to any of our walks!): the swinging of the *Botafumeiro* in the cathedral, a giant incense burner that swings from the rafters, reaching a height of 65 feet and achieving a speed of 45 miles per hour. The tradition began in the eleventh century, and some think it was designed to

Over its 500 miles across northern Spain, the Camino leads pilgrims through a variety of landscapes; here, walkers pass through a quiet forest.

This simple, romantic *albergue*,
Hospital Para Peregrinos San
Nicolas de Puente Fitero, is without
electricity and uses only candlelight.

mask the smell of pilgrims, many of whom had walked hundreds or even thousands of miles. The ceremony surrounding the *Botafumeiro* provided a powerful, even magical finale to our walk.

Most walkers acknowledge the pilgrimage by honoring several important traditions, one of which is the custom of identifying yourself as a pilgrim. Historically, pilgrims used a staff, and most walkers continue this tradition, though most have updated it with contemporary trekking poles. And most walkers hang a scallop shell from their pack signifying that they are on a pilgrimage; scallop shells were found on the beach where St. James's body was discovered and have become the symbol of the pilgrimage. Most importantly, each walker carries a passport or "credential" (*Credencial del Peregrino*) and collects stamps along the walk—at local churches, *albergues*, cafes, and other locations. The passport is then presented to the church office in Santiago as proof of the journey so that a *Compostela* may be awarded.

In medieval times, walking the Camino was an extraordinary, often dangerous undertaking. Many of the larger rivers had to be crossed at the mercy of unprincipled ferrymen, Spain was at war with the Moors of North Africa, bandits made a living by robbing pilgrims, and wolves occupied the region. Today's pilgrims have it much easier, but there are still several logistical concerns. The busy season on the Camino is July and August, and it can be very busy indeed; it's better to walk in the spring, early summer, or fall, if possible. A few short sections are along busy roads, requiring attention to safety.

Most pilgrims stay in *albergues*, hostel-like accommodations with communal sleeping and bathing facilities. They're operated by churches, towns, and as private businesses and are inexpensive, but there are few frills and they tend to fill quickly during the busy season. Because of this, many pilgrims walk very early in the day to claim a bunk or room at the next town. Many towns also have B&Bs and small inns. Along the way, walkers soon develop a rhythm to their journey; the Camino is especially well marked (look for the scallop shell motif and accompanying yellow arrows everywhere), footing is easy, and climbs and grades are not excessive. Though there can be many pilgrims on the trail during the busy season, it's interesting to meet like-minded people from all over the world, and since the Camino is essentially a one-way trail, it doesn't feel quite so crowded.

Be advised that the Spanish have a long tradition of eating dinner late; many restaurants don't open until 9 p.m. This might be a problem for walkers who are tired and hungry at the end of the day, but many cafes offer a "pilgrim's meal" that usually starts at 7 p.m. and includes a limited (but adequate) menu, including wine, at a reasonable cost. You should not expect locals to speak English (and many don't), so it's advisable to bone up on Spanish (including key words like *panaderia* (bakery), *bocadillos* (sandwiches), *cerveza* (beer), and *vino tinto* (red wine), and bring along a phrase book.

Because the original pilgrims started their journeys to Santiago from their homes, there are many routes, but the Camino Francés is the most well known and heavily traveled. There are others, including the Camino Norte (along the northern coast of Spain) and the Camino Portugués (starting in Porto, Portugal). In fact, there are a number of pilgrimages from around the world, and we've walked several of them, including the Camino Portugués and Japan's Kumao Kodo (we describe these in our book *Walks of a Lifetime: Extraordinary Hikes from Around the World*), and the Via Francigena (described in a later chapter of this book).

The Camino is one of the oldest and most significant walks in the world. We were reminded of this in one of our guidebooks that said the trail "still passes through the same villages, climbs the same hills, crosses the same rivers, and visits the same chapels, churches, cathedrals and other monuments as did the route taken by our predecessors in centuries gone by." Another guidebook pointed out that some of the deeply incised sections of trail in Galica and elsewhere have been eroded "by millions of pilgrims over many centuries of walking." It was a privilege and joy to follow in the footsteps of so many pilgrims who have walked the trail for over a thousand years. We hope you'll consider joining in this tradition. *Buen camino.*

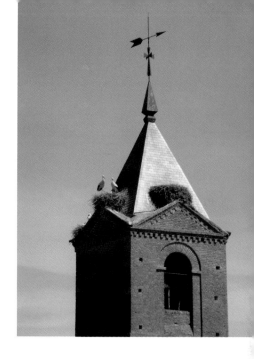

Storks nest in church steeples and other high places, delighting pilgrims.

Resources

Websites

American Pilgrims on the Camino: https://americanpilgrims.org
The Confraternity of St. James: www.csj.org.uk

Guidebook

John Brierley, *A Pilgrim's Guide to the Camino de Santiago (Camino Francés)*, 2021

Map

John Brierley, *Camino de Santiago Maps (Camino Francés)*, 2022

Walkers travel through lovely vineyards that sit at the base of the dramatic Hottentots Holland Mountains.

Cape Winelands Walk

The second day of our walk started in Lourensford, one of the oldest and largest wine estates in South Africa, and, the guidebooks say, one of the most beautiful in the world. Apple, pear, and plum orchards complemented the extensive vineyards, and the estate has provided the setting for a number of national and international films. We walked across the estate through the vineyards as we climbed toward a pass in the surrounding Hottentots Holland Mountains that would lead us to another wine estate and our next night's accommodations. Soon the carefully cultivated vineyards gave way to the wilder fynbos, the biologically rich shrublands that make this area famous in the plant world. The weather was warm—in the 80s—but the full summer sun made it feel hot. We lingered in the shade of eucalyptus trees along several mountain streams that crossed the trail and ate our packed lunch at the pass as we peered into the next valley to the north, where we were headed. We celebrated our ascent of the pass by pouring one of our water bottles over our heads and felt instantly cooler. After lunch, we followed farm roads down to the smaller, family-owned Dornier Wine Estate, where the historic manor house has been converted to a lodge and restaurant. We were the only guests that evening and toasted our day at dinner with a cold, crisp bottle of Sauvignon Blanc made from grapes grown on the estate.

LOCATION
South Africa

LENGTH
60 miles

ACCOMMODATIONS
Commercial (e.g., Inns, B&Bs):
Yes
Huts/Refuges: No
Backpacking/Camping: No

BAGGAGE TRANSFER
Yes

OPTION TO WALK IN SECTIONS
All

DEGREE OF CHALLENGE
Low–Moderate

———— ≈ ————

There are many reasons to walk the Cape Winelands—the wine, the culture, the distinctive plants and animals, and the rich history of the local area and of Africa more generally. Let's start with the wine. While wine has come to dominate agriculture in a number of regions around the globe, they've been doing it—and doing it well—for more than 300 years in the Western Cape of South Africa, a wide swath of some of the world's most productive farmland located about 50 miles north of Cape Town. Here you can follow firsthand the story of winemaking from vineyard to glass. There are more

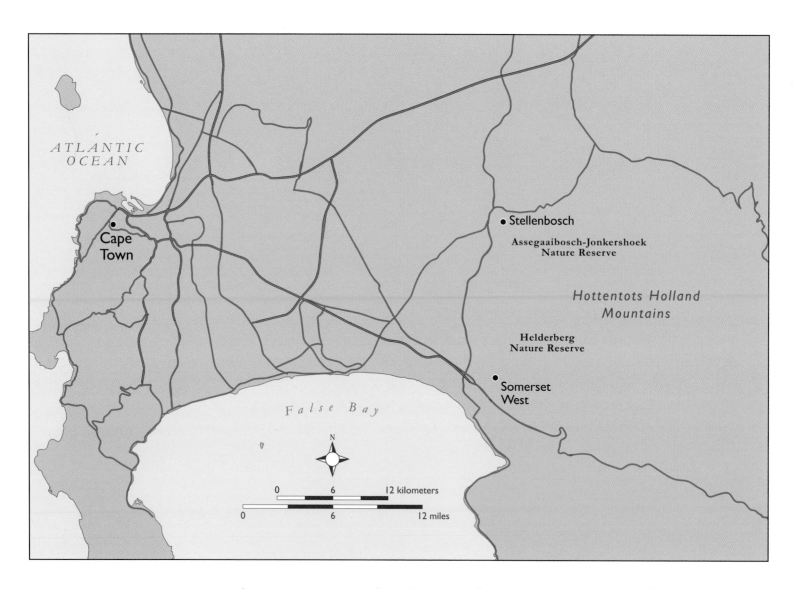

Atlantic Ocean

Cape Town

False Bay

Stellenbosch

Assegaaibosch-Jonkershoek Nature Reserve

Hottentots Holland Mountains

Helderberg Nature Reserve

Somerset West

N

| 0 | 6 | 12 kilometers |
| 0 | 6 | 12 miles |

than 200 wine estates in the region, many offering tours, tasting, dining, and lodging. The wine—and the region's other agricultural products, including fruits, vegetables, and cheese—offers a terroir that contributes to the area's distinctive and appealing sense of place. Our walk took us to several of the most famous wine estates, including Lourensford, Vergelegen, Dorrnier, and Vriesenhof.

The Cape Winelands Walk also has a wilder side that features the distinctive and important fynbos vegetation and an impressive, associated collection of animals. In the world of plant biology, the earth is divided into six plant kingdoms, the smallest and biologically richest of which (on a per acre basis) is the fynbos, geographically restricted to the Western Cape of South Africa. This shrubland comprises an estimated 10,000 species, many of which are endemic (found naturally nowhere else in the world). Primary plant families include large, broad-leafed *Proteas* (the showy king protea is the national flower of South Africa), *Ericas* (small plants with needlelike leaves evolved to conserve water), and *Restios* (grasslike plants that have historically been used for thatching roofs). Many fynbos plants are "serotinous"—that is, they're adapted to survive periodic fires. These adaptations include seeds that persist for long periods of time and open in response to the heat of wildfires. This Cape Floral Region is a World Heritage Site. Our walk took us to several parks, forests, and nature reserves, including the Helderberg, Jonkershoek, and Assegaaibosch Nature Reserves and the Jonkershoek State Forest, and through three mountain ranges—Hottentots Holland, Helderberg, and Stellenbosch.

The mountains and fynbos provide habitat for a variety of interesting and exotic animals, many of which will be seen by walkers, including baboons, bontebok, sugar birds, and sunbirds. Leopards are rarely seen, though their tracks and droppings offer clear evidence of their presence. Several species of venomous snakes, including the puff adder and Cape cobra, inhabit the area, though we didn't see them (despite watching carefully!).

The Cape Winelands has a rich history that is a microcosm of much of Africa. Colonized by the Dutch and other Europeans over 300 years ago, much of the country prospered economically but

(ABOVE LEFT) Vergelegen Winery is one of a series of historic wine estates linked by the Cape Winelands Walk.

(ABOVE) Lovely and lively Stellenbosch, the "City of Oaks," marks the end of the Cape Winelands Walk; we suggest taking an extra day here.

(ABOVE) Showy proteas are an important component of the distinctive and diverse fynbos vegetation in the Cape Wineland's region.

(ABOVE RIGHT) Cape Wineland's walkers often see and hear baboons and other exotic wildlife.

to the disadvantage of the native Black population, which experienced active discrimination. This long apartheid era in South Africa ended officially in 1994 thanks to the sacrifice and leadership of Nelson Mandela and many others, but the country is still plagued by racial problems, including continuing tension between the Black majority and the White minority and large-scale immigration of Blacks from surrounding countries. Sprawling squatters camps are found along the main road from Cape Town, and even in more rural areas such as the outskirts of Stellenbosch. However, the complicated history of the area has left an unusual and fascinating culture that blends elements of European and African architecture, arts, food, and language.

The Cape Winelands Walk is about 60 miles, though there are a number of options that can shorten or lengthen it. Our walk began in the town of Somerset West and included a short guided tour of the adjacent Helderberg Nature Reserve, an excellent place to learn about the area's natural history, which enabled us to more fully appreciate this unusual landscape. We completed the walk six days later in the lovely town of Stellenbosch. Founded in 1679, Stellenbosch is the second-oldest town in South Africa, second only to Cape Town, the "Mother City." Stellenbosch is the geographic and historic heart of the Cape Winelands region. Nicknamed the "City of Oaks," many of the town's streets are lined with 300-year-old oak trees, some of which have been declared national monuments. The prestigious University of Stellenbosch is embedded in the town and features rows of attractive buildings with red tile roofs, an impressive botanical garden, and its famous Coetzenburg Sports Grounds, including a rugby stadium and historic rugby clubhouse. Other attractions in town include the historic and picturesque Lanzerac Hotel, Rupert Museum, Kweekskool Theological Seminary, Oliver Art Center, a small African market, and the Institute of Culinary Arts (which we

This attractive and comfortable guesthouse was one of our accommodations along the Cape Wineland's Walk.

recommend for lunch or dinner). We spent an extra day in Stellenbosch, which happened to be a Saturday, and that night we enjoyed the town's lively downtown streets, which were closed to traffic and featured live music and dining under the oaks.

The Cape Winelands Walk is an excellent introduction to southern Africa and its distinctive landscape, history, and culture. The walk encompasses impressive public nature reserves with exotic plants and animals, private lands in the form of wine and other agricultural areas, and lively and attractive towns. Most of the walking is on country roads, farmland tracks, and mountain paths, and accommodations include upscale wine estates, small hotels, and more modest guesthouses and family stays. This part of South Africa has a Mediterranean climate—warm, dry summers and cool, wet winters—thus the best months for walking are October through April. Parts of the walk traverse private lands where rights-of-way have been negotiated, and because of this, the walk must be arranged through a walking company such as those noted in the "Resources" section below. We saw very few other walkers, but always felt secure. Our walk left us glad we had chosen this hike—and we have a strong desire to return to this part of the world.

Resources
Information and maps are provided by the following commercial companies:
Trails and Travel: www.trailsandtravel.co.za/walking-tours-south-africa/cape-winelands-walk/
World Walks: www.worldwalks.com/holidays/south-africa/self-guided/the-cape-winelands-walk/

The 185-mile Chesapeake and Ohio (C&O) Canal features a series of seventy-four historic locks, eleven large aqueducts, restored lockkeepers' houses, and a towpath where mules pulled 90-foot-long canal boats laden with cargo and passengers.

Chesapeake and Ohio (C&O) Canal Towpath

What has seventy-four locks but no doors? Given the trail we're describing, this riddle isn't very challenging, but we enjoyed watching the elementary school group at one of the National Park Service visitor centers along the trail try to puzzle it out. These visitor centers are located at the two ends of the trail (Georgetown and Cumberland) and at Brunswick, Williamsport, and Hancock. National Park Service visitor centers are also located at the nearby attractions of Harpers Ferry and Antietam Battlefield. These visitor centers are rich sources of information about the C&O Canal and the surrounding area, including its human and natural history. They have interesting displays, are staffed by knowledgeable rangers and volunteers, and offer books and other materials. And they're even free! While the C&O Canal is fortunate to have such a rich stock of visitor centers, many of the long-distance trails included in this book have similar facilities, and walkers should take maximum advantage, as these will make your walking more interesting (and sometimes even entertaining!).

───── ≈ ─────

The Potomac River is one of the largest in the eastern United States and was important to Native Americans as well as colonists and others who traveled westward along its banks. Following the Potomac on its journey from the Chesapeake Bay to its headwaters is like reading a record of the colonial expansion of the nation. The lands surrounding this important river have seen it all—peace and warfare, cooperation and confrontation, boom and bust. For years, the river marked the western frontier of the emerging country and separated North from South during the Civil War.

Along the river's northern bank runs the Chesapeake and Ohio (C&O) Canal and its delightfully walkable towpath extending 185 miles from the trendy neighborhood of Georgetown in

LOCATION
Maryland and Washington, DC, United States

LENGTH
185 miles

ACCOMMODATIONS
Commercial (e.g., Inns, B&Bs): Some
Huts/Refuges: No
Backpacking/Camping: Most

BAGGAGE TRANSFER
No

OPTION TO WALK IN SECTIONS
All

DEGREE OF CHALLENGE
Low

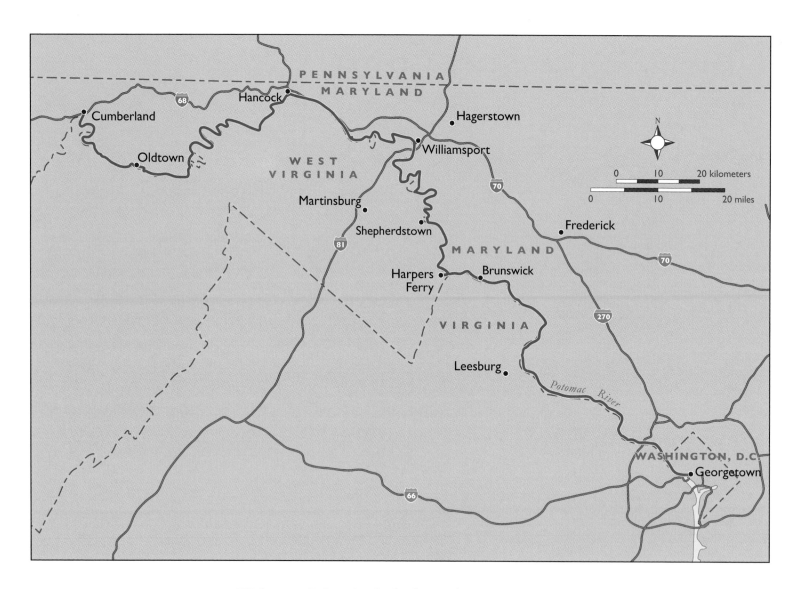

Washington, DC, to Cumberland in rural western Maryland. The C&O Canal has been called "the most delightful and varied greenway in America," and we can't argue with that. With a total change in elevation of only about 600 feet, the towpath is essentially flat, and the surface is packed clay and gravel and well groomed, all making for easy walking (or biking). The towpath and its immediate environs compose the Chesapeake and Ohio National Historical Park, a unit of the National Park

System, and has been called "America's most distinctive national park." (For more great walks in the US national parks, see our book *Walks of a Lifetime in America's National Parks*.)

But the C&O Canal didn't have its origins as a park. Early Americans hoped the Potomac River would provide a way westward to the Pacific Ocean. George Washington first wrote of the river's potential when helping with a survey party traveling upriver to the Ohio Valley when he was only 16. As early as 1774 he introduced legislation in Virginia to build skirting canals around the Great Falls area to make navigation of that part of the river possible, and in 1785 he became the first president of the Potowmack Canal Company. Because of these early efforts, he's thought of as "Father of the C&O Canal." Later politicians and industrialists continued to dream of a way to connect the Chesapeake Bay with the Ohio River to make navigation and trade possible between the eastern United States and the Midwest. The Potomac River was promising, but the powerful and treacherous rapids made navigation along its length impossible. But a canal incorporating a series of locks to raise and lower boats could work, and a towpath constructed beside the canal would allow mules to pull boats along.

The canal was started at the Georgetown end in 1828 just as the Industrial Revolution was coming to a head in America; President John Quincy Adams broke ground. But the project turned out

(ABOVE LEFT) The Potomac River parallels much of the canal, but some sections are too steep and rough to accommodate commercial navigation; thus, the canal was constructed in the nineteenth century for commercial boat traffic.

(ABOVE) Fall is a great time to walk the C&O Canal Towpath.

(ABOVE) Large aqueducts were constructed to contain the canal as it passed over the largest tributaries of the Potomac River.

(ABOVE RIGHT) The southern end of the canal runs through the historic Georgetown section of Washington, DC, where it flows into the Potomac River.

to be harder and more expensive than imagined (sound familiar?). The terrain was tough in places; challenges included the need for a nearly mile-long tunnel and negotiation of many small and large streams flowing into the Potomac. Way behind schedule (and way over budget), the canal didn't reach Cumberland until 1850; by that time the Baltimore and Ohio (B&O) Railroad was completed along roughly the same route, making the canal nearly obsolete before it could even begin to reach its imagined potential.

By the mid-1920s, the canal had been abandoned and fallen into disrepair. The federal government purchased the canal in 1938 with the intent of making it a recreation area. After World War II, priorities had changed, and Congress considered developing it into a parkway for automobiles. This plan was met with indignation by conservationists, and Supreme Court Justice William O. Douglas led an eight-day protest march along the canal in 1954, calling the towpath "a long stretch of quiet and peace." The canal was proclaimed a national monument in 1961 and established as C&O National Historical Park in 1971. The park now draws millions of thankful visitors a year, though most are concentrated near the Washington metropolitan area.

The prehistory of the area includes use of the Potomac River by several tribes of Indigenous Americans, including the Potomac, Iroquois, Piscataway, and Shawnee, though there is little physical evidence of this today. The word "Potomac" may be a derivation of the Algonquian name for a tribe in the area and may mean "place of trade." The river was a bountiful source of food throughout the seasons, as well as a transportation corridor.

The canal runs directly through much of the military history of America, including the French and Indian War and the Civil War. The impressive Fort Frederick, just off the towpath at mile 112 (the full length of the canal has mileage markers), is an impressive stone structure (most forts at the time were wooden) that was built to defend the western frontier during the French and Indian War. Oldtown, at mile 161, was a key location for both the French and Indian War and Civil War; it had previously served as a wilderness trading post for hundreds of years.

But the town of Harpers Ferry at mile 61 is the historical jewel of the walk. Set just above the impressive confluence of the powerful Potomac and Shenandoah Rivers, this town was the site of abolitionist John Brown's famous raid on the federal armory in an attempt to arm a slave uprising, and the location of the largest surrender of US forces in the Civil War. The Confederate Army used the surrounding heights to shell the town and the Union troops in it, and an empathetic Confederate General Stonewall Jackson said he'd rather "take the town 50 times than defend it once"; in fact, Harpers Ferry changed hands eight times during the war. Other spots along the Potomac saw many troop crossings, skirmishes, and battles. Union and Confederate troops clashed again later at Antietam, the bloodiest battle in US history. The battlefield is just 2.5 miles off the canal near mile 70. Both Harpers Ferry and Antietam are units of the National Park System.

The walk includes the fascinating story of the construction and engineering of the canal, and walking the towpath allows close inspection of this wonder of its time. The seventy-four locks raised and lowered boats along the course of the canal; the swinging miter gates at the ends of each lock were derivations of designs by Leonardo da Vinci. The locks were usually lined with locally quarried rock, and much of the stonework is elegant (though some of it has been damaged by flooding). At every lock there was a house for the lockkeeper and his family, and some of these structures remain. The National Park Service has restored a lockhouse and its associated buildings, including a mule barn, at Four Locks (mile 108.8). Several of the lockhouses are now available for overnight stays by walkers, which we recommend; see the website of the C&O Canal Trust (found below under "Resources") for information and to make reservations.

There were other impressive feats of engineering and construction. Large culverts were constructed under the canal to allow for the many tributaries of the Potomac to reach the river. A series of eleven large aqueducts were built to contain the canal as it passed over the larger tributaries of the Potomac. The grandest of these is the Monocacy Aqueduct, which is supported by seven lovely stone arches. The Paw Paw Tunnel between miles 155 and 156 was the canal's largest construction

The nearly mile-long Paw Paw Tunnel took fourteen years to construct and nearly bankrupted the company that developed the canal.

The National Park Service operates replica canal boats at some locations along the canal.

project, taking fourteen years (instead of the two that had been estimated) and nearly bankrupting the company that developed the canal. This was also the site of numerous labor disputes when Irish, English, and German workers staged walkouts because they were poorly treated (and sometimes not even paid). The tunnel is nearly a mile long and was built as a shortcut to avoid several miles of a winding section of the Potomac. Because construction was so difficult, the tunnel was not built wide enough to allow boats to pass one another. There's a story that two boats stayed in the Paw Paw Tunnel for days because neither captain would grant the right-of-way, and this backed up canal traffic for miles. Finally, canal officials flushed them out by building a smoky fire at one end.

Boats were specially built to navigate the canal; these wooden boats were 90 feet long and 14 feet wide, the maximum that could be accommodated by the locks. A small mule barn was located on the bow and a small cabin on the stern for the captain and his family. Two teams of two mules could keep 120 tons of boat and cargo moving at 4 miles per hour. Much of the cargo was coal mined in the Allegheny Mountains to be delivered to the Washington, DC, metropolitan area; produce moved upstream. If you'd like to ride in a replica boat, the National Park Service operates canal boats at some locations, and there's another canal boat on display just south of Cumberland.

Although most people consider the C&O Canal a historical trail, don't overlook its natural history. Landforms change dramatically and include tidewater at Georgetown where the Potomac empties into the Chesapeake Bay, the fertile rolling Piedmont farmlands (called "the sugar lands" by European settlers), the Great Valley of Maryland, and the Appalachian Mountains of western Maryland. The 20,000 acres composing the park are highly biodiverse. There is good birding along the canal with bald eagles, red-tailed hawks, turkeys, owls, several kinds of woodpeckers (including flickers and hairy, downy, and pileated), warblers, and other migrating songbirds in the spring and fall; and lots of waterbirds, including ospreys, great blue herons, ducks, and geese. It's common to see whitetailed deer, but less common to see foxes and beavers, though there's lots of evidence of the latter. Much of the area is heavily forested, primarily in hardwoods, and we especially enjoyed the Osage orange trees with their distinctive fall fruits (look for them on the ground).

Other highlights for us were the Great Falls area at mile 15, where we took a short detour on the Billy Goat Trail to see the impressive rapids on the Potomac (this side trail is rough); a short section of the trail near Harpers Ferry that is part of the Appalachian Trail; and the Potomac rapids at mile 41.6, where US Olympic kayakers often train. Several restaurants made the highlights list as well, including Betty's across the bridge in Shepardstown, West Virginia (where we enjoyed the bean soup with country ham and rivels, a closely guarded recipe); Weaver's in Hancock, Maryland (where the chocolate pie and other delicacies are worth the weight in the pack); and the School House Kitchen in Oldtown, Maryland (funky but friendly). You can probably tell we were often hungry!

Logistics for walking the C&O Canal are relatively easy. The walking season is long, with the summer months of June through August generally hot. Long springs and falls offer great opportunities for less crowded conditions; spring includes showy dogwood and redbud, and the foliage in the fall is pleasant. Even winter offers good opportunities for walking sections of the canal when there is no snow on the ground. The entire towpath is very well marked, and the mile markers make it easy to keep track of where you are. A series of camping areas are spaced roughly every 5 to 7 miles; see the National Park Service website for the park for more information, including a downloadable "Recreational Guide." The towpath meets roads periodically, and this provides access to B&Bs and other commercial lodgings and services, though you'll need to arrange for occasional rides because these services may be a little way off the towpath. The walk can be done in either direction, though if you start at the eastern end you walk along with the canal's twenty-two-year history of construction; walking west to east leads you (slightly) downhill. Walkers, lots of bikers, and occasional equestrians enjoy the towpath, and the canal itself is used in a few places by canoeists and kayakers (though most of the canal is dry). Commercial shuttle service is available, and there is train service between Washington, DC, and Cumberland.

The C&O Canal is a wonderful resource for walkers from the busy Washington, DC, metropolitan area and leads ambitious walkers into the hinterlands of rural Maryland. The C&O follows the course of the impressive Potomac River with all its natural history and traces the eventful and important human history of this area over the last several hundred years. With a number of road crossings, it's an ideal trail to walk in sections. The C&O Canal Association offers occasional group hikes, and these are a good option. And be sure to take advantage of the visitor centers along the way, as they'll make your walk more informative (and keep you entertained!).

Resources

Websites
Chesapeake and Ohio Canal National Historical Park: www.nps.gov/choh
C&O Canal Association: www.candocanal.org
C&O Canal Trust: www.canaltrust.org

Guidebook
Mike High, *The C&O Companion*, 2015.

App
C&O Canal Explorer Mobile App (recommended by the C&O Canal Trust)

After climbing the "Golden Staircase" over challenging Chilkoot Pass, prospectors followed a series of lakes and rivers through British Columbia, where they ultimately carried their gear on homemade boats to the Yukon goldfields.

Chilkoot Trail

Our first day's walk of the Chilkoot Trail traced the length of the Taiya River, from its ocean inlet to Sheep Camp, just below the start of the serious climb over Chilkoot Pass. We'd walked 12 miles through the rich rain forest on the western slope of the coastal mountains, gaining about a thousand feet in elevation. Our plan was to stay at Sheep Camp that night and walk over Chilkoot Pass the next day. We were tired but excited as we pitched our tent and cooked our dinner. After dinner, the National Park Service ranger (we'll call him "Rick") gathered all the campers (about twenty of us) for the evening talk. He did a good job of explaining the natural and cultural history of the Chilkoot Trail and preparing us for the next day's hike. He cautioned us about the potential dangers, and at the end of his talk admonished us not to die on the hike "because it creates too much paperwork." He continued, "But if you do die, make it epic." We all laughed—he did a good job of breaking the tension we were feeling about the historic and challenging climb we were about to do.

The once popular and distinctive Alaska centennial automobile license plate featured a stylized representation of a long string of hikers climbing up and over a high mountain pass—sort of like ants climbing a gigantic hill. This is the Chilkoot Trail, an important part of the history of Alaska, British Columbia, and, ultimately, the Yukon Territory. The Klondike Gold Rush of 1898 found thousands of Americans and others traveling frantically to reach the goldfields to the north. The standard route took them by boat to the head of the Taiya River and the boomtown of Dyea, but this was as far as the boats could travel. From there, prospectors had to hike over Chilkoot Pass to the promise of riches beyond. And this is where the real drama began.

The Chilkoot Trail is 33 miles long and connects Dyea, Alaska, and Bennett Lake, British Columbia, now two ghost towns. The pass marks the halfway point and is the boundary between the United States and Canada. Prospectors were subject to the "ton of goods" rule imposed by Canada and enforced at Chilkoot Pass by the Northwest Mounted Police; prospectors were

LOCATION
Alaska, United States, and British Columbia, Canada

LENGTH
33 miles

ACCOMMODATIONS
Commercial (e.g., Inns, B&Bs): No
Huts/Refuges: No
Backpacking/Camping: Yes

BAGGAGE TRANSFER
No

OPTION TO WALK IN SECTIONS
No

DEGREE OF CHALLENGE
High

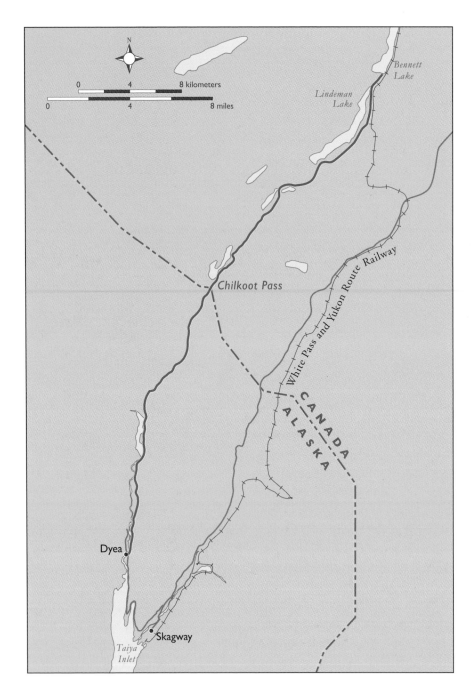

required to carry one ton of equipment and supplies into Canada to help ensure they would survive the journey north and a year in the wilderness. However, as it turned out, carrying these supplies over the pass may have been just as difficult as surviving the journey beyond. The "Golden Staircase," as this long pitch was euphemistically called, rises 2,800 feet in the 3.6 miles from Sheep Camp to the pass, with the final push a nearly 45-degree scramble up a huge talus slope. Some "stampeders," as they were called, needed as many as thirty trips to get their outfits across the pass. From the pass, the stampeders walked on frozen lakes and rivers in winter; in summer they used boats and wagons. Over 100,000 people started off for the Klondike goldfields, but fewer than 30,000 made it.

The rush over Chilkoot Pass transformed the area overnight, with Dyea growing to be one of the biggest towns in Alaska, boasting a population of nearly 10,000 and featuring 150 businesses catering to prospectors. Sheep Camp boasted sixteen hotels, fourteen restaurants, three saloons, two dance halls, a bathhouse, a lumberyard, and a post office. At the other end of the trail, the town of Bennett Lake swelled to 20,000 as prospectors built boats and waited for ice-out. On May 29, 1898, the ice broke, and within a week more than 7,000 boats departed for the Yukon town of Dawson. Hiking the wilderness of the Chilkoot Trail today, it's hard to believe the number of people the area attracted and the associated level of development, most of which has melted back into the earth. The next year, the White Pass and Yukon Route Railroad was completed, opening a new and easier route north, and the boomtowns died as quickly as they grew. Today the Chilkoot Trail is jointly administered by the US National Park Service and its Canadian

equivalent, Parks Canada, and commemorates the Klondike Gold Rush that caught the imagination of the world and stimulated a mass migration of humanity.

Few trails in the world offer more dramatic changes in landscape over such a short distance. On the American side, the trail begins at sea level, climbs through the rich Alaskan coastal rain forest, and then emerges above tree line into alpine tundra to reach Chilkoot Pass at 3,525 feet. It then descends through the subalpine boreal forest of British Columbia, past wild rivers and a chain of large lakes, reaching the shores of Bennett Lake. All this in just 33 miles! It's a strikingly beautiful and varied landscape that provides habitat for a rich diversity of animals including black and grizzly bears, mountain goats, river otters, wolves, moose, marmots, pikas, porcupines, wolverines, bald eagles, ptarmigan, ruffed grouse, arctic ground squirrels, seals, and pink and chum salmon.

Of course the trail has an important cultural component as well—it's "littered" with artifacts of the Klondike Gold Rush. As you walk the trail, it's common to find picks and shovels, boot soles, and tin cans discarded by discouraged prospectors. We even saw a wood-burning cookstove abandoned along the trail. These items are important evidence of the gold rush and should not be disturbed; the Chilkoot Trail is sometimes referred to as "the world's longest museum." But long before the gold rush of 1898, Chilkoot Pass was used as a trading route by the First Nations Tlingit people, who traded with inland tribes for moose and caribou hides, copper, and other goods unavailable along the coast. Chilkoot Pass is one of only three glacier-free corridors through the coastal mountains of Alaska.

(ABOVE LEFT) The British Columbia segment of the Chilkoot Trail follows the shores of lovely lakes and rivers.

(ABOVE) At Bennett Lake, travelers built boats to carry their requisite "ton of goods" for the onward journey to the Yukon.

(ABOVE) The Chilkoot Trail begins outside the historic boomtown of Dyea, where it follows a series of lakes and wetlands on an extended system of boardwalks.

(BELOW) The Chilkoot Trail is littered with artifacts left by overladen "stampeders" as they hurried to get to the Yukon goldfields.

There were several other highlights of our hike. A short side trail leads to Canyon City, one of the boomtowns along the trail where many historic artifacts still exist. Of course our hike over Chilkoot Pass was challenging, but very exciting and rewarding. It was cold (32 degrees at the pass—in the middle of August!) and foggy, and we carefully followed poles marking the route over large snowfields. We were the first walkers over the pass that day, arriving at the Parks Canada cabin on top in late morning. No one was there, but a thoughtful warden had left insulated jugs of hot tea. The second half of the trail leads hikers along mountain streams, around scenic lakes, and through deep forests to the shores of large Bennett Lake. Here, nearly all hikers ride to Skagway, the tourist-friendly gateway town just a few miles from Dyea, on the historic White Pass and Yukon Route Railroad. Many also purchase a box lunch to eat on the journey. The train ride is especially scenic, passing over high, dramatic wooden trestles and through tunnels. (Backpackers are relegated to a special car, presumably so as not to offend the tourists riding the train.) When we got back to Skagway, we celebrated with a pizza and enjoyed the "Days of '98 Show," a local musical comedy production (with audience participation) about the history of the area.

There are a number of logistical issues associated with hiking the Chilkoot Trail. Skagway itself is a little off the beaten track. We enjoyed a spectacular ride in a six-seat airplane from Juneau to Skagway and back again. Another option would be to arrive by ferry; the Alaska Marine Highway ferries operated by the state serve the coastal communities of Alaska, transporting people and freight. Unlike some of these coastal communities, however, Skagway also boasts road access, and it has become a popular cruise ship destination.

While the Chilkoot Trail is not long—most walkers take three to five days—this is a backpacking trip through a wilderness area. The weather on the Alaskan coast can be bad—lots of rain and wind and snow can fall in any month, and much of the trail is above tree line, exposing hikers to the weather. The trail can be rough with mud, roots, standing water, and slick and unstable rocks. In some places it is a route rather than a maintained trail. Large snowfields persist throughout the summer on both sides of Chilkoot Pass, and avalanche hazards persist through mid-July. Hikers may need as long as 12 hours to walk the 8 miles from Sheep Camp, over Chilkoot Pass, and to the next available campground at aptly named Happy Camp. Only walkers who are both physically fit and experienced backpackers should attempt this trail.

A permit (and nominal fee) is required from Parks Canada, and campsites must be reserved; see the websites listed in "Resources" below for details. Hikers are required to watch the film on bear safety and related matters before being issued a permit, and the permit must be picked up in person at the Trail Center in Skagway. Almost all hikers walk from south to north to keep the prevailing weather and wind at their backs and to replicate the historic hike. Camping is restricted to nine designated campgrounds where food storage facilities (metal lockers or poles) are provided to keep food away from bears (and bears away from the campgrounds!). No fires are allowed, and all cooking must be done on backpacking stoves in communal areas away from tent sites. Documentation of identity and citizenship must be carried to cross the international border.

The Chilkoot Trail may be unique and is a bit of a paradox. It represents the hardship of the tens of thousands of stampeders, but offers a recreational opportunity of the finest quality to today's walkers in the form of one of the world's most distinctive long-distance trails. It's both a natural and cultural resource, the detritus of the Klondike Gold Rush history deeply embedded in an outstanding natural landscape. And it is an interesting blend of unity and diversity—the trail representing the integrity of the Klondike Gold Rush era, but being managed by two countries that administer it in somewhat different ways. In the United States, the trail is part of Klondike Gold Rush National Historical Park and is administered by the US National Park Service, and in Canada, the trail is part of Chilkoot Trail National Historic Site and is managed by Parks Canada. Upon completing the hike at Bennett Lake, nearly all hikers ride the White Pass and Yukon Route Railway back to Skagway (see information on reservations at the website in the "Resources" section below); air service is also available. The hiking season is generally considered to be from June through early September. (For more great hikes in the US national parks, see our book *Walks of a Lifetime in America's National Parks*.)

We encourage walkers to prepare carefully and enjoy the Chilkoot Trail, one of the most unusual and interesting walks in the world. We don't know of any trail of this length that includes so much natural diversity along with such a rich and substantive history. Pretend you're a stampeder and try to imagine such a journey with your year's supply of goods. And remember—be considerate of the park rangers and wardens and don't create extra paperwork for them.

Resources

Websites
Chilkoot Trail National Historic Site: www.pc.gc.ca/en/lhn-nhs/yt/chilkoot
Klondike Gold Rush National Historical Park: www.nps.gov/klgo
White Pass and Yukon Route Railroad: https://wpyr.com

Map
National Geographic Trails Illustrated Map 254, *Chilkoot Trail, Klondike Gold Rush National Historical Park*, 2019

(ABOVE) The White Pass and Yukon Route Railway eventually offered a quicker and easier way for stampeders to carry their supplies into Canada; today, Chilkoot Trail hikers use the railroad for the dramatic return trip to Skagway.

(BELOW) Stampeders built wooden boats on the shores of Bennett Lake to carry their supplies north; boats were launched as soon as the ice melted.

The lovely town of Manarola, one of the five villages that compose Cinque Terre, made a great "base camp" for our week of walking in the region.

Cinque Terre

It had been a pleasant high-speed train ride from Rome to La Spezia, where we changed to the local train serving the dramatic coastal villages that compose Cinque Terre. When we arrived at the town of Manarola, our destination, it was the end of the day and starting to get dark. We walked into the historic town square, where a warren of narrow, winding streets and footpaths went in what seemed like every direction, and we wondered how we were going to find the way to our accommodations. As we stood there trying to figure out what to do, we heard someone call out our names in a lovely Italian accent. We turned and saw Marcella standing at the railing of the street above and behind us, motioning for us to meet and follow her. She greeted us warmly and we walked with her to the apartment we'd reserved. There she proceeded to show us around the tiny, spotless apartment with its endless view of the Mediterranean Sea. It's a stereotype that Italians talk with their hands, but Marcella was fluent in this way. She spoke no English and we spoke no Italian, but when Marcella left us we knew exactly what she'd said: how to operate the quirky refrigerator, where to shop for groceries, and how to fasten our wash tightly to the clothesline so it didn't blow out to sea (as she gestured dramatically). Our apartment served as our base of operations for the next week as we walked the spectacular trail that connects the communities of Cinque Terre and explored the network of trails that wander up, down, and across the impossibly steep slopes covered in olive and lemon groves and vineyards that rise above the seaside towns.

≋

Cinque Terre means quite literally "the five lands"; these are the five towns strung out along this historically isolated region of Italy, hard on the shores of the Ligurian Sea, a large bay of the Mediterranean. The region is often called the "Italian Riviera." These medieval fishing and farming villages rest at the base of steep cliffs that plunge into the waves. Over the centuries, much of the land above

LOCATION
Italy

LENGTH
Variable

ACCOMMODATIONS
Commercial (e.g., Inns, B&Bs): Yes
Huts/Refuges: Some
Backpacking/Camping: No

BAGGAGE TRANSFER
No

OPTION TO WALK IN SECTIONS
All

DEGREE OF CHALLENGE
Low–Moderate

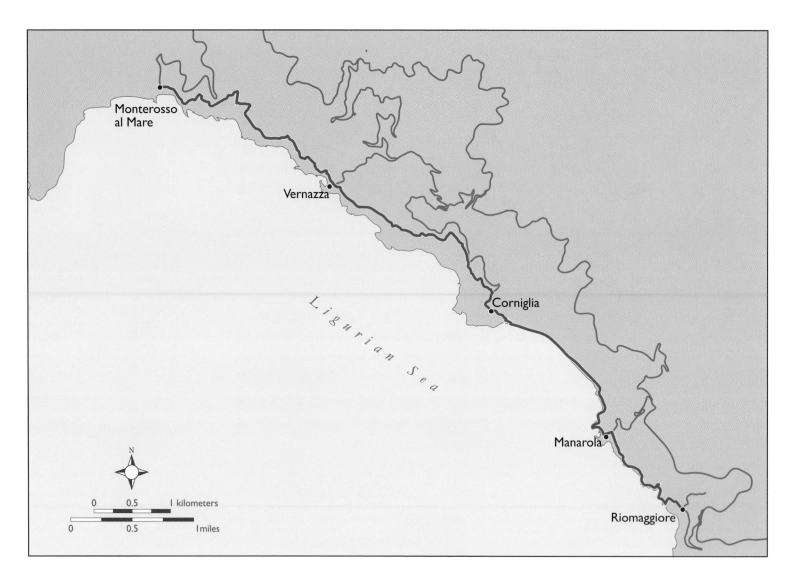

the towns has been terraced to support local agriculture, primarily olive and lemon trees, and grapes for wine. The area is so strikingly beautiful and historic that it has been declared a national park and a World Heritage Site.

The most famous trail is the Sentiero Azzurro (Blue Trail) that connects the five towns via the shortest route. Though the trail is only about 11 miles, it includes the occasional elevation gain and

loss. Moreover, most visitors take several days to walk it, admiring the spectacular views at every turn and exploring and lingering at each of the five towns. Indeed, this is the only way to fully absorb the rich, elegant atmosphere, and to sample the local foods, including fresh seafood, wine, pasta with local pesto, produce, focaccia, farinata, limoncino, and plenty of gelato. A local train provides frequent service between the towns, so it's easy to walk from one to the next and return at the end of the day by train. Small ferries also shuttle back and forth and offer a different perspective on the landscape. The streets and walkways of each village wind in complex and pleasing patterns, and buildings are painted in shades of pastel that seem to glow in the reflection of the azure-blue Mediterranean. The overall effect is stunning and almost magical.

But walking in Cinque Terre has become more challenging over the past decade. A torrential rainstorm caused extensive damage to the Sentiero Azzurro in 2011, closing sections of the trail, including the iconic Via dell'Amore (the "Love Walk," or the more Americanized "Lover's Lane"). Subsequent rain and rockslides have continued to cause problems. Walkers should consult online sources, particularly the website for Cinque Terre National Park (noted in the "Resources" section below), for updated information, and confirm trail conditions with local tourist offices upon

(ABOVE LEFT) Cinque Terre National Park offers 75 miles of trails through the terraced headlands above the five famous towns along the sea; on this day, we took a shuttle bus to the small village of Volastra, then walked down through olive groves and vineyards and a small pine forest to Corniglia, a delightful day trip.

(ABOVE) A large network of ancient paths lace the Cinque Terre region.

(ABOVE) The village of Vernazza includes a small, dramatic harbor and the medieval Belforte castle and watchtower.

(BELOW) The Sentiero Azzurro (Blue Trail) connects the five towns and clings to the steep cliffs over the Ligurian Sea.

arrival. However, there are 75 miles of trails in Cinque Terre National Park alone, so rewarding hiking opportunities are readily available. And the trains still run.

The Sentiero Azzurro connecting the five towns is linked to a much larger network of trails above the towns. There's a continuous ridgetop trail and many other "donkey tracks" that connect to the coastal path. Since a system of shuttle and local buses serve many of the higher locations, we sometimes took a bus uphill and walked down, enjoying seeing more of the landscape and the local culture. One day we rode from Manarola up to the inland village of Volastra and walked down through olive groves, vineyards, and a small pine forest to Corniglia, then took the train back to Manarola, a delightful day trip. All five towns have "sanctuary walks" that lead to religious retreats perched high on the cliffs overlooking the sea. For example, we rode a bus from Monterossa up to the interesting Nostra Signora de Soviore (Sanctuary of Our Lady of Soviore) and walked back to town, a half-day outing. The legendary Alta Via delle Cinque Terra (also known as the Sentiero Rosso, or Red Trail) is an ambitious 22-mile route that runs high above the Cinque Terre villages.

Riomaggiore is the southernmost village of Cinque Terra and some say the prettiest. It was established in the eighth century around a small natural harbor, and today fishermen "park" their brightly painted and highly varnished dories on the streets surrounding this harbor. The walk starts here and leads north for a short distance to Manarola. It's an easy, flat section where sweethearts can often be seen sitting on benches enjoying the unobstructed views of the sea and the striking shoreline (as well as enjoying each other's company, of course!). Manarola is the oldest of the five towns, small and especially scenic; we made it our "base camp," walking each day and returning each night, and this worked well. Walking north, the next village is Corniglia, which is distinctly different from the others. An ancient Roman village, the town is set above the sea and has no direct access to the water. The walk to Corniglia is not long, but it requires climbing the Lardarina Steps—nearly 400 of them—to reach the town. Local artists cluster on the steps, selling their paintings of the area. The walk continues north to Vernazza, founded about 1000 CE, the town some people think of as the best of Cinque Terre. It's a fishing village with a small, dramatic harbor and the medieval Belforte castle and watchtower jutting into the sea. Open to the public, this historic tower offers sweeping views of the whole length of the trail. The town includes a tiny port and charming piazza lined with restaurants and bars. The last section of trail leads to beautiful Monterossa al Mare. This is the largest town and has the only swimming beach, so it's always bustling with visitors. The section of the trail from Corniglia to Monterossa is a little steeper and rougher in places than the trail to the south.

Cinque Terre is an interesting blend of old and new. Because the landforms isolated these communities and kept modernity out, the communities have retained their old-world charm; many residents have multi-generational ties. Local people still fish and farm the area, and it's fascinating to watch them go about their daily activities. And, of course, the local foods they produce are a delight.

This is the birthplace of pesto sauce made with basil, cheese, garlic, pine nuts, and olive oil. These wonderful local foods are served in the restaurants and can be purchased in agricultural cooperatives in each town. Arrival of train service in the late nineteenth century provided easy access to this area, and it has become an increasingly popular tourist destination. However, strict regulation of development has maintained the special character of the area. For example, cars are not allowed in the five towns composing Cinque Terre. Many of the historic buildings are now used for tourist accommodations and restaurants, some of them very upscale.

(ABOVE) Monterossa al Mare is the largest of the five towns and the only one with a large swimming beach; it's always bustling with visitors.

(BELOW) Local fishermen "park" their colorful boats at the Riomaggiore town harbor.

Cinque Terre can be walked in any season, but early spring and fall are recommended. Summers can be hot and will certainly be crowded, perhaps overly so as the world discovers this region's appeal. There is a fee for walking the Sentiero Azzurro (Blue Trail), but it's nominal and may include unlimited use of the local train (depending on what type of pass is purchased). Passes can be bought locally and can cover one or more days; be sure to purchase one, as revenues help support management of the area (and they are required!). Since the towns are so close to one another, we recommend picking a village and making it your home base, eliminating the need to move your accommodations. We walked all of the Sentiero Azzurro and another 30 miles in the headlands of Cinque Terre National Park over a five-day period.

Cinque Terre is a marvel. In many ways it's a model of sustainability—it produces local and distinctive foods, it's interconnected by train, cars are banned from most towns, and development is controlled to preserve its history and cultural heritage. Walking is the ideal way to contribute to this sustainability and enjoy one of the finest and most distinctive cultural landscapes in the world.

Resources

Website
Cinque Terra National Park: https://national-parks.org/italy/cinque-terre

Guidebooks
Gillian Price, *Walking in Italy's Cinque Terre: Monterosso al Mare, Corniglia, Manarola, and Riomaggiore*, 2019
Rick Steves, *Rick Steves' Pocket Italy's Cinque Terre* (2nd edition), 2020

Maps
Freytag Berndt, *Cinque Terre - Portofino*, 2019
Cinque Terre Map + Guide to Trails, 2017
Paper maps are available at trail stations.

The classic Coast to Coast Walk across England begins on the Irish Sea at St. Bees and travels 190 miles across the country to Robin Hood's Bay on the North Sea.

Coast to Coast Walk

We were tingling with excitement as we arrived by train that afternoon in St. Bees, England, ready to engage the Coast to Coast Walk across the country, a hike we'd been planning for a year. We rose early the next day, enjoyed the traditional English breakfast (eggs, bacon, fried tomatoes, baked beans, mushrooms, and, of course, strong tea—good food to power a long day of walking) and ventured to the beginning of the trail hard on the shore of the Irish Sea. Tradition has it that walkers are supposed to dip the toes of their boots in the Irish Sea, a ritual to be repeated at the North Sea in two weeks' time. (Another version of the tradition has walkers carrying a stone from one shore to the other, but we didn't want to carry any extra weight!) It was a great feeling of accomplishment when we arrived at Robin Hood's Bay at the conclusion of our walk, and we made our way directly down to the shore for the ceremonial dipping of the toes—a fine celebration of our two-week walking adventure across England.

There's something very satisfying about walking all the way across a country, perhaps even more so when you walk from coast to coast. The Coast to Coast Walk, a 190-mile trek across northern England (admittedly, the "skinny" part of the country) is a transect of the national landscape: Much of the walk is routed through three large and distinctive national parks. National parks in England are not isolated tracts of public land as they often are in North America; instead, expect a working landscape with lots of character and historical depth, but with occasional moments of solitude.

The patron saint of this route is Alfred Wainwright, who "pioneered" it in the early 1970s by creatively linking a series of existing footpaths, bridle ways, minor roads, and other rights-of-way. The trail is locally known as "Wainwright's Way," a tribute to this folk hero of the British walking tradition. (It seems as though nearly everyone walks in England—we saw grannies with baby strollers on one section of the Coast to Coast Walk, and even encountered a very elderly man maneuvering his walker.) Curiously, the Coast to Coast Walk is not included in England's extensive system of

LOCATION
England

LENGTH
190 miles

ACCOMMODATIONS
Commercial (e.g., Inns, B&Bs):
Yes
Huts/Refuges: Some
Backpacking/Camping: Some

BAGGAGE TRANSFER
Yes

OPTION TO WALK IN SECTIONS
All

DEGREE OF CHALLENGE
Moderate

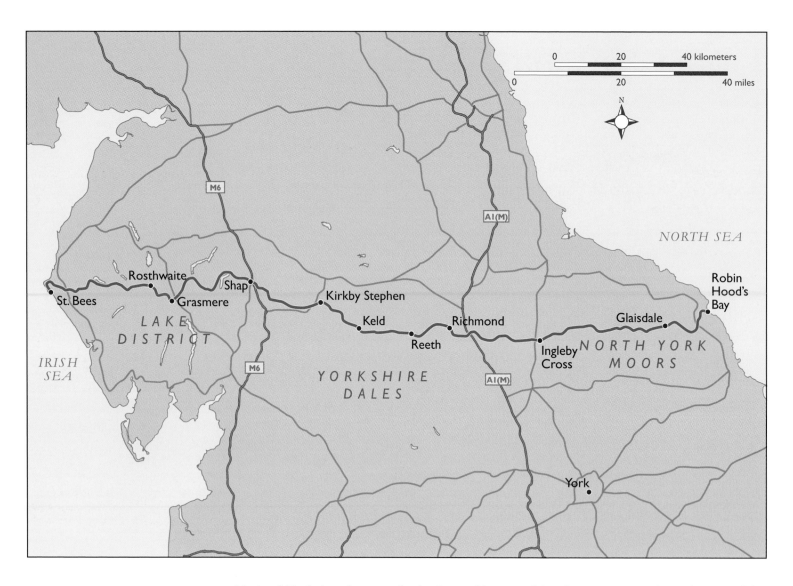

National Trails (see, for example, the Cotswold Way and South Downs Way in later chapters of this book), even though it may be the most popular trek in the country. Elevations along the trail vary from sea level to around 2,500 feet. Although most days involve a modest climb or two, the footing is good and the degree of challenge is rarely more than moderate.

The walk leads hikers over historic and graceful bridges that span the landscape's many "burns" (British for creek); this one is of medieval origin.

What will it be like? On the first day, as you ascend the dramatic headlands, you're introduced to sheep and then more sheep—and stiles of all designs, all forms of openings through (or over) the rock and wooden fences that define so much of the British countryside. You'll pass through both public and private lands. Public rights-of-way have a long tradition in Great Britain—as does the public's Code of Conduct when using another's land. (Essentially, the code says to leave things as you found them, and this includes closing farm gates you've opened.) Over the course of your journey, you'll walk on paths, quiet roads, through barnyards and towns, along recreational paths, and on an ancient Roman road, the northernmost one around. You'll walk through pastures with placid livestock (though the occasional bull will increase your heart rate a few ticks), around the perimeter of fields, and right down the middle of towns—the variety is energizing and joyful. We were never bored as we watched the landscape evolve on our long walk eastward.

At the end of the first day, you'll have entered the Lake District National Park, the most celebrated landscape in all of England. The Lake District includes some of the most "rugged" (by English standards) mountains in the country—and this means a relatively challenging first few days of walking. But the mountains (locally called "fells") are softened by the hill-farming culture, whitewashed cottages, and flocks of sheep that flow within the remarkable and striking networks of stone walls constructed over hundreds of years of human habitation. And true to its name, the Lake District is dotted with charming "waters," as lakes are known. Grasmere, heart of the Lake District and home

(ABOVE) Nine Standards is a collection of giant cairns, thought by some to have been built by Viking raiders.

(ABOVE RIGHT) Drystone walls and simple "Monopoly-style" barns characterize the lovely Swaledale region near the town of Keld.

to William Wordsworth, the famous Romantic poet, is an ideal spot for a "zero day," a no-hiking day to rest up from an ambitious start to the walk. It's a beautiful and tourist-friendly town, and offers a pilgrimage to Dove Cottage, Wordsworth's home.

Continue on to Yorkshire Dales National Park. "Dales" is British English for valleys, and these strikingly beautiful landforms were carved by glaciers some 10,000 years ago. The local culture is straight out of James Herriot's *All Creatures Great and Small* books and associated television series. The characters are everywhere, and we're sure we saw Tristan visiting one of the local pubs. Here the trail climbs up and over the Pennine Hills, which bisect the country on a north–south axis. Highlights of this section are Nine Standards, a series of giant rock cairns thought by some to have been built by Viking raiders; tidy "Monopoly piece" barns that dot the landscape; and the historic hamlet of Keld, the halfway point of the hike. Here, you'll cross the Pennine Way, the first of England's National Trails and the most iconic (see our book *Walks of a Lifetime: Extraordinary Hikes from Around the World* for a firsthand description of this and other National Trails in England and Wales).

The trail emerges from the Yorkshire Dales at Richmond, the largest town on the walk—and one of the most historic in all of England. There are many Richmonds around the world, but this is the original and maybe the best. Richmond boasts an impressive Norman castle, several museums, cobbled streets, and historic inns; about two-thirds of the way along the trail, it makes an ideal layover.

A long day's walk beyond Richmond, the trail enters the North York Moors National Park for the last several days of walking. Sometimes described as a bleak landscape, this is an inaccurate notion for these dramatic moorlands cloaked in heather, though civilization is spotty through this area. The tops of the moors offer exciting first views of the North Sea and the sheer cliffs beside the charming village of Robin Hood's Bay. Down the steep cobbles you go to the water's edge and the ceremonial dipping of the toe.

The Coast to Coast Walk is serviced throughout its length by a ready and varied stock of B&Bs, guesthouses, and country inns, and the ubiquitous pubs serve hearty meals, good beer, and lots of local color. The primary walking season is July and August, when you must book your reservations well ahead. However, walking can be done in the shoulder seasons as well, with September an especially good choice. Many of the towns along the trail are well connected by a network of local trains and buses. For a modest fee, you can avail yourself of baggage transfer service and walk with only a daypack.

It's easy to get to the start and back from the finish of the Coast to Coast using public transportation, primarily trains. Several walking companies can assist you in planning your trip. If walking the whole trail isn't possible, your walk could be a single day, a section, or a series of "best of" sections. Two weeks is the minimum recommended if you choose to cover the whole distance, though Wainwright would suggest more time to "stand and stare" at this quintessential English landscape.

This is England, not the wilderness, at least not by North American standards, and the nearest road is rarely more than an hour or two away. However, you must be prepared. A good guidebook, maps, and an app are a necessity, as the trail is not well marked in places. And the weather can (and will) change quickly, limiting visibility and threatening hypothermia, so dress and pack accordingly, including a jacket, "waterproofs" (as the British say), and a hat. This is a splendid walk, long enough to relax into the adventure and varied enough to stimulate a high level of energy, excitement, and enthusiasm. With definitive starting and ending points, it's deeply satisfying. It's one of our favorites, and we recommend it in the highest terms.

Resources

Guidebooks

Henry Stedman and Stuart Butler, *The Coast to Coast Path*, 2022
Terry Marsh, *The Coast to Coast Walk: St. Bees to Robin Hood's Bay*, 2017

(ABOVE) Each village along the Coast to Coast Walk seems to outdo the last with classic English gardening.

(BELOW) Hikers are treated to a rich stock of B&Bs, small hotels, and pubs along the Coast to Coast Walk.

High-elevation alpine meadows along the Colorado Trail are filled with wildflowers; the blue columbine is the Colorado state flower.

Colorado Trail

We had camped that night in rugged and dramatic Elk Creek Canyon, a narrow gorge with an abundance of cascades, waterfalls, and inviting campsites. As usual, we were up at dawn, scrambling out of our tent into the chilly mountain air, getting back on the trail as quickly as possible to warm up. But there was a little more urgency than usual in our steps as we headed for Elk Park, a large meadow in the middle of the Weminuche Wilderness. Here, we were told, the Durango-Silverton Narrow Gauge Railroad stops for hikers—if you know the right signal—and we wanted a ride into Silverton, where we had a reservation at a bed-and-breakfast that included the hot tub we'd been dreaming about. The signal? Don't wave your arms over your head or the conductor will think you're simply sending a greeting. Cross your arms back and forth across your knees (sort of like doing the Charleston) and the train will stop. So when we saw the train approaching, we did our dance in the wilderness and, sure enough, the train stopped for us—to the obvious amusement of the tourists riding the train. It's a beautiful 45-minute ride from Elk Park along the Animas River (the "river of lost souls") into colorful and historic Silverton, where we enjoyed a welcome respite from backpacking—clean sheets, a dinner that hadn't been freeze-dried, and a long soak in the hot tub—on our monthlong walk of the glorious Colorado Trail.

Planning our walk of the Colorado Trail was a bit intimidating. First, the trail itself is challenging; it wanders well over 500 miles through the Rocky Mountains between Denver and Durango. Like the mountains themselves, the trail rises and falls, but many of its miles are spent above 10,000 feet, often well above (the highest point on the trail is 13,334 feet, and the full distance of the trail includes nearly 90,000 feet of elevation gain). Second, much of the trail is wild, traversing eight ranges of the Rocky Mountains and five major river systems, crossing six national forests and six wilderness areas. But like most long-distance trails, there are a number of roads that cross the Colorado Trail as well as

LOCATION
Colorado, United States

LENGTH
567 miles

ACCOMMODATIONS
Commercial (e.g., Inns, B&Bs): Some
Huts/Refuges: No
Backpacking/Camping: Yes

BAGGAGE TRANSFER
No

OPTION TO WALK IN SECTIONS
Some

DEGREE OF CHALLENGE
Moderate–High

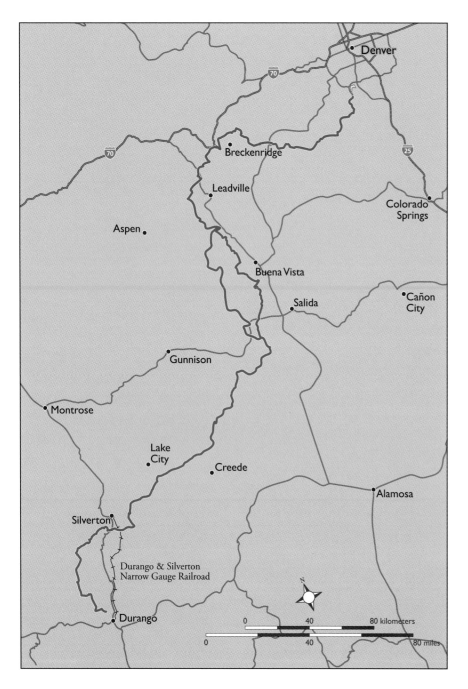

Durango & Silverton
Narrow Gauge Railroad

0   40   80 kilometers

0   40   80 miles

side trails that feed into it, and these offer relatively easy access to a string of colorful Colorado towns, including Breckenridge, Leadville, Buena Vista, Salida, Creede, Lake City, and Silverton. These towns offer access to the trail and are resupply stations as well. We planned our five weeks of walking (spread over successive summers) to hike as many miles of the trail as possible, but also to take advantage of the region's small towns, learning about the area's history and culture and meeting its people.

Much of the trail follows the Continental Divide, a long section of which coincides with the roughly 3,100-mile Continental Divide National Scenic Trail (CDT). And much of it is above tree line, crossing meadows filled with world-class displays of wildflowers, including the striking blue columbine, the state flower. The trail passes through pure stands of aspen, isolated clusters of ancient bristlecone pines, stunted krummholz vegetation (trees that have adapted to harsh growing conditions by staying close to the ground), and many square miles of alpine tundra. It also passes through historic Camp Hale (now abandoned), home of the famous 10th Mountain Division of the US Army that trained here and fought so heroically in Italy in World War II; this area is now a national monument.

There were many other highlights of walking the Colorado Trail: Hiking the high Collegiate Range, whose peaks—Mounts Princeton, Harvard, Yale, and Columbia—were named in honor of the Ivy League geologists who spent summers with their students studying the area. The southern portion of the Sawatch Range, where the names of the mountains honor another era of their history—Mounts Antero, Shavano, Ouray, and Chipeta—Ute Indian Nation chiefs and notables. The elk on Sargent's Mesa. Camping at Baldy Lake. Our layover day in Creede, a town directly off the pages of

(ABOVE LEFT) Hikers share the Colorado Trail with equestrians and must yield the right-of-way.

(ABOVE) The Rocky Mountains were thoroughly explored for valuable minerals, and the trail features many artifacts of this historic period, including this miner's cabin.

Western history books, its "downtown" composed of several blocks of nineteenth-century buildings that sprang up overnight with the discovery of silver in the late 1800s. Celebrating that night with a pizza and bottle of wine on the balcony of our room at the Creede Hotel overlooking Main Street. Crossing the headwaters of the famous Rio Grande. Walking through the high San Juan Range, what many people feel is the most striking part of the Rocky Mountains because the peaks are high and dramatic, their location on the western side of the Rockies collecting more rain and snow and supporting the greatest abundance of wildflowers. Fred and RJ, who gave us rides when we needed them.

The Colorado Trail represents the best of the natural history of the Rocky Mountains, but it's also a great cultural landscape. The towns adjacent to the trail are a reflection of the engaging history of the region, including its architecture, institutions, food, arts, and mythology. The people we met were as genuine and trustworthy as they were colorful. They and the folks before them shaped the landscape over the years, and the reciprocal is just as true. This process continues today, and institutions like the Colorado Trail Foundation (which maintains the trail and produces its guidebook) and Gudy Gaskill (the trail's founder) are the latest and maybe greatest chapters.

Walking the full length of the trail normally requires six weeks or more, though this is a little complicated. The trail includes a large loop as it passes through the dramatic Collegiate Range, and walkers must choose between the Collegiate East and West routes (both routes are about 80 miles, though the western route is co-located with the CDT and generally considered more challenging; the full Colorado Trail overlaps 235 miles of the CDT). Thus, the Colorado Trail has 567 miles of

(ABOVE) High alpine tundra is lush and supports lots of wildflowers.

(ABOVE RIGHT) We camped in the Weminuche Wilderness and caught a ride the next morning on the Durango-Silverton Narrow Gauge Railroad to Silverton, where we enjoyed a night in a B&B and a welcome soak in a hot tub.

trails, but a thru-hike is about 485 miles. We walked the 72-mile section from the beginning of the trail near Denver to Kenosha Pass, and the next year walked 330 miles of the trail between Kenosha Pass and Durango (using the eastern option around the Collegiate Peaks), skipping a few segments as time constraints demanded.

We recommend several sections in particular. The 12.5-mile walk from CO 9 to Copper Mountain is strenuous and well above tree line, but offers stunning views and lush wildflowers. The free Summit Stage shuttle bus serves the local communities and offers convenient transportation back to your starting point, making it quite easy to hike without a car. Later, the trail makes a sweeping turn around the town of Leadville, which features access to several of the state's 14,000-foot mountains and a number of high mountain lakes. The day hike from San Luis Pass to CO 149 is the Rocky Mountains at their best. Much of the trail traverses the La Garita Wilderness, where the trail is faint in some areas and seems isolated everywhere; in fact, we saw no one along the trail that day. In places, the trail is marked with historic stone cairns that were built to guide a famous stock drive, and you feel like you're experiencing the true West. (We experienced some drama as well—thunderstorms built up early that day, menaced us with hail as we hurried across a broad saddle just under 13,000 feet, and then chased us all the way across 3-mile Snow Mesa.) We recommend any of the sections

The iconic Collegiate Range of the Rocky Mountains is named for the Ivy League geologists who studied the origin of these 14,000-foot mountains.

along the San Juan's for gorgeous mountain scenery. And the last day's walk to the end of the trail near Durango was bittersweet, but an extra day in lively Durango, plus the clean clothes we had mailed ourselves there, softened the blow of ending our adventurous hike.

Primary issues associated with walking all or part of the Colorado Trail concern its length and elevation. Of course, the trail can only be walked in summer, with some of the higher passes retaining snow well into June. It's common for thunderstorms to build on warm summer afternoons, so it's important to plan your hike to avoid high elevations above tree line after lunch. Take time to acclimate to the high elevations and lower levels of oxygen—arrive in the area a few days early and start your walk with short days, building distance as your body adjusts by producing more red blood cells. And be sure to drink plenty of water. Be prepared for warm, sunny days and use sunblock liberally, and remember that temperatures drop rapidly at night due to high radiational cooling. A permit isn't needed for the Colorado Trail, though the US Forest Service generally asks walkers to complete a self-service permit when entering the wilderness areas through which much of the trail traverses. Most thru-hikers start their walks on the eastern end of the trail because elevations are a little lower.

The Colorado Trail Foundation, a nonprofit group that helps steward the trail, maintains an extensive, authoritative, and helpful website that should be consulted closely by all Colorado Trail

Dramatic mountains and lovely forests make the San Juan Range one of the favorites for many hikers on the Colorado Trail.

hikers. The organization's *The Colorado Trail: The Official Guidebook of the Colorado Trail Foundation* is the bible of the trail; read it carefully. The foundation also offers some guided walks each year. Consider joining the organization to help support all its good work.

The Colorado Trail is long and full of potential adventures, but don't be intimidated. There's a lot of wisdom in the old saying in the hiking community: "Walk your own walk." No one says you have to walk all 485 miles (or is it 567 miles?), though the thought of a grand thru-hike is tantalizing. Pick an appealing section or two and start from there. The Colorado Trail is one of the finest long-distance walks in the United States, combining nature and culture in a harmonious whole. Whether you're looking for a backpacking trip or want to walk one day at a time, this trail's variety guarantees it'll have what you want. See for yourself.

Resources

Website
Colorado Trail Foundation: https://coloradotrail.org

Guidebooks
Colorado Trail Foundation, *The Colorado Trail* (9th edition), 2017
Colorado Trail Foundation, *The Colorado Trail Databook*, 2021

Map
National Geographic Trails Illustrated Map, *Colorado Trail Map Pack*, 2017

App
Colorado Trail by FarOut (recommended by the Colorado Trail Foundation)

Sheep are synonymous with the Cotswold region; in Anglo-Saxon times, sheep were grazed in enclosures called "cots" on the region's hills, called "wolds."

Cotswold Way

March was approaching, and we had a window of opportunity—ten days available for an adventure. Of course we wanted to do a walk, but where? The Cotswold Way had been on our "to-do" list for several years, but early spring is hardly the traditional walking season in England. But the long-range weather forecast looked promising—cool, but little chance of rain (or snow!)—so we decided to go for it. Soon we were delighted to be back on the trail, cold-weather gear close at hand, and we were enjoying the benefits of off-season walking. Yes, it was brisk, but walking keeps you warm! Our nightly pub meals tasted better than ever, and we always managed to find a table close to the fire. And, it seemed, we had the trail to ourselves. The trees had not yet leafed out, so the views across the landscape were expansive and striking. March is lambing season in this country of sheep, and we stopped time and again to watch the newborns running and jumping for the pure joy of it, playfully butting heads, and returning to nuzzle with their mothers when they were tired and hungry. Our recommendation? Consider walking in the off-season when the weather allows—it expands the walking year and offers a different kind of adventure.

―――――― ≈ ――――――

The Cotswold Way is one of England's National Trails, running 102 miles in the west-central region of the country between the Roman city of Bath in the south to the lovely English market town of Chipping Campden in the north. It wanders along the ridge of the Cotswold Hills, dropping down into the valleys to visit a series of historic towns and villages. Though the elevated features of this landscape are popularly called hills, the principal geologic feature of the region is more technically a very large escarpment—an elevated, tilted layer of rock. The Cotswold escarpment is nearly 100 miles long, rises gradually from the east to elevations around 900 feet, and drops off dramatically (the "scarp") to the west. The escarpment forms the eastern edge of the valley of the Severn River, the longest river in Britain, and the Cotswold Way offers outstanding views of this lovely valley from the raised land on which it's sited. Between Bath and Chipping Campden, the route deliberately

LOCATION
England

LENGTH
102 miles

ACCOMMODATIONS
Commercial (e.g., Inns, B&Bs): Yes
Huts/Refuges: No
Backpacking/Camping: Limited

BAGGAGE TRANSFER
Yes

OPTION TO WALK IN SECTIONS
All

DEGREE OF CHALLENGE
Moderate

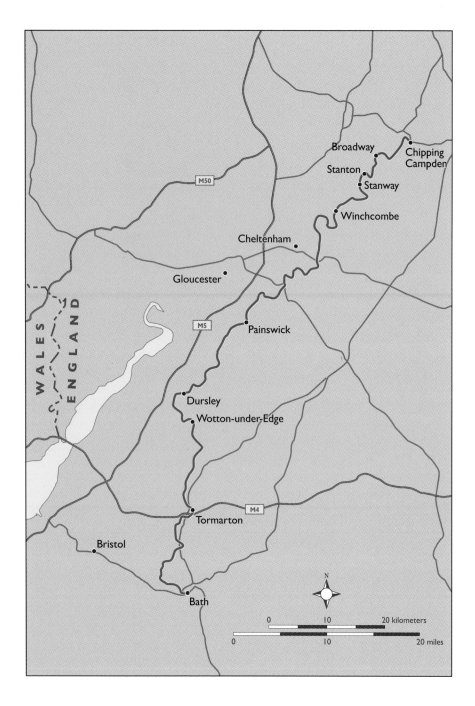

meanders, visiting historic towns, stately homes, and other cultural sites, along with rolling pastures and farmlands divided by drystone walls, and old-growth beech forests.

If there were an "England National Park," it would be in the Cotswolds. History has flowed over Britain in successive waves since about 8,000 BCE, but time seems to have stopped in the Cotswold region around 1800 CE, when the area's wool industry began to collapse. The Industrial Revolution mostly bypassed the Cotswolds and left behind a living history of prosperous farms, thatched-roof cottages, well-to-do villages, and large market towns. And all of this is set against the Cotswold Hills, the Severn River, and the surrounding pastoral valleys. For many people, this is the idyllic, picture-postcard vision of rural England, which is validated by designation of the Cotswolds as the largest Area of Natural Beauty in England and Wales.

Of course the walk can be done in either direction, but we chose to start in Bath and walk north to keep the sun and wind at our backs. Stunning Bath is a World Heritage Site. Celts worshipped there during the Iron Age, Romans built an elaborate bathing complex and enjoyed the natural hot springs for 400 years, and later the Georgians erected magnificent buildings around and over the baths. It's easy to imagine you are in one of Jane Austen's novels because the center of town has changed so little since she lived and wrote there. Later still, fashionable Victorians traveled to Bath to "take the waters." Take the time to spend a couple of hours on one of the free guided historical and architectural walks of the town. You'll undoubtedly find places that demand further exploration (the baths themselves or the Jane Austen Museum, for example), so it's best not to rush onto the trail itself. Stonehenge, one of the most famous archaeological sites

in the world, is a short drive from Bath, and it's easy to book a reasonably priced half-day tour if you wish to include this diversion.

The trail starts from the southern terminus of Bath Abbey and leads through a parade of charming villages and towns. Painswick is known as the "jewel of the Cotswolds," and its church boasts the area's largest collection of carved tombs. The hamlet of Stanway reveals a small cluster of historic buildings, including a Jacobean manor and a twelfth-century church. Nearby Stanton has been restored and is considered "the perfect Cotswold village" with its thatched-roof cottages. Broadway boasts one of the most photographed main streets in England, and the Broadway Tower outside the town is an iconic folly designed to suggest the remains of a castle. Chipping Campden is an elegant old market town at the northern terminus of the trail, and its High Street and "wool" church are showpieces. Most of the historic buildings along the walk are constructed from the native oolitic limestone (formed when dinosaurs roamed) that composes the escarpment. This is a rich honey-colored stone that almost glows, and the buildings seem to be extensions of the very land on which they were built.

Just as geology has helped shape the Cotswolds, so have sheep. The Romans developed sheep farming on large estates in this region, and this farming expanded in Anglo-Saxon times. The sheep

(ABOVE LEFT) The history of the Cotswold Way is deep; Neolithic burial sites are scattered along the trail.

(ABOVE) The southern end of the Cotswold Way is in Bath with its Roman heritage.

(ABOVE) Several towns along the trail feature historic homes with thatched roofs.

(ABOVE RIGHT) These ruins and many other historic buildings in the Cotswold region are constructed of native honey-colored limestone that almost glows.

were grazed in large "cots," meaning enclosures, on the "wolds," or hills. But these weren't just any sheep, they were Cotswold Lions—big, fast-growing, hornless animals with white faces and, most importantly, heavy, long fleece. These sheep were the foundation of the English wool trade with Europe and brought great prosperity to the Cotswold region. The Norman saying was "In Europe the best wool is English; in England the best wool is Cotswold." In the thirteenth century there were half a million sheep in Britain, four times the human population. Most human landscapes along the route (towns, churches, manor houses, markets) can be traced to this wool trade and the money it generated. When the Industrial Revolution in the north of England offered more efficient means of production, the Cotswold wool economy declined precipitously. Fortunately, several flocks of Cotswold Lions still graze in the region's pastures, and the breed is making a comeback.

You'll see evidence along the trail of habitation and prosperity that are much older than the sheep trade. Nearly one hundred Neolithic long barrows mark ancient burial sites; the most impressive of these is Belas Knap, started around 3,000 BCE. There are Iron Age hill forts that attest to the need for protection from warring tribes. There are ruins of Roman villas and fragments of Roman roads. There are medieval farming terraces and foundations of Norman buildings, sometimes reused by later Britons. The history rolls on and on—sometimes on top of itself, as sites have layer upon layer of use. Various places along the trail are associated with some wonderful legends and myths—some Saxon, some Norman, some English. And the names of places leave no doubt you're in England—Birdlip, Crickley Hill, Old Sodbury, Wotton-under-Edge.

Allow a minimum of seven days to do this walk—and a few more would offer time to explore the many highlights of this cultural landscape, including some delightful short walks off the main trail. Well served by delightful B&Bs and pubs along the route, the walk is not really appropriate for camping (though it's allowed in a few commercial campgrounds). The main gateway cities and towns are Bath, Gloucester, Cheltenham, Oxford, and Stratford-upon-Avon, with good train links and bus service and some local taxis. The Cotswold Way is one of the most effectively way-marked trails in England (look for the iconic acorn symbol that marks all of England's National Trails). The gentle route is sometimes on paths that were traveled by shepherds, priests, and tradesmen through the ages, and sometimes on more modern country lanes and roads. The Cotswold Way is not for someone who seeks solitude and wants a sense of wilderness; it's a walk for those who appreciate the human touch upon a welcoming land. And remember to consider walking the Cotswold Way (and other trails) during its extended shoulder seasons.

Resources

Website
National Trails of England/Cotswold Way: www.nationaltrail.co.uk/cotswold

Guidebooks
Andrew McCluggage, *Trekking the Cotswold Way, Two-way Trekking Guide with OSI 1:25K Maps*, 2022
Kev Reynolds, *The Cotswold Way: Two-Way National Trail Description*, 2016

(ABOVE) Ancient oak trees are a highlight along the Cotswold Way, and are especially dramatic in winter without their leaves.

(BELOW) Tea shops in villages along the trail offer hikers well-deserved refreshment.

The historic town of Pavlov is viewed from the ruined castle in the surrounding Pavlovske Hills; the town was established in the twelfth century and is known for its well-preserved castle complex and large fishponds.

Czech Greenways

We were excitedly walking through the medieval town of Cesky Krumlov when we spotted a brochure advertising "Romantic Classic Concerts." And there was one that night! What a perfect celebratory nightcap to our lovely day on the trail. We arrived that evening at candlelit Jesuit Hall, a small performance space in the town's former sixteenth-century Jesuit Dormitory, well before the appointed hour and found ourselves the first to arrive, choosing front-row seats. When the concert began, there were only about a dozen people in attendance. The concert by the small chamber orchestra featured a selection of classical pieces by Mozart, Bach, Vivaldi, Dvorak, and others. It was magical, the music providing a lovely aural dimension to our walk through historic central Europe. And the orchestra seemed to be playing just for us.

———— ≈ ————

The Czech Greenways is an extensive and diverse system of trails through the Czech Republic that connects the great European capitals, Vienna, Austria, and Prague, Czech Republic. This web of trails and country roads totals approximately 350 miles and wanders through historic towns and cities, lovely forests and vineyards, along rivers and around lakes, and to the doorstep of many impressive castles, churches, chateaus, follies, and other architectural monuments. It passes through several UNESCO World Heritage Sites and Biosphere Reserves. Much of the trail network consists of centuries-old salt, silver, and amber trade routes and trails established by the Czech Hiking Club over the last one hundred years or more. A portion of the trail network takes walkers behind the Iron Curtain, where the remaining barbed-wire fences and watchtowers are reminders of the draconian restrictions on freedom of movement imposed by the Communist Party of Czechoslovakia in the 1930s and 1940s. Communist control was peacefully overthrown in what is commonly called the Velvet Revolution in 1989, and the nation was subsequently divided into two countries, the Czech Republic and the Slovak Republic (popularly known as Slovakia).

LOCATION
Austria and Czech Republic

LENGTH
350 miles

ACCOMMODATIONS
Commercial (e.g., Inns, B&Bs): Yes
Huts/Refuges: No
Backpacking/Camping: No

BAGGAGE TRANSFER
Yes

OPTION TO WALK IN SECTIONS
All

DEGREE OF CHALLENGE
Moderate

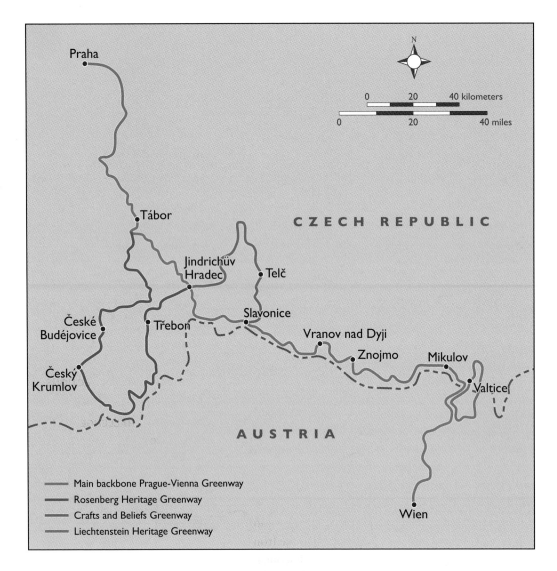

Praha

Tábor

CZECH REPUBLIC

Jindřichův
Hradec

Telč

Slavonice

České
Budějovice

Třebon

Vranov nad Dyji

Znojmo

Mikulov

Český
Krumlov

Valtice

AUSTRIA

—— Main backbone Prague-Vienna Greenway
—— Rosenberg Heritage Greenway
—— Crafts and Beliefs Greenway
—— Liechtenstein Heritage Greenway

N

0   20   40 kilometers

0   20   40 miles

Wien

The nonprofit organization that helps manage the network of trails, Czech Greenways, was founded in the early 1990s by a group of Czech and American citizens who were catalyzed by their mutual interest in preserving the unique and powerful natural and cultural landscape of the Czech Republic. The trail network is modeled after the Hudson River Valley Greenway in New York State. Generally, the route follows the Dyje River in southern Moravia and the Vltava River in southern and central Bohemia, with Vienna and Prague marking the two ends of the trail network. Walks of any length can be taken along the Greenways, but walking trips tend to average about a week and use public transportation to link various sections of the trail network. Vienna and Prague are the usual starting/ending points. We contacted Czech Greenways Travel Club, and they helped us arrange a seven-day walk that started in Vienna and finished in Prague, using public transportation—a bus, a taxi, and a train—where needed. It's not feasible for most people to walk the approximately 350 miles of the trail network, but our weeklong experience of approximately 100 miles included many of the highlights of this historic cultural landscape. We spent a few additional days walking in both Vienna and Prague and strongly recommend these add-ons.

Vienna is the capital of Austria and is located near the Czech border. The city center is a UNESCO World Heritage Site (though proposals to construct skyscraper buildings has put this designation in jeopardy). Vienna is known as the "City of Music" for its musical legacy that includes

luminaries Beethoven and Mozart. Major visitor attractions include the imperial palaces of the Hofburg and Schönbrunn; we especially enjoyed walking the grounds of the Upper and Lower Belvedere baroque palaces, a historic complex of buildings and extensive gardens.

After a short train ride out of Vienna, our first day of walking on the Greenways trails took us through the heart of the Lednice-Valtice Cultural Landscape, a UNESCO World Heritage Site that encompasses over 100 square miles and highlights the Lednice Chateau, surrounded by extensive parklands designed according to English romantic traditions. Parklands include the lovely Temple of Diana and the smaller "Minaret," classic examples of architectural "follies," large garden buildings constructed primarily for decoration. The town of Valtice is known as the center of winemaking in Moravia and has a network of large fishponds that attract a variety of birdlife.

The next two days of walking took us over the Pavlovske Hills, around lakes, and through vineyards, connecting the towns of Mikulov, Vranov, and Pavlov. Highlights were the Archeopark Pavlov (a contemporary archaeological museum), the ruins of the Maidenburg and Orphan Castles, and the Vranov nad Dyji Castle. Much of the walk was through the Podyji National Park. The historic town of Mikulov (and its distinctive castle) is the center of Czech winemaking. The town of Pavlov was established around the middle of the twelfth century and includes a historic town center and a well-preserved castle complex. Known for its large system of fishponds built between 1585 and 1589, it features the largest fishpond in the world. Along this walk, we encountered elaborate barbed-wire fences and watchtowers left over from the Communist period and designed to keep citizens from escaping Czechoslovakia and into Austria. Now, however, the Austrian border is an optional short,

(ABOVE LEFT) The culturally rich city of Vienna, Austria, anchors one end of the extensive trail network that runs through the Czech Republic to Prague; the Upper Belvedere is one of the many historic palaces built here.

(ABOVE) The town of Telc is known for its stately homes featuring colorful Renaissance facades.

(ABOVE) Barbed wire and guard towers are left on purpose to remind citizens of the repression that was forced upon them during the Communist era.

(ABOVE RIGHT) The trail segment that leads out of the town of Trebon follows the shoreline of a large fishpond.

peaceful walk on a bridge across the Dyje River and into the small, lovely Austrian town of Hardegg; we enjoyed this little side trip.

Our walk the next day was in the south Bohemia region and featured the dramatic town of Telc, a UNESCO World Heritage Site that features Telc Castle and a central square (in the shape of a long rectangle) that looks like a movie set. The original wooden homes that lined the streets burned in 1530 but were rebuilt by Italian craftsmen to incorporate pink, yellow, and blue Renaissance facades with high gables and arcades, and the result is stunning.

The next few days of walking took us through beautiful countrysides of woods, open fields, and a series of lakes, ponds, and rivers, and to historic sites that included the towns of Trebon (with its dramatic Chateau Trebon) and Jindrichuv Hradec. This landscape is a part of the global system of UNESCO Biosphere Reserves.

A final day of walking led us to one of the highlights of the trip, the south Bohemia town of Cesky Krumlov, an area that has become an especially popular destination for tourists in the Czech Republic. This is another UNESCO World Heritage Site and features a sprawling castle complex, one of the largest in Europe, that was founded in the thirteenth century and rebuilt 300 years later in Renaissance style; the complex includes forty richly decorated Renaissance and baroque buildings and palaces (including the elaborate Baroque Theatre, several courts, and an extensive garden). The charming old-town section of this small city sits directly along a large bend in the Vltava River.

From Cesky Krumlov, we took a bus to Prague and finished our hike on the Czech Greenways with a couple of days of walking and sightseeing in this political, cultural, and economic center of central Europe. Prague is the largest city in the Czech Republic and is its capital, and is walker friendly.

Popular attractions in this UNESCO World Heritage Site include Old Town Square with its famous astronomical clock (installed in 1410), Prague Castle, the Jewish Quarter, St. Vitus Cathedral, the Vltava River (a short cruise is a good way to see much of the city and the surrounding area), and the fancifully decorated Charles Bridge that crosses the river, connecting the city and Prague Castle.

Thanks to Czech Greenways for stewarding its namesake network of trails in central Europe. Much of this part of the world was relatively new to us, and walking proved to be a great way to experience and appreciate it. We found the trails to be easy to follow and well maintained, and to offer a steady supply of lovely countryside and rich history. Accommodations typically provided breakfast, and towns offered lots of choices for evening meals. We usually bought supplies for picnic lunches at small shops along the way. Wine and beer are made in large quantities in the region and are readily available. In fact, the Czech people joking call beer "liquid bread."

Resources

Website
Friends of Czech Greenways: www.pragueviennagreenways.org

(LEFT) Lovely and historic Cesky Krumlov includes a sprawling castle complex and a medieval town center, and is a favorite of visitors to the Czech Republic.

(ABOVE) Prague is the highly walkable capital city of the Czech Republic at the eastern end the Czech Greenways; its astronomical clock was installed in 1410.

(BELOW) The opulent dining room is just one of many rooms that fill the landmark Valtice Chateau.

The Twelve Apostles, an iconic group of sea stacks at the west end of the Great Ocean Walk, is the scenic symbol of this dramatic trail.

Great Ocean Walk

We've stayed in lots of mountain huts/refuges and hostels (you don't have to be a "youth" to do so). They were often rugged structures in remote places with, at best, a semi-private room, toilet and shower facilities, hearty dinners and breakfasts prepared by the hut master, and, of course, the company of fellow hikers. What hostels may lack in amenities they make up for in terms of location—and the food and company are always welcome. But the Eco Beach Youth Hostel in Apollo Bay, Victoria, Australia, neatly situated at the edge of a lively fishing and tourist town that serves as the gateway to the Great Ocean Walk, breaks all the traditional rules. This is a relatively new structure that is leading hostels into the twenty-first century. It's an architecturally designed passive solar structure built to use 50 percent less water and energy than comparable accommodations, and it combines guest comfort with functionality to generate a big "wow" factor. There are two communal kitchens complete with everything a traveler could want (and some things a traveler might not even think of, such as bread making machines), comfortable lounges around a fireplace, internet service, laundry facilities, a rooftop terrace, and patio space with grills. Oh, yes, there are also private rooms with balconies and spotless shared baths. We stayed at the Eco Beach Youth Hostel both before and after our Great Ocean Walk and found it to be (as one reviewer commented) "eco-tastic."

≈

An encouraging trend in contemporary travel is the increasing interest in all things "eco," and the Great Ocean Walk, a 68-mile route along the dramatic coast of Victoria, Australia, is a good example. The walk itself was built to be "green." The trail is located to minimize degradation of the land, and sometimes travels inland to avoid sensitive areas or to eliminate the need for elaborate engineering. Providing designated campsites reduces the overall impact of camping—and the Great Ocean Walk's campsites are tucked away to be visually unobtrusive.

LOCATION
Australia

LENGTH
68 miles

ACCOMMODATIONS
Commercial (e.g., Inns, B&Bs):
Some
Huts/Refuges: Some
Backpacking/Camping: Yes

BAGGAGE TRANSFER
Yes

OPTION TO WALK IN SECTIONS
Yes

DEGREE OF CHALLENGE
Low–Moderate

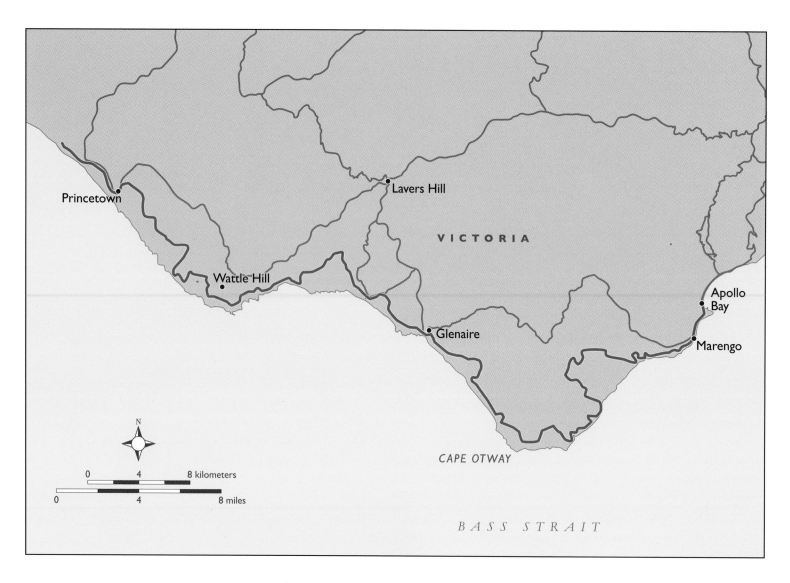

Another good example of focus on the environment is the Great Ocean Ecolodge where we stayed one night along the walk. It's an environmental research and education center as well as a refuge for injured wildlife—and the ecolodge has several comfortable bed-and-breakfast-style rooms. Extensive grounds include both eucalyptus forests and open areas. The dusk wildlife walk was wonderful, but perhaps more impressive was the mob of kangaroos casually feeding outside the lodge.

There was even a baby wallaby housed in an incubator in the living room! Income from the bed-and-breakfast helps fund the center, and, of course, staying there allows guests the time to appreciate the good work that's being done.

The Great Ocean Walk would be spectacular even without the ecological slant it showcases. Australia is known for its stunning coastline and wild beaches, and the Great Ocean Walk offers some of the country's finest. The route passes through two national parks—Great Otway and Port Campbell—and overlooks the Twelve Apostles Marine National Park and Marengo Reefs Marine Sanctuary. This relatively isolated geography on the southern coast of Victoria is tucked between the Otway Mountain Range to the north and the Bass Strait and Southern Ocean to the south. Some of the waves you'll see washing ashore started in Antarctica—respect their power and temperature; swimming is not advised. Basically, the Great Ocean Walk follows some of the same coastline featured on the famous Great Ocean Drive, a 151-mile stretch of road in the southeast of the continent. The walk has been called the "back stage" of the road because it goes to the shore when the road heads inland, and the trail offers a much more intimate experience than driving. Or perhaps you'd like to combine driving and walking.

(ABOVE LEFT) The Great Ocean Walk is a delightful blend of coastal beaches and high headlands.

(ABOVE) Cape Otway Lighthouse was built to improve safety along what is locally called the "Shipwreck Coast"; it offers hikers great views from its high, circular walkway.

Australian wildlife is iconic; we enjoyed watching many kangaroos along the trail.

This walk was designed so that you can easily "step on/step off" the trail. Many walking segments are less than 3 hours long, and it's easy to tailor the walk to your fitness level and interests. Because there are often low tide and high tide options (beach vs. headlands), "out and back" walks can easily become loop trails, an added bonus. Choose your type of overnight accommodations as well. Parks Victoria provides a system of walk-in campgrounds with tent pads and tanks of rainwater (treat before using), or you can stay in bed-and-breakfasts or hotels. Whether you prefer camp food with a view of the ocean or candlelit dining in a romantic getaway, this is your trail.

Coastal beaches are isolated and deserted; be sure to build in plenty of time for lingering and beachcombing here. Our favorite beaches were Station Beach with its magnificent waves and waterfall, and aptly named Wreck Beach with the protruding anchors of two ships grounded there in the nineteenth century. Headlands offer open areas with wildflowers. There are windswept dunes and cliffs and patches of thick forests of eucalyptus, ancient myrtle, beech, mountain ash, and blue gum trees. And in the rain forests there are tree ferns similar to those that were around when dinosaurs roamed this part of Australia. Inland portions of the route curve around rivers and bays, crossing biologically rich estuaries and occasionally climbing to higher elevations that offer sweeping views of the seemingly endless coastline—our favorite was Gable Lookout, one of the highest sea cliffs on mainland Australia.

It's pretty exciting to see kangaroos and wallabies along the trail, and you've got a good chance of seeing both around the Aires River Escarpment and Hordenvale Wetlands. You also may be lucky enough to see koalas and echidnas. Sooty oystercatchers, king parrots, peregrine falcons, and cockatoos will delight even walkers not usually interested in birding. If the season is right, look for migrating whales (in winter), and dolphins sometimes frolic in the waves.

The walk includes two especially iconic features. Cape Otway Lighthouse was the first lighthouse built in Victoria, and was designed to improve safety on what is locally called the "Shipwreck Coast." The lighthouse, scenic symbol of the state of Victoria, hovers nearly 300 feet above the sea and is topped with a circular walkway that's open to the public. It offers striking views up and down the coast, though strong, gusty winds can make it difficult to hold the camera still. At the west end of the walk lie the Twelve Apostles, just offshore from Port Campbell National Park; the Apostles are an exceptionally dramatic series of sea stacks just off the coast. (Interestingly, when the official name was bestowed, there were only eight stacks in the grouping.) These stacks (the largest of which is roughly 150 feet high) were originally part of the mainland cliffs, but the stormy ocean and blasting winds have gradually (over 10 to 20 million years) eroded the soft limestone. One stack crashed in 2005, but others are slowly forming. This may be one of the most strikingly scenic views in all of Australia, and more than 2 million people visit each year.

The Great Ocean Walk is highly accessible, with several roads providing periodic access to the trail, making it easy to break the longer route into shorter walks. There are commercial shuttle services, and lodgings will sometimes provide rides for walkers. Those wanting to experience the whole trail should allow a week or more. If you're camping, a permit must be obtained from Parks Victoria, and campers must travel from east to west (from Apollo Bay to the Port Campbell area) to maximize campsite availability (this offers better views and easier gradients, as well). Campfires are not allowed. There are also several drive-in campsites. As with all coastal trails, walkers must be mindful of tides and not find themselves stranded (or worse) by high tides—carry and use tide tables. Parks Victoria has thoughtfully provided signs noting "Decision Points," where the low tide and high tide trails diverge. Drinking water can be scarce, so be sure to carry plenty of water, particularly in summer. Apollo Bay, a 2.5-hour drive southwest of Melbourne, is the gateway town for the walk and is a lively, friendly place. We used the good bus service between Melbourne and Apollo Bay—and the driver was even kind enough to stop the bus to point out a family of wallabies in the trees beside the road. Several walking companies offer services to walkers, allowing for self-guided and guided hikes.

We're partial to coastal walks, and the Great Ocean Walk lives up to its name, offering some of the best of Australian coastal life—its magnificent scenery, wild beaches, rich and exotic wildlife, and friendly, fun-loving people. It's a trail that offers lots of choices—we hope it's one you'll choose.

Resources

Websites

Parks Victoria: www.parks.vic.gov.au/places-to-see/parks/great-otway-national-park/things-to-do/great-ocean-walk

Great Ocean Walk: www.greatoceanwalk.info

(LEFT) The Great Ocean Walk is a beachcomber's paradise.

(CENTER) The headlands offer walking through lush rain forests that feature several species of tree ferns that evolved when the dinosaurs roamed.

(RIGHT) Some of the waves that wash ashore on the Great Ocean Walk had their origin in Antarctica (and the water is still cold!).

The first view of Machu Picchu from the Sun Gate
near the end of the Inca Trail is a thrill.

Inca Trail

Like most people who walk the Inca Trail, we traveled to the small city of Cuzco, sometimes referred to as the "Katmandu of the Andes" and the jumping-off point for walking in this part of the world. Translated as "navel of the world," Cuzco was once the capital of the vast Inca Empire and home to an estimated 15,000 nobles, priests, and servants. The city sits at a little over 11,000 feet, and it's highly recommended that walkers stay here for a few days to acclimate to the thin air that will be encountered along the Inca Trail. Cuzco has its own impressive attractions—the Inca ruins of Sacsayhuaman, Pukapukara, and the Sun Temple; a historic Spanish cathedral; a thriving market and a large central square; and local people in colorful dress—so three days passed quickly. We had booked our walk of the Inca Trail with a local guiding service as required by the Peruvian government to help ensure that the tourist economy benefits the local population. On our last night in Cuzco, we met with our guide and were surprised to find that we were the only two people to sign up for this particular trip. Thus, our "group" included our guide, a cook, a waiter, two porters, and us! On the trail, our guide explained the natural and cultural history of what we saw, we ate our excellent meals (prepared from local foods, including several of the many varieties of potatoes grown in Peru, and served by our white-coated cook and waiter) in the "dining tent," we enjoyed hot water in the morning and evening for washing, and, of course, the porters carried nearly everything in enormous packs, leaving us with only daypacks. On our last night in camp, our cook made us a cake to celebrate our successful walk of the Inca Trail and our impending arrival the next morning in much anticipated Machu Picchu. What a luxurious alternative to conventional backpacking!

The Inca Trail (sometimes called the Camino Inca) and Machu Picchu are among the most iconic places in the world. The trail is one of the world's most famous walking routes and leads hikers

LOCATION
Peru

LENGTH
30 miles

ACCOMMODATIONS
Commercial (e.g., Inns, B&Bs): No
Huts/Refuges: No
Backpacking/Camping: Yes

BAGGAGE TRANSFER
Porters

OPTION TO WALK IN SECTIONS
No

DEGREE OF CHALLENGE
Moderate–High

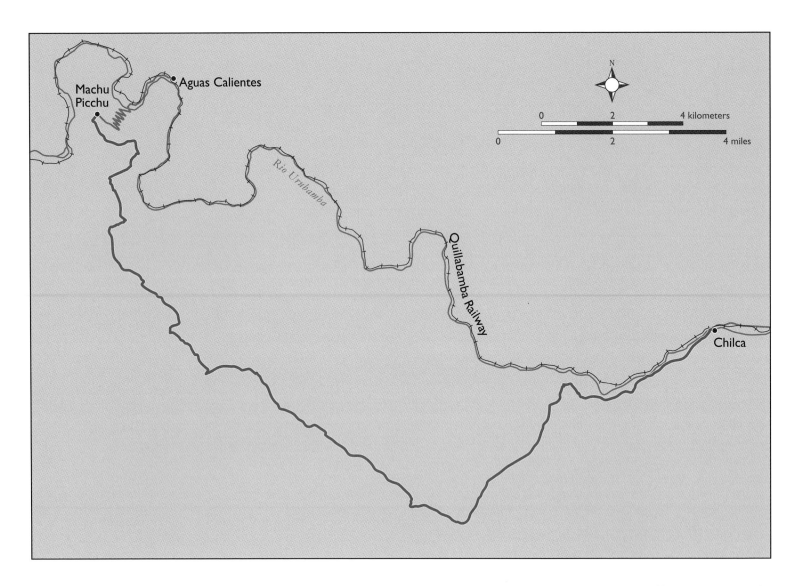

Machu
Picchu

Aguas Calientes

Río Urubamba

Quillabamba Railway

Chilca

N

| 0 | | 2 | | 4 kilometers |

| 0 | | 2 | | 4 miles |

to Machu Picchu, the mysterious "Lost City of the Incas," a UNESCO World Heritage Site. The approximately 30-mile trail is actually just a fragment of the elaborate system of roads and trails that connected the Inca Empire across much of what is now Ecuador, Peru, Argentina, and Chile. Though there are no written records, archaeological evidence documents that the vast and power-ful Inca civilization reached its zenith between 1100 and 1530, when it finally succumbed to Spanish

conquest. The trail is a marvelous example of the engineering prowess of the Incas, navigating the impossibly steep Andes, and the route reveals remains of an astonishing civilization clinging to the sides of soaring mountains. It was an improbable, fascinating empire.

We were driven about 3 hours from Cuzco across the Sacred Valley to the trailhead at the tiny town of Chilca. Along the way we stopped at the authentic Inca town of Ollantaytambo to pick up our porters. The last 20 minutes were along a one-lane road (with two-way traffic!). At the trailhead the Peruvian government has established a checkpoint where all walkers must show their permit and get their passport stamped. Porters pass through a separate checkpoint where their loads are weighed to ensure they are not too heavy. We then crossed a swinging bridge over the Urubamba River and were excited to start our trek to Machu Picchu. The first several miles were through lower-elevation, arid lands, and the trail was busy with Inca Trail walkers, a variety of farm animals, and occasional farmers from surrounding hamlets. But then the trail began to climb toward the high mountain passes, and the traffic (and the air!) thinned out. We camped the first night in a pasture that showed clear evidence of recent grazing animals. The stars of the Southern Hemisphere put on a great show, but we were asleep in our tent shortly after dinner.

(ABOVE LEFT) Hikers are advised to acclimate to the high elevations of the Inca Trail by staying in the 11,000-foot town of Cuzco for several days before starting the hike; there's lots to see and do here in the "Katmandu of the Andes."

(ABOVE) Hikers climb toward Dead Woman's Pass at nearly 14,000 feet.

Long stretches of trail are "paved" with local stones as part of the vast network of roads constructed throughout the Inca Empire.

We walked and camped for three more days. The trail quickly climbs out of the arid lands of the Urubamba Valley through high, open grasslands and ultimately into extensive and impressive rain forests with tree ferns, mosses, lichens, bromeliads (members of the pineapple family with short stems and rosettes of stiff leaves), and 250 species of orchids. Animals include nearly 400 species of birds (we saw Andean condors and listened to screeching parakeets) and lots of butterflies. Views toward the tops of the surrounding mountains reveal glaciers and massive snowfields. Most of the trail is above 10,000 feet, and there are three high passes to negotiate; the highest—colorfully named "Dead Woman's Pass" (from the right angle, it looks like a woman lying down)—is just under 14,000 feet. Guides often offer walkers coca tea as a mild stimulant to help with overcoming the elevation, but we passed on this option. The trail isn't excessively steep or rough; in fact, it's "paved" in stone in some places. At one point, walkers descend 2,800 stone steps in a 0.5-mile section of trail, all fashioned by the Incas.

But the stars of the show are the world-class archaeological sites along the way—Llaqtapata, Runkurakay, Sayamarca, Winawayna, and more. Nearly all of the ruins are well preserved thanks to the remarkable engineering and construction by their builders. The stonework is impressive, especially when you realize no mortar was used and the rocks were worked by hand. In some places, steps and tunnels were fashioned out of solid rock. Many of the ruins are sited on the flanks of seemingly unbuildable slopes and include extensive terracing for stability and to support agricultural production. Visitors are allowed to walk freely through these sites, and our guide helped us understand their history and significance.

On the final evening walkers tingle with excitement about entering fabled Machu Picchu the next morning. Everyone rises early to reach the famous Sun Gate for the unforgettable first view of Machu Picchu in the rising sun. From the Sun Gate it's about an hour's walk into Machu Picchu proper, a truly magical site, and there's ample time to enjoy it in relatively uncrowded conditions before the first busloads of visitors arrive from the nearby town of Aguas Calientes. The extensive ruins are on a high saddle and seem even more impossibly sited than the previous archaeological sites. Llamas graze placidly among plazas, aqueducts, baths, and tiers. Archaeologists still don't agree on the original use of Machu Picchu—was it an astronomical observatory, religious retreat, city, or palace? They do agree that it was abandoned and the memory of it lost before the Spaniards came to South America. Yale historian Hiram Bingham found the ruins of Machu Picchu in 1911 and spent several years supervising the clearing of the area; he's a local folk hero. Not surprisingly, Machu Picchu is usually crowded, and most visitors arrive in the nearby town by train. From Machu Picchu, hikers and day-trippers alike use a shuttle bus to travel down to Aguas Calientes, a funky tourist town where we saw chickens casually scratching in front of luxury hotels. Visitors return to the Sacred Valley by train, an enjoyable and interesting 3-hour ride along the Urubamba River that provides another perspective on the region—and views of even more ruins.

As noted earlier, walkers on the Inca Trail must use the services of a local guiding company, and there are many to choose from. These companies help hikers appreciate the trail and make sure visitors don't disturb the ruins, and the policy also allows local people to enjoy more of the benefits of the tourist economy. Only a limited number of people are allowed to start the walk daily, so it's advisable to make your arrangements well in advance. Our sense is that this number is too high, as camping areas were often crowded and toilet and other facilities overtaxed. Walking is allowed in one direction only to lessen perceived crowding. The trail is open all year, but the best weather is from May to October, with the peak season from June to August. The classic Inca Trail walk is conducted in five days, including the return trip by train. This is a camping trip, but guides, cooks, and porters take much of the burden off walkers; these people work hard, so consider tipping generously. The primary challenges are the elevation and the potential for bad weather in the form of rain. We found hiking poles to be helpful in wet areas and on steep slopes and steps, but be sure to use rubber tips on the poles. Recently, an alternative route called the Camino Salcantay has become popular; this is also part of the vast Inca Trail network, but is served by a system of recently constructed upscale lodges (this is not the classic Inca Trail that we describe here).

Read all you can about the Incas and Machu Picchu before your trip—you'll be more appreciative of the spectacular adventure that's the Inca Trail. Just realize that you still won't be fully prepared for the magic of this place.

Resources

Website
Inca Trail: www.incatrailperu.com

Guidebook
Ryan Dubé, *Moon Machu Picchu*, 2016

(ABOVE LEFT) Machu Picchu, the "Lost City of the Incas," is a UNESCO World Heritage Site.

(ABOVE) There are many elaborate archaeological sites along the Inca Trail.

The John Muir Trail can be a life-changing backpacking trip through the iconic Sierra Nevada; camping beside unnamed lakes is a true marker of wilderness.

John Muir Trail

"I'll trade a mac and cheese dinner for a bag of Peanut M&M's." "Anyone want a package of beef jerky?" We were in the midst of a mini-marketplace at Muir Trail Ranch, the last resupply opportunity along the famous John Muir Trail. We'd backpacked just over a hundred miles and had another hundred or so to go—about nine more days at our current pace. Like all hikers, we'd mailed ourselves a resupply package to this remote outpost in the wilderness. Supplies had to be mailed in five-gallon plastic buckets (with handles) because they were carried the last several miles to the ranch on the backs of pack animals. So here we sat, going through our new supply of food and a few other things—socks, toothpaste, Band-Aids—thinking hard about what to take and what to leave behind. This is the eternal dilemma of backpackers: the luxury of food and other supplies versus the need to lighten the pack. There were two other groups sorting through their new supplies, and we were all comparing notes, swapping things back and forth, and making painful decisions about what to leave behind in the donation barrel. The most popular solution, of course, was to eat as much as possible now, and we were doing a pretty good job of that. We calculated carefully what we thought we needed and added a little more for the sake of safety, repacked our gear, and walked south in the warm summer sun, the summit of Mount Whitney still unseen, but beckoning.

——— ≈ ———

Everyone knows about the beautiful, iconic sights of Yosemite National Park—towering granite cliffs and domes, some of the world's highest waterfalls, lush meadows, rivers rushing through virgin forests, high mountain lakes. Now imagine a trail that winds its way through more than 200 miles of this landscape, taking walkers on a spectacular, roller-coaster ride along the "High Sierra." That's the John Muir Trail. John Muir felt the Sierra Nevada was the most beautiful mountain range in the world, and we have no reason to disagree. "His" trail starts in Yosemite Valley and works its

LOCATION
California, United States

LENGTH
211 miles

ACCOMMODATIONS
Commercial (e.g., Inns, B&Bs):
Few
Huts/Refuges: No
Backpacking/Camping: Yes

BAGGAGE TRANSFER
No

OPTION TO WALK IN SECTIONS
Some

DEGREE OF CHALLENGE
High

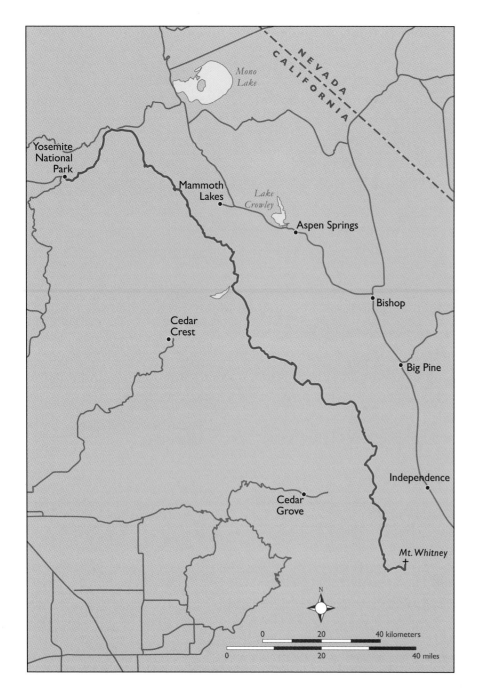

way over a series of high mountain passes to the summit of Mount Whitney, the highest peak in the contiguous United States, passing through Yosemite, Sequoia, and Kings Canyon National Parks and the Ansel Adams and John Muir Wildernesses. This is one of the world's great walking adventures, and it may change your life; it did for us.

The trail starts at well-named Happy Isles along the Merced River in Yosemite Valley and immediately climbs toward the high country. The nearly 40 miles of the trail in Yosemite National Park are packed with scenery of the highest order, including Vernal and Nevada Falls, Half Dome, the Cathedral Peaks, Tuolumne Meadows, and Lyell Canyon. Take time for a daylong side trip to the top of Half Dome, but only if you're prepared to pull yourself up the cables that lead to the summit, a challenge for those of us who are even just a little afraid of heights. Impossibly beautiful Lyell Canyon, its rich meadows fed by meandering Lyell Creek, leads walkers south, then it's up and over 11,000-foot Donahue Pass, out of Yosemite, and into Ansel Adams Wilderness.

Ansel Adams is America's most famous landscape photographer, and the High Sierra was his favorite subject. The trail passes along the shores of Thousand Island Lake with striking Ritter and Banner Peaks in the background, the scene of some of Adams's most well-known photographs. Ruby, Emerald, and Garnet Lakes are among the collection of "jewel"-like lakes in the 23-mile stretch of trail through this wilderness area. This area is also noted for its impressive evidence of volcanic activity, including hot springs, cinder cones, and Devil's Postpile National Monument with its unusual columns of basalt formed by cooling magma.

The next 50 miles of the trail run through the massive John Muir Wilderness. Muir wandered extensively

through the Sierras in the late nineteenth century, making many first ascents of the tallest peaks, successfully lobbying for creation of Yosemite National Park, and eloquently preaching the gospel of conservation. When many Americans seemed more concerned about material things, Muir wrote, "Everybody needs beauty as well as bread, places to play in and pray in." He called the Sierras the "Range of Light," not just because of the whitish color of the exposed granite peaks, but because they offered an opportunity to find higher, spiritual truths. Muir is the father of national parks in America, and this trail and the wilderness it traverses are powerful monuments to all his good work. This portion of the trail is classic High Sierra with towering snowcapped peaks, sparkling streams, patches of deep forest, and Virginia, Purple, and Marie Lakes, some of the most beautiful in all the Sierras. Be sure to look back occasionally to see Ritter and Banner Peaks fading 50 miles and more into the distance as evidence of your progress along the trail. And look off to the east and west into vast, seemingly untouched granite canyons. This extensive complex of national parks and forests offers many lifetimes of exploration.

Just past the 100-mile mark, the trail enters Kings Canyon National Park and then Sequoia National Park. Much of the trail through these parks is especially remote, and we were thrilled to

(ABOVE LEFT) Hikers follow delightful Lyell Creek south out of Yosemite National Park.

(ABOVE) Dramatic Cathedral Peak marks the end of the long climb out of Yosemite Valley and into the High Sierra.

(ABOVE) Known for some of the world's highest and most beautiful waterfalls, the JMT takes hikers to the brink of Nevada Falls.

(ABOVE RIGHT) Lovely Lyell Creek in its namesake canyon leads hikers south out of Yosemite National Park and on toward Mount Whitney, the highest point in the lower 48 states.

camp on the shores of unnamed lakes, a marker of true wilderness. A highlight of this area is Evolution Basin, an especially dramatic 8-mile stretch well above tree line. The surrounding 13,000-foot peaks are named for famous scientists in the field of evolution—Mendel, Darwin, and Huxley. Nearly devoid of vegetation due to its elevation, this area looks much like it must have when the last glaciers retreated some 10,000 years ago. Just south are Rae Lakes, a chain of five lakes that offer plentiful campsites with five-star views. Speaking of stars, the night skies all along the trail are world class. And the meadows are the finest in the Sierras—every shade of green and sporting lush wildflowers, including lupines and Indian paintbrush. As walkers make their way south, the passes rise higher and higher: Muir Pass at 11,955 feet, Mather Pass at 12,100 feet, Pinchot Pass at 12,130 feet, and finally Forester Pass at 13,120 feet.

And then there's Mount Whitney at 14,505 feet. As you approach the mountain, look east and south for breathtaking views (if you have any breaths left to take) of the Great Western Divide. Most walkers make their last camp at Guitar Lake and wake early for the final push to the summit. About 2 miles from the top, the trail splits from the route that will be used to descend the mountain, so this is a good place to stash your pack and lighten your load for the final pitch. Short steps and frequent breaks are advised in this thin air. The summit is a sea of rocks with magnificent views

The John Muir Trail leads hikers to a series of lakes that offer plenty of drinking water, refreshing swims, and rich beauty.

in every direction. Be sure to sign the hiker's register at the small stone building housing meteorological equipment. We found ourselves with mixed emotions as we sat and luxuriously ate nearly all of our remaining stock of snacks — elated to have completed the trail, but sad to see our adventure come to an end. But there wasn't much time to romanticize because it's a 10-mile walk descending 6,000 feet from the summit to the nearest trailhead at Whitney Portal. And we wanted to get down in time for dinner and that cheeseburger we'd been dreaming about lately.

This trail offers an abundance of human and natural history. The place names celebrate the birth of America's conservation movement: Muir; Gifford Pinchot, first director of the US Forest Service; and Stephan Mather, first director of the National Park Service. Tectonic forces followed by centuries of glacial action and the eroding forces of water shaped the landscape. Forests of Jeffrey, white, lodgepole, and other pines and hemlock cloak the lower elevations. Animals include eagles, marmots, mule deer, and rarer mountain sheep and mountain lions. Walkers see fewer black bears than they used to because the long-term program of keeping human food away from them has been largely successful.

The primary logistical concerns for walking the trail are its length and elevation. The trail is accessible only by backpacking, and there are only a few reasonable options to get resupplied, so careful planning is required. It's wise to allow about three weeks to walk the trail in its entirety. Elevations are high. With the exception of the trailhead in Yosemite (at about 4,000 feet), the trail rarely

The JMT crosses high-elevation Evolution Basin; the area looks much like it must have when the glaciers retreated some 10,000 years ago.

drops below 8,000 feet and is usually substantially higher. The combined ascent over the length of the trail is about 46,000 feet. But the trail is well maintained and marked, and the grades over the passes are generally moderate. Because of high demand, a permit is required. The good news is that the agencies that manage the parks and wildernesses that the trail traverses have developed a coordinated permit system; the bad news is that permits are very difficult to obtain. Permits are allocated primarily through a lottery system; see the website for Yosemite National Park for up-to-date information. Campers must use bear canisters, hard plastic containers that keep food and other aromatic items away from hungry or inquisitive bears. Nearly all walkers start at the northern end of the trail, acclimating gradually to the elevation as the passes increase in height (this diminishes the likelihood of altitude sickness). It's wise to camp within a few hours' walking distance of the higher, exposed passes so you can get up and over them the next day before the chance of afternoon thunderstorms.

With a little creative map work, the trail lends itself to a number of section hikes of varying lengths, such as Tuolumne Meadows to Yosemite Valley (nearly all downhill in this direction!), Tuolumne Meadows to Reds Meadow, and a loop hike that includes the Rae Lakes area. The hiking season is short—from July through most of September—due to heavy snows that start early and continue to clog the higher passes well into the summer. Summer days are usually sunny and warm, but nights are cold. Walkers are blessed over most of the trail with plentiful supplies of water for drinking (which should be purified), swimming, and fishing. There are commercial shuttle services that will provide rides at the southern end of the trail, but they can be expensive.

Way above tree line, the last few miles of the JMT lead hikers to the summit of Mount Whitney.

The John Muir Trail makes nearly everyone's top ten list, including ours. *Backpacker* magazine says, "Step for scenery-packed step, nothing else compares." We concur. Late in his life, Muir wrote, "I only went out for a walk and finally concluded to stay out till sundown, for going out, I found, was really going in." Take the time to follow Muir's advice about what's really important in life. (For more great walks in US national parks, see our book *Walks of a Lifetime in America's National Parks*.)

Resources

Website
Yosemite National Park: www.nps.gov/yose

Guidebook
Elizabeth Wenk and Kathy Morey, *John Muir Trail: The Essential Guide to Hiking America's Most Famous Trail* (5th edition), 2007

Maps
National Geographic Trails Illustrated Map 1001, *John Muir Trail Topographic Map Guide*, 2014
Erik Asorson, *John Muir Pocket Atlas*, 2020

The renowned Kaibab Trail leads walkers across the Grand Canyon and through nearly 2 billion years of geologic history.

Kaibab Trail

Grand Canyon is one of our favorite US national parks. Like most of the park's several million annual visitors, we were awestruck the first time we saw the canyon—its jaw-dropping scale and complexity seemingly beyond human imagination. The global importance of the Grand Canyon is clearly manifested in its designation as a World Heritage Site. But to more fully appreciate Grand Canyon, you must walk below the rim, ideally all the way to the Colorado River, the living heart of the park. This walk takes you roughly a mile beneath the surface of the earth, revealing nearly 2 billion years of geology in an orderly, step-by-step, layer-by-layer story more graphic than any written description. It's estimated that each step on the trail descending into the canyon represents 100,000 years of geologic history, and there are correspondingly dramatic changes in climate, plants, and animals. On our most recent walk of the Kaibab Trail, we met a young family on their first hike into the canyon. They were so excited about what they were seeing and experiencing, they could hardly find the words to express their feelings, and that's how we've felt sometimes, too. For many people, there's an emotional, even spiritual, component of the Grand Canyon—an overwhelming sense of humility that only comes with walking through it. One writer calls walking the canyon the "physical price of admission," but it's well worth the cost.

———— ≈ ————

Grand Canyon National Park was established in 1919 and is one of the "crown jewels" of the US National Park System. Of course it's most famous for its massive gash in the earth—about 275 miles long, 5 to 15 miles wide, and about a mile deep—revealing much of the geologic history of the earth. The canyon was formed by a combination of the uplift of the Colorado Plateau (an elevated area that composes much of the southwestern United States) and the downward erosive force of the powerful Colorado River. The resulting exposed cross section reveals all three of the basic forms

LOCATION
Arizona, United States

LENGTH
21 miles

ACCOMMODATIONS
Commercial (e.g., Inns, B&Bs): Limited
Huts/Refuges: No
Backpacking/Camping: Yes

BAGGAGE TRANSFER
No

OPTION TO WALK IN SECTIONS
Some

DEGREE OF CHALLENGE
High

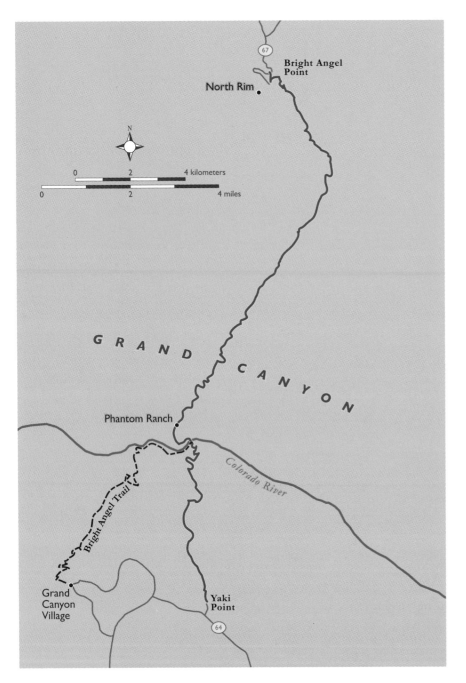

of rock that make up the earth: sedimentary (formed by deposition), igneous (formed through cooling and solidification of magma or lava), and metamorphic (changed molecularly by intense heat and pressure). The upper half of the canyon lays bare a succession of sedimentary rocks: deposits of marine organisms on the floor of deep seas (forming limestone) and windblown sand dunes (forming sandstone). The harder limestone erodes more slowly into steep cliffs, while the softer sandstone weathers more quickly, forming more gradually sloped layers. Over the eons, the upper canyon has taken on a distinctive "stepped" appearance. Rocks at the bottom of the canyon, in what's called the Inner Gorge, are estimated to be as much as 1.7 billion years old and include volcanic intrusions (igneous rock) and schist (metamorphic rock). You'll want to spend some time at the National Park Service interpretive exhibits, particularly the Trail of Time geology exhibit on the South Rim; learning about the geology certainly makes experiencing the canyon more meaningful.

The word *kaibab* is Paiute and means "mountain lying down," their term for the Grand Canyon. The South Kaibab Trail descends from the 7,000-foot South Rim of the canyon just over 7 miles to the Colorado River; its steepness has led to its description as "a trail in a hurry to get to the river." It leaves the rim at Yaki Point, just east of Grand Canyon Village. Much of the trail follows a natural ridge line in the canyon, which results in some of the most expansive views in the park. However, the trail has been highly engineered (using dynamite and jackhammers where needed) and is steep in places. Notable points along the trail include aptly named Ooh Ahh Point, Cedar Ridge, Skeleton Point (named for the remains of a mule that fell to its death here), and the Tip Off (where the trail enters the canyon's Inner Gorge).

The North Kaibab Trail drops off the 8,000-foot North Rim of the canyon at Bright Angel Point and follows the natural fault line of Bright Angel Creek, an ancient Native American route through the canyon. It's considerably less steep, but consequently takes longer—slightly over 14 miles—to reach the Colorado River and join the South Kaibab Trail by means of a suspension bridge over the river. Notable points along the trail include Coconino Overview, Supai Tunnel (blasted out of the rock), Roaring Springs (a large natural spring that serves as the source of fresh water for most residents and visitors to Grand Canyon), Cottonwood Camp, Manzanita Rest Area, Ribbon Falls, and Phantom Ranch and Bright Angel Campground, the latter two located on the substantial delta formed where Bright Angel Creek enters the Colorado River. This delta is a delightful oasis—a perennial source of water and shady cottonwood trees, willows, and tamarisk—for hikers who have just walked through miles of hot, desert conditions.

The only lodging in the canyon, Phantom Ranch is a rustic "resort" opened in 1922, designed by architect Mary Elizabeth Jane Colter at the behest of the Fred Harvey Company and the Santa Fe Railroad. The railroad helped open Grand Canyon to public use by building a spur line to the South Rim in the early 1900s, and the route from Williams, Arizona, has recently been restored (a ride that many visitors now enjoy). Phantom Ranch has a series of cabins, a bunkhouse, and a dining room,

(ABOVE LEFT) Just past the Tip Off, the South Kaibab Trail offers walkers entry into the Inner Canyon and views of the Colorado River, the beating heart of the Grand Canyon.

(ABOVE) The North Rim offers visitors lovely views out over the Grand Canyon.

The South Kaibab Trail descends toward the Colorado River through a dramatic series of switchbacks.

and it serves hikers and mule riders. The National Park Service manages nearby Bright Angel Campground.

The North and South Kaibab Trails are among the most storied, historic, and popular trails in the US National Park System and have been designated as part of the National Trails System (they constitute the most iconic section of the much longer Arizona National Scenic Trail described earlier in this book). The earliest trails in Grand Canyon were built by private individuals and companies primarily for mineral prospecting. Enterprising entrepreneurs charged a toll for use of these trails by the public. In response, the National Park Service constructed the Kaibab route in the 1920s. The Colorado River was a primary obstacle, and early crossings were made by ferry and then a cable car. Today, there are two bridges (for hikers and mule/horseback riders only) that cross the river in the vicinity of Bright Angel Creek, the only crossings of the Colorado River within the nearly 300 miles of the river in the national park. The Kaibab Suspension Bridge (often called the "Black Bridge" because of its dark color) includes eight 550-foot braided steel cables that support the bridge, each weighing more than a ton; forty-two men of the local Havasupai Tribe carried each large strand down from the rim. Construction of this route was rarely easy!

Experiencing the Colorado River is one of the principal rewards for Kaibab Trail walkers. This mighty river drains much of the southwest quadrant of the United States and is a vital source of water in this arid land. It rises in the Rocky Mountains and flows 1,450 miles before emptying into the Gulf of California. The portion of the river that flows through Grand Canyon was first run in four wooden boats by one-armed Civil War veteran John Wesley Powell and his crew of ten men in 1869, one of the great American adventure stories. Powell was surveying the river and surrounding lands to help ensure wise use of the river's scarce water. Today, thousands of people raft the river each year for recreation, and Kaibab Trail walkers are likely to see one or more of these river trips.

Colorado is Spanish for "red river," and references the natural color of the river as a result of all the sediment that is washed into the river from the surrounding arid lands. However, the section of the river that flows through Grand Canyon is now often clear as a result of the Glen Canyon Dam, constructed just upstream of Grand Canyon in the 1960s. The dam slows the flow of the river, causing most of the sediment to be deposited at the bottom of the reservoir; when water is released through the dam, it's clear and cold.

At 8,000 feet, the North Kaibab Trailhead lights up with the golden fall foliage of the area's extensive aspen forests.

While geology and the Colorado River are the stars of the show for Kaibab Trail walkers, other elements of natural and human history add considerable interest. Walkers making the nearly 5,000 to 6,000 feet of elevation change from the canyon's rims to the river (and back!) pass through five of the seven North American life zones, representing highly unusual biological diversity in such close proximity. For every 1,000 feet of elevation loss from the canyon rims, air temperature rises 4 to 5 degrees. Snow is common on the canyon rims in winter, and temperatures at the bottom of the canyon can approach 120 degrees F in summer. Because of this extreme temperature differential, plants and animals are highly varied. You can find mule deer, elk, and coyotes along with fir, spruce, and ponderosa pines on the canyon rims, and desert bighorn sheep and rattlesnakes along with cactuses and yucca deep within the canyon. California condors have been reintroduced into the Grand Canyon area and are sometimes seen soaring. Utah agaves are also common, and they are a favorite of ours. This remarkable low-growing plant stores energy for about twenty-five years, then grows a stalk up to 12 feet high in a single season, flowers, and then dies, completing its life cycle.

Archaeological evidence suggests that Native Americans settled in and around the canyon roughly 11,000 years ago. These people, called Ancestral Pluebloans by contemporary archaeologists,

The North Kaibab Trail falls steeply off the Grand Canyon's North Rim; a long series of switchbacks ease the grade.

built small settlements and raised crops over a thousand years ago, but abandoned the area in about 1140. A 900-year-old pueblo can be seen near the Kaibab Suspension Bridge. Spanish explorers looking for gold "discovered" Grand Canyon in 1540, but quickly moved on because the canyon presented such an impediment to travel. American prospectors combed the canyon in the 1800s but found little of economic value. The canyon was first protected by Executive Order of President Teddy Roosevelt, who, in a famous speech on the South Rim, admonished Americans: "Leave it as it is. You cannot improve on it. The ages have been at work on it, and man can only mar it." It was designated a national park in 1919.

The North and South Kaibab Trails are well designed and maintained to a high level. While they are necessarily steep in some places, the trail tread is wide and generally well groomed, making them a pleasure to walk. You're likely to see mule trains moving up and down the canyon carrying visitors and supplies to Phantom Ranch. Walkers should follow directions given by wranglers, usually to stop and be still and quiet while the mules pass.

There are several options for walking the Kaibab Trail, and the Grand Canyon more broadly. The preferred option is to start on the North Rim of the canyon and walk down the North Kaibab Trail to the Colorado River and then ascend the South Kaibab Trail to the South Rim. Traversing the canyon from north to south saves walkers about a thousand feet of elevation gain (since the North Rim is higher than the South Rim). Most walkers leave their car at the South Rim and take a long commercial shuttle to the North Rim to begin their hike. Be aware that this will take time: The North Rim is only about 10 miles from the South Rim as the crow (condor in this case) flies, but the drive around the canyon is about 215 miles! Also note that car access to the North Rim is usually available only from about mid-May to mid-October, as snow closes the road the rest of the year.

Plan on spending at least one night at either Phantom Ranch or Bright Angel Campground on this hike, and preferably more; walking the North Kaibab Trail can be broken into two days by camping at Cottonwood Camp. If the North Rim is not open, an alternative is to hike down the South Kaibab Trail and back up to the South Rim via the Bright Angel Trail. Less steep than the South Kaibab Trail, the Bright Angel Trail is about 10 miles long. Again, at least one night should be spent at Phantom Ranch or Bright Angel Campground; there is also a campground about half-way up the Bright Angel Trail. Some visitors do this walk (down the South Kaibab Trail and up the Bright Angel Trail) in one day, but the National Park Service strongly discourages this. Walking in Grand Canyon is like mountain climbing in reverse; you walk downhill first, but then have to climb up (way up!) out of the canyon. As some of the locals say, walking down the trail is optional, but walking back up is mandatory; this is a demanding hike that requires lots of water, especially in extreme summer temperatures.

You must always be prepared for hiking in desert conditions; don't be fooled if the air temperature is cool on the canyon rims; it will get much warmer as you descend. Hikers are advised to drink a gallon of water per day on the trail. There's no water and little shade on the South Kaibab Trail, but water is available at several locations on the North Kaibab and Bright Angel Trails. It's wise to hike early in the day, starting your hike out of the canyon at sunrise or even earlier. Some walkers don't follow this advice and wind up needing assistance, and some have even died in the canyon. From July through September, monsoon thunderstorms can bring rain and lightning to the canyon. Winter snows can result in dangerously icy conditions at higher elevations. No matter how tempting, don't swim in the Colorado River—its current is strong and dangerous and the water is cold. Reservations for accommodations at Phantom Ranch and at the campgrounds must be made well in advance. There is limited parking at the North Kaibab Trailhead and Bright Angel Trailhead and no parking at the South Kaibab Trailhead (use the park's free shuttle bus system to access the latter two trailheads).

A number of years ago, epic Grand Canyon walker Colin Fletcher wrote a book called *The Man Who Walked Through Time*. Walking the Grand Canyon and taking your own trip back in geologic time is one of the great walking experiences in the world. If walking all the way to the Colorado River is not advisable, then consider doing a day hike to any of the waypoints along the North or South Kaibab Trails noted above. Good destinations include Supai Tunnel on the North Kaibab Trail, Cedar Ridge on the South Kaibab Trail, and Mile-and-a-Half House on the Bright Angel Trail; all of these hikes will allow you to experience the magic of walking below the rim of Grand Canyon. And we bet you'll be left speechless! (For more great walks in US national parks, see our book *Walks of a Lifetime in America's National Parks*.)

Resources

Website
Grand Canyon National Park: www.nps.gov/grca

Guidebooks
Scott Thybony, *Grand Canyon South Kaibab Trail Guide*, 2006
Scott Thybony, *Grand Canyon North Kaibab Trail Guide*, 2005
Elizabeth Wenk, *One Best Hike: Grand Canyon*, 2010

Hikers are rewarded at Kalalua Beach with a mile of golden sand and crashing surf at the mouth of a tropical valley; we camped on the beach that night and slept especially well.

Kalalau Trail

It was late afternoon by the time we reached the end of the trail, and we were tired. The Kalalau Trail had been a harder hike than we expected, both physically and emotionally. But here we were at Kalalau Beach, a mile of golden sand and crashing surf at the mouth of a lush tropical valley. We pitched our tent in the shade of a cluster of trees and waded (carefully) into the surf. That evening, we walked to the far end of the beach and rinsed ourselves under a waterfall. At night we watched the stars in the clearest night sky we'd seen since we were kids and let the surf lull us to sleep (which didn't take long). You have to work some to experience this iconic bit of Hawaiian paradise, but we found it to be more than worth the effort.

≈

Kauai is the "garden isle" of the Hawaiian Islands. Sounds like paradise, and in many ways it is. Lush rain forests and hanging valleys cling to steep 3,000-foot cliffs that rise out of the turquoise Pacific Ocean. The 11-mile (one-way) Kalalau Trail is the only land access to the famous Na Pali Coast, immortalized in dozens of Hollywood movies, including *Blue Hawaii* and *Jurassic Park*. But as usual, paradise comes at a cost. This is an adventurous, hard, and even occasionally scary walk—and remember that it must be walked again to return to the trailhead. The trail follows the folds in the cliffs, climbing in and out of deep, narrow valleys, rising and falling from beaches to more than a thousand exposed feet above the ocean, and seeming to periodically double back on itself. But the reward is some of the most beautiful scenery in the world, exotic vegetation, rugged grandeur, and camping at a world-class beach with a waterfall as your personal shower (use only biodegradable soap; better yet, skip the soap and just rinse).

Formed by lava from deep undersea volcanoes, Kauai was the first of the Hawaiian Islands to rise out of the Pacific Ocean. The island is estimated to be about 5 million years old—relatively young geologically—but this has allowed development of dense and rich vegetation that covers nearly every square inch of the island that will support it. The Kalalau Trail was originally built in the late

---

LOCATION
Hawaii, United States

LENGTH
22 miles (round-trip)

ACCOMMODATIONS
Commercial (e.g., Inns, B&Bs):
No
Huts/Refuges: No
Backpacking/Camping: Yes

BAGGAGE TRANSFER
No

OPTION TO WALK IN SECTIONS
No

DEGREE OF CHALLENGE
High

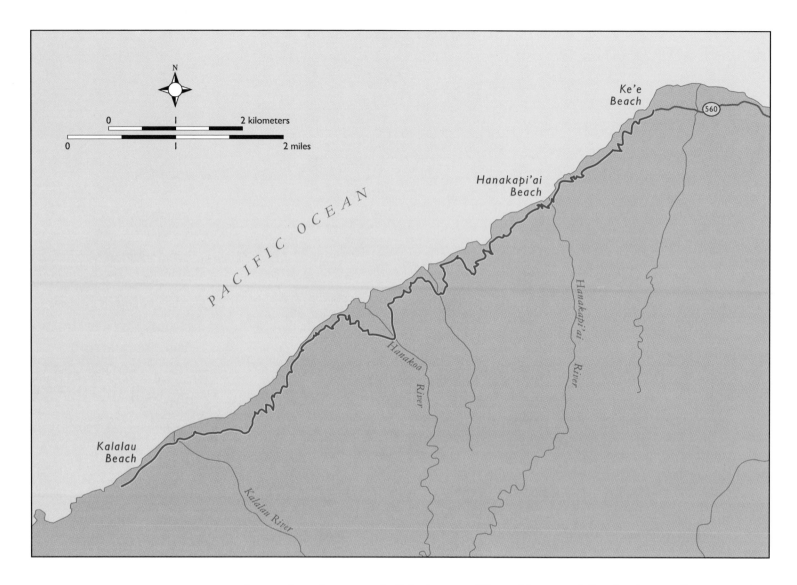

1800s, and portions were rebuilt in the 1930s. The trail is easy to follow, but is not well maintained. In several places, the path is very narrow with steep drop-offs to the ocean, and we found these places a little unnerving; we relied heavily on our hiking poles to get us through these sections.

Pali is Hawaiian for "cliffs." The sheer, towering cliffs of the Na Pali Coast are cut by waves made by wind and water that collect over a vast expanse of Pacific Ocean, while its steep valleys are shaped by the many streams and waterfalls along its face. The rain forests that cover the cliffs are supported by prodigious precipitation—the summit of nearby Wai'ale'ale' Mountain holds the world record for rain, at more than 600 inches in a year (it averages 420 inches). The trail starts at Ke'e Beach, often rated as the most beautiful on the planet, and traverses five valleys, ending at Kalalau Beach, where further travel is blocked by a sheer, fluted *pali* that juts into the sea. Extensive stone-walled terraces can still be found in several of the valley bottoms; Hawaiians once lived there and cultivated taro (an Asian starchy root vegetable) and coffee. Many rare plants grow on the trail's inaccessible cliffs, and wild goats roam. There are two campgrounds along the trail, including the one at the end of the trail, and camping is restricted to these areas. We strongly recommend spending at least two nights camping at Kalalau Beach to reward yourself, to rest and prepare for the return journey, and to fully appreciate "paradise."

Even though this is a relatively short walk, it requires preparation, both physical and psychological. One might be tempted to try to walk out and back in one long day, but this would be a mistake. First, it would not allow for the time needed to fully appreciate this magical place. Second, it's a demanding walk, requiring nearly 10,000 feet of accumulated elevation gain (round-trip) in a hot and humid environment, on a trail tread that's sometimes narrow and rough, and that includes fording several (usually small) creeks. Frequent rain can cause these streams to flood, and walkers should wait for the water to recede before attempting to cross (these small, steep streams tend to rise and fall quickly). Drinking water can be taken from streams but must be treated. The bacterium *leptospirosis* exists in several creeks along the trail and can invade the body through small cuts and cause a sometimes fatal hepatitis-like sickness; be cautious about swimming in these waters. Caution is also needed regarding swimming at all ocean beaches because of unpredictable surf and dangerous currents and riptides.

A permit (and fee) is needed for the hike, and the number of permits is limited. The rules for obtaining a permit are somewhat convoluted and periodically change, so pay close attention to the website noted at the end of this chapter. However, walking the first 2 miles of the trail (to

Lush rain forests and hanging valleys cling to the steep 3,000-foot cliffs that rise from the deep blue waters of the Pacific Ocean.

Pali is Hawaiian for "cliffs"; the sheer, towering cliffs of the Na Pali Coast are cut by wind and water, while its steep valleys are shaped by streams and waterfalls along its face.

Hanakapi'ai, a lovely beach) does not require a permit (though you will need a parking reservation at Ha'vena State Park) and offers an appealing sample of the trail. In fact, just walking the first half mile of the trail offers stunning views of the Na Pali Coast. Walking the Kalalau Trail beyond Hanakapi'ai requires a permit. Other day-hiking options include walking 4 miles to Hanakoa and then hiking up this valley to a waterfall, but the trail in the valley is very rough, and this would make for an especially long day hike. Camping is allowed at Hanakoa. The primary hiking season is May through September when there is less rain, but it can be walked any time of the year, as temperatures rarely drop below 60 degrees F, even in winter. We walked in March.

Choosing to walk the Kalalau Trail is serious matter. Not only is it challenging, but it can be perilous; both *Backpacker* and *Outside* magazines list the trail as one of the most dangerous in the world. After reaching Hanakoa, the trail narrows, leaving hikers exposed to steep drop-offs that fall hundreds of feet to the ocean below. One of these sections is appropriately called "Crawlers Ledge." Moreover, the trail crosses several streams that often flood in response to the abundant rainfall; when in flood, crossing these streams should not be attempted. Even though it's only 11 miles from Ke'e Beach to Kalalau Beach, this is a hard, all-day hike.

(LEFT) Walkers who are uncomfortable with heights must steel themselves along stretches of the trail that include steep drop-offs to the ocean; we found trekking poles to be especially helpful.

(RIGHT) The red rocks and soil are manifestations of Kauai's volcanic origins.

In response to the tension between the beauty of the trail and the potential danger it represents, the Kalalau Trail has been described as having a strong spiritual component—*mana* in Hawaiian, meaning "big medicine." Carefully consider walking the Kalalua Trail and getting a strong dose of this medicine. We feel we're better for it.

Resources

Website

Hawaii Division of State Parks (Kalalau Trail): https://dlnr.hawaii.gov/dsp/hiking/kauai/kalalau-trail

King Ludwig commissioned construction of Neuschwanstein; the castle reflected his fanciful interests in art and architecture.

King Ludwig's Way

It was day five of our eight-day walk across Bavaria, following in the footsteps—literally and figuratively—of charismatic and eccentric King Ludwig, the nineteenth-century ruler of Bavaria when it was still an independent country. We were enjoying the rural character of the region—small-scale farms scattered across a rolling, pastoral landscape and dotted with a series of charming villages, each featuring a baroque church with an interior seemingly more ornate than the last. But on this August afternoon a thunderstorm was building and clearly heading our way. As the storm broke we were fortunate to find a small barn beside the country road we were walking, doors open and beckoning us to take shelter. Hay bales offered us comfortable seating and a good view of the lightning and accompanying sheets of rain. After an hour, the storm ended as quickly as it began and we continued on our way, the storm and our picturesque shelter another memorable and romantic moment of our delightful Bavarian adventure.

Popularly called the "Dream King," Ludwig ascended to the throne of Bavaria in 1864 at the vulnerable age of 18. He ruled erratically for twenty-two years until his mysterious death at age 40. While he was politically naive and spent money lavishly (and beyond the country's means), he made lasting and increasingly valuable contributions in the areas of art and architecture. He was also an avid walker, and the trail that bears his name is an especially appropriate way to honor his legacy. This trail is one of Germany's best-known footpaths.

The two ends of the trail mark the beginning and ending of Ludwig's reign, and the trail is usually walked in reverse chronological order, saving the best for last. It starts in the village of Leoni on the shores of Lake Starnberg, where Ludwig drowned just a few days after he was removed from power for mental incompetence. Did he jump into the lake or was he pushed? This remains one of the great mysteries of European history. A simple cross in the lake and a small votive chapel on the shore mark the site of Ludwig's death. From the lake, the trail wanders south for 75 miles, stopping

LOCATION
Germany

LENGTH
75 miles

ACCOMMODATIONS
Commercial (e.g., Inns, B&Bs): Yes
Huts/Refuges: No
Backpacking/Camping: Some

BAGGAGE TRANSFER
Yes

OPTION TO WALK IN SECTIONS
All

DEGREE OF CHALLENGE
Low-Moderate

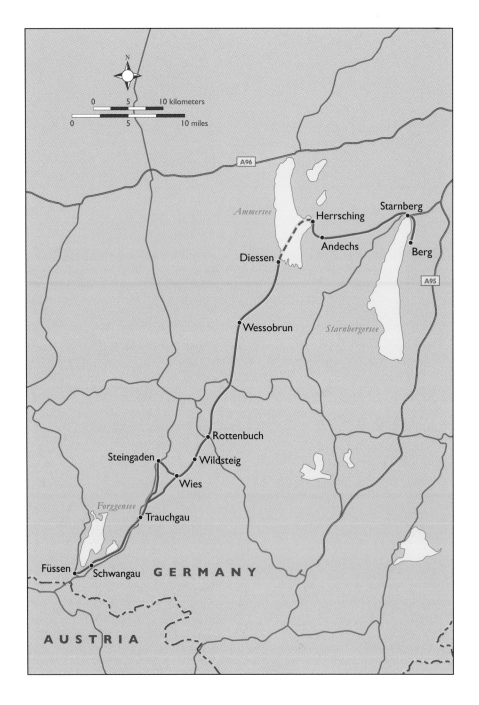

just short of the Austrian border. The end of the walk features the fairy-tale castles that are the most tangible manifestations of Ludwig and this period of Bavarian history.

The track wanders through the green countryside that sits at the base of the Alps, passing through a dozen towns and villages that are attractive, offer numerous opportunities for accommodations or a hot meal, and allow the trail to be walked in any number of days. Our favorite towns were Andechs, Diessen, Rottenbuch, Wildsteig, and Füssen. Andechs was founded in 1455 by Benedictine monks and sits on a hill, the "Holy Mount." The impressive abbey church is a historic pilgrimage site and is approached by a long lane featuring the Stations of the Cross. Today, most visitors drive to Andechs, attracted by the Andechs Monastery Brewery (is this an oxymoron?) with its restaurant and beer garden. Famous Andechs Bockbier, brewed by enterprising monks, is served by the traditional *mass*, a liter container shaped like a great vase, and, judging by the crowds the day we visited, the monks are good brewers, indeed. Diessen is an attractive lakeside town that's reached by ferry over Ammersee Lake and features the Diessen Monastery Church, a striking example of Bavarian baroque architecture. Rottenbuch is a tiny but delightful monastery town, dominated by a grand church set on one side of a cobbled square and reached through a stone gateway. Wildsteig is an agricultural hamlet; the day we were there, the town was celebrating its 900th anniversary, complete with antique tractors, residents in traditional costume, and an oompah band. Füssen is the largest town on the trail, a walled city located less than a mile from the Austrian border and featuring a castle, medieval streets, and a fine church. It's visitor friendly, offering all services

that walkers might need. All along the route nearly all houses (many of them traditional chalets) feature elaborate window boxes stuffed with geraniums.

The last day of walking presents the highlight of the trail, the two castles that mark the beginning and ending of Ludwig's reign. Hohenschwangau is the family castle where Ludwig was born. It's an impressive structure that features variations of the royal family's swan motif on everything. But Ludwig yearned for something more than his birth home—a castle reflecting his fanciful interests in art and architecture, and he commissioned the building of Neuschwanstein, located in an improbable setting on the crest of a hill towering above the surrounding plains. It's a mix of architectural styles, including Romanesque, Byzantine, and many forms of Gothic (Neuschwanstein is rumored to be the model for Cinderella's Castle at Disney World). To illustrate the lavish style in which the castle was created, fourteen wood-carvers worked for four years on the bedroom furniture alone. More than 2 million visitors come to Neuschwanstein annually, so be prepared for long lines to purchase tickets. The trail approaches the castle through the steep Pollat Gorge at the base of the hill, and leads to the Marie Bridge spanning the gorge and offering classic views of the castle. Tours of both castles are offered in several languages.

Other features of the trail include grand views of the surrounding Alps, two lakes (crossed by ferry), grand maypoles with the symbols of traditional occupations marking the entrance to all towns, Ammer Gorge (Bavaria's "Grand Canyon"), and the summit of Hofenpeissenberg Hill, which offers what many think is the finest view in Bavaria. We especially liked the pilgrimage church at Wies (a UNESCO World Heritage Site), built in the eighteenth century and dramatically set in the midst of agricultural fields without any surrounding town; it's popularly called the "Meadow Church."

(ABOVE LEFT) Quiet walks through old-growth beech forests are a highlight of King Ludwig's Way.

(ABOVE) This pedestrian bridge offers iconic views of Neuschwanstein, the fairy-tale castle of King Ludwig.

(ABOVE) Many of the churches along King Ludwig's Way may appear plain on the outside, but have much more elaborate and impressive baroque interiors.

(ABOVE RIGHT) Hohenschwangau is the family castle where Ludwig was born; the swan motif of the royal family is featured throughout the elaborate building.

While most of the trail follows farm and rural roads, portions of the track cross patches of dense forest—beeches in the lower elevations and fir and pine at higher locations. Forests, or *walds*, are important in German folklore as places of wildness, beauty, and legend. Contemporary damage to these areas by air pollution and acid rain is taken very seriously by many Germans and is a contentious political issue.

King Ludwig's Way is a pleasant walk presenting only modest challenges. There are no long or steep climbs, and daily walking distances average 8 to 12 miles, or even shorter if desired. This is a "lowland" walk, surrounded by the Alps but traveling through the valleys and forests at their base. All towns offer *gasthofs* (guesthouses), which are usually a combination of pub, hotel, and restaurant, and baggage transfers can easily be arranged. Part of the fun is eating traditional German food such as *Weiner schnitzel*, *sauerkraut*, *spätzle*, and *apfelstrudel*, and, of course, drinking German beer. However, ordering can sometimes be an adventure, as little English is spoken in some of the rural areas the trail traverses. Although our language skills were challenged, we always found the people we met to be friendly, helpful, and welcoming. The trail is well maintained and easy to follow—marked by a

stylistic "K"—and access to the trail is easy by train from Munich and Diessen. The peak walking season is June through August, but the shoulder months of May and September offer appealing options; October is also a possibility, though accommodations may be scarce during Octoberfest, a tradition started by King Ludwig in celebration of his wedding.

Before this walk we didn't fully understand what an interesting figure King Ludwig was, nor did we appreciate his legacy for Germans in particular and Europeans more generally. King Ludwig's Way is an opportunity to experience the idyllic Bavarian landscape and enjoy its modern rural character and people. Consider walking with King Ludwig across his beloved native Bavaria.

Resources

Guidebook

Cassandra Overby, *Explore Germany's King Ludwig's Way on Foot: Berg to Füssen*, 2018

(ABOVE LEFT) Walkers enjoy peaceful valleys and lovely lakes along King Ludwig's Way.

(ABOVE) King Ludwig's Way ends in the visitor-friendly walled city of Füssen, less than a mile from the Austrian border.

The Kungsleden traverses thousands of square miles of arctic tundra, deep forests, glacier-filled mountains, and big northern rivers.

Kungsleden

Our first day on the Kungsleden was just what we'd hoped—glorious scenery, beautiful weather, and a good night's sleep in a warm, cozy hut. Unfortunately, day two offered up an entirely different experience. We stepped out of our hut and back on the trail just as the rain started—and then came the wind. We walked (and occasionally slogged) all day across vast stretches of arctic tundra, finally reaching our next hut about four o'clock that afternoon. We were cold and beat. But then came an unexpected reward. After the hut master checked us in, he casually asked if we would like to take a sauna before dinner. A sauna?! As it turns out, some of the more enterprising hut masters have built saunas for their guests, and this sounded like just what we needed. Of course we didn't know exactly what a genuine Swedish sauna was, but it sounded like a place to get clean and warm. And it was—for everyone at the hut—at the same time—co-ed, naked. This was a real cultural experience for two prudish New Englanders. We entered the sauna and washed with buckets of water heated on the woodstove and then sat on tiered benches soaking up the hot steam. When we were finally too hot, we dashed out of the building and plunged into the adjacent river, returning to the sauna to repeat the whole process. Our walk along the Kungsleden instilled in us a genuine appreciation for the tradition of the sauna.

Kungsleden is translated as the "trail of kings" and sometimes the "king of trails." Both of these worked for us, as the drama of the vast and stark landscape of Lapland is truly regal in scale and character. This 270-mile trail connecting Abisko in the north to Hemavan in the south traverses the Lapponia World Heritage Site, the largest area of wilderness left in Europe, and wanders through four national parks and a nature reserve—in all an area larger than some European countries. The Kungsleden is often referred to as the "national trail" of Sweden. The northern portion of the trail (from Abisko to Kvikkjokk, about 110 miles and all sited north of the Arctic Circle) is acknowledged as the most

LOCATION
Sweden

LENGTH
270 miles

ACCOMMODATIONS
Commercial (e.g., Inns, B&Bs): Some
Huts/Refuges: Yes
Backpacking/Camping: Yes

BAGGAGE TRANSFER
No

OPTION TO WALK IN SECTIONS
Some

DEGREE OF CHALLENGE
Moderate–High

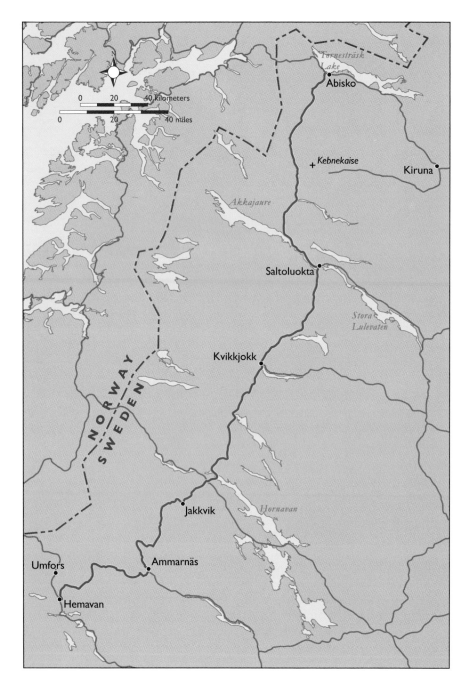

scenic section, and that's what we walked, taking nine days.

This is a vast and dramatic landscape capped by an endless sky. Huge, shallow valleys lie at the foot of rolling, low-lying, snowcapped mountains with glaciers clinging to their sides. Big, fast-flowing rivers connect large, icy lakes. Deep forests of pine, spruce, and stunted birch cover much of the landscape the farther south you go. The trail is well marked with stone cairns and red blazes, and wayfinding is not difficult.

The trail tread is often wet, but miles of boardwalk have been constructed, and walking is easy in these places. However, other portions of the trail are rough with occasional steep, but short, climbs. All in all, this trail is of only moderate difficulty, though the weather and the trail's remoteness can add a substantial layer of challenge.

We enjoyed the wildlife: willow grouse, ptarmigan, golden eagles, and moose (what Swedes call elk). As we made our way along the edge of a small lake, an arctic tern dove at us repeatedly, protecting its young in a nest near the trail. And of course there are reindeer—herds of them flowing across the landscape. One afternoon we were taking a break, sitting on some rocks sunning ourselves, when a herd of reindeer walked slowly toward us, enveloping us, then moving on—a truly enchanting moment. We didn't see some of the more secretive wildlife, such as lynx, wolverines, wolves, and bears.

The Sami, northern Scandinavia's indigenous people who have lived in this area for 10,000 years, herd reindeer. Small clusters of Sami huts are seen periodically along the trail, and the Sami provide walkers with goods and services—local fish and food, and ferries across lakes. Their knowledge of this land is so intimate

that they divide the year into eight seasons. The Sami continue to practice reindeer husbandry, and hikers should be careful not to interfere.

Walking the trail offers adventures every day. Near the beginning, the trail takes walkers through the dramatic saddle known as Lapporten, the "Gates of Lapland." Four large lakes must be crossed along the trail, and this can be done in self-service rowboats. There are three rowboats at each lake. If there are two boats on your side, then you simply row one across, pulling your boat up on shore at the end. But if there is only one boat on your side, then you row to the other side, tow a boat back, and then row across again. This honor system ensures that there is always a boat for walkers approaching from either the north or the south. However, you must exercise caution in crossing these lakes—they're broad, deep, and icy. Local Sami guides will ferry walkers across the lakes in motorboats for a nominal fee, and this is a good idea if the water is rough or you're not experienced with boats.

Side trails lead into even more remote areas, and there are two especially attractive alternatives. At 6,932 feet, Kebnekaise is the highest mountain in Sweden (and all of Arctic Scandinavia), and it is accessible by a steep but not too difficult trail. Skierfe is not as high, but is especially dramatic and offers outstanding views into the heart of the wild and rugged mountains of Sarek National Park. Wild bilberries, cloudberries, and blueberries are more than plentiful (but can be sour!). The region is so pristine that water can be consumed directly from rivers and lakes (one of the few places we've done this). Local smoked fish can sometimes be purchased for dinner. Take time to look closely—on

(ABOVE LEFT) The Kungsleden follows several wild rivers on its long journey above the Arctic Circle.

(ABOVE) Low-lying mountains covered in glaciers and snowfields, along with big northern lakes, offer dramatic scenery.

(ABOVE) Miles of boardwalk protect tundra vegetation, keep hikers' feet dry, and make for easy walking.

(ABOVE RIGHT) Hikers must boat across five large lakes encountered along the northern half of the Kungsleden; local Sami people provide rides when it's too rough for self-service rowboats.

hands and knees—at the tundra you're walking across and appreciate this biologically diverse, miniature "forest." Enjoy the midnight sun, meet walkers from around the world, and embrace the challenge of reading trail signs written in Swedish.

An elaborate system of huts and lodges is scattered along the trail, an easy day's walk apart, and this means walkers don't have to carry tents, cooking equipment, and other camping gear (though camping is allowed in most places). Huts are simple, but clean and efficient, providing bunks and communal kitchens stocked with gas stoves, pots and pans, and dishes. Some huts sell limited provisions. Hut etiquette demands that walkers take their boots off before entering, gather clean water for communal use, sweep floors, sort trash, shake and fold duvets, and store stools on tables before leaving. Walkers should also split wood when needed. Lodges (called *fjallstations*) are less common (there are three along the section of the trail we walked—Abisko, Saltoluokta, and Kvikkjokk) and are much more elaborate, offering hotel-like rooms, hot showers, and full-service restaurants. Lodges are the only places along the trail that have road access. The Swedish Touring Association (STF) operates most huts and lodges; because we had joined the organization prior to our trip, we received a substantial discount on fees.

As might be expected, the walking season is short on the Kungsleden—late June through some of September (depending on weather). (The trail also serves cross-country skiers in the winter.) Our walk was in the second half of August, and temperatures dipped below freezing on a few nights. June and July can be wet, bringing out mosquitoes, but offer wildflowers in profusion. September displays fall colors. Huts and lodges take credit cards, but bring some cash for ferries and trade with the Sami. Camping is allowed along the trail with few restrictions, but nearly everyone uses the

huts. Positioning for the Kungsleden takes a day or two on both ends of the walk. We took the 18-hour overnight train from Stockholm (an adventure in itself—our advice is to reserve a sleeping car because the train may be crowded). You can also fly to Kiruna and use buses to reach the beginning and ending points of the trail. Most people walk from north to south to keep the sun's warmth on their face. While in Stockholm, we mailed ourselves a resupply package that was delivered to one of the lodges. Study maps and apps carefully, both for wayfinding (which was not difficult) and to find road access, if you wish a shorter or longer version of the trail than we walked.

Our walk on the Kungsleden was one of our favorites because the landscape and culture were so distinctive and appealing. The trail is really a bit of a paradox; it tends to make lists of the world's best trails, but relatively few people actually walk it. On many days of our walk, we saw no one on the trail and relatively few at the huts. In fact, most walkers haven't even heard of the Kungsleden. We suggest you walk this trail soon before the rest of the world discovers it.

(ABOVE LEFT) The indigenous Sami people of far northern Sweden have been herding reindeer for 10,000 years.

(ABOVE) Cozy huts offer accommodations, well-equipped kitchens, and the company of like-minded hikers from all over the world.

Resources

Website
Swedish Tourist Association: www.swedishtouristassociation.com

Guidebooks
Mike Laing, *The Kungsleden—Walking Sweden's Royal Trail*, 2019
Danielle Fenton and Wayne Fenton, *Plan & Go | Kungsleden*, 2017

Stratton Pond is one of many lakes along the trail that offer swimming in the summer and reflections of Vermont's iconic fall foliage.

Long Trail

We love our *Long Trail Guide*. It's the compact source of all the information needed to walk this remarkable trail, the first long-distance trail in America. It provides detailed descriptions of the trail, including mileages, hiking times, difficulty ratings, locations of overnight shelters and campsites, water sources, and elevation profiles. It includes directions to trailheads and parking and even a small map. And it's designed to fit easily into the pack. There's only one problem with the guide—it's written in code. After a few days of walking, we figured it out. For example, when the guide describes the terrain as "rolling," it means get ready for a series of significant ascents and descents. When the trail "drops steeply," hang on to exposed roots and whatever else is available. When it "climbs steeply," get ready for a half hour of anaerobic breathing. "Uneven" means extremely rough. "Rough going" means nearly impassable. "Wet area" means this bog will suck your boots off. Learning the understated language of Vermonters is just part of the fun of walking this trail. And the trail reflects its history. Developed prior to contemporary trail-building methods, the route tends to go from Point A (the trailhead) to Point B (a mountain summit) in the most direct line, without consideration of such niceties as switchbacks. But that's part of the adventure of the Long Trail—remember, the trail is "rolling."

———————≈———————

The aptly named Long Trail is a 272-mile roller-coaster ride along the ridgeline of Vermont's Green Mountains, connecting Massachusetts to Canada, crossing the state's highest peaks, and exposing much of its most beautiful scenery. It was conceived in 1909 by James P. Taylor, a teacher at Vermont Academy, who liked to take his pupils on hikes but was frustrated that there weren't more trails connecting the major peaks of the Green Mountains. The Green Mountain Club (GMC) ultimately achieved his vision of a "long trail" linking all the major mountains in 1930. When the trail was officially opened that year, flares were lit from the tops of the mountain peaks along the route, a signal to

LOCATION
Vermont, United States

LENGTH
272 miles

ACCOMMODATIONS
Commercial (e.g., Inns, B&Bs):
Some
Huts/Refuges: Three-sided
shelters
Backpacking/Camping: Yes

BAGGAGE TRANSFER
No

OPTION TO WALK IN SECTIONS
Yes

DEGREE OF CHALLENGE
Moderate–High

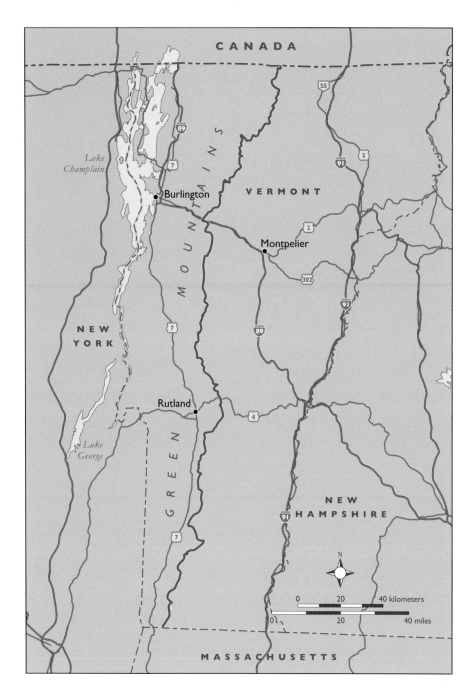

all Vermonters. Today, the Long Trail, popularly called "A Footpath in the Wilderness," is one of the iconic features of Vermont and attracts thousands of hikers each year. The trail offered inspiration and a model for the 2,200-mile Appalachian Trail that runs from Georgia to Maine; in fact, a 100-mile section of the Long Trail is part of the more famous "AT."

The Green Mountains are the geologic backbone of Vermont and give the Long Trail its distinctive "rolling" character. Part of the greater Appalachian Mountain system, the Greens run the length of the state, extending into Massachusetts and Canada, and ranging from 20 to 35 miles wide. The original mountains are thought to be over a billion years old and once rose to heights of 10,000 to 20,000 feet. But erosion, glaciation, and other geologic forces have reduced heights to around 4,000 feet. The glaciers have given the mountains and surrounding landscape their distinctive form—mountains with relatively gentle north-facing slopes and steep south faces (rock "plucked" away by glaciers advancing to the south), smooth exposed peaks, broad U-shaped valleys, frequent ponds and bogs, and rocks everywhere. Two impressive rivers, the Winooski and Lamoille, bisect the range.

Long Trail walkers climb up and over all the major peaks—Glastonbury Mountain, Stratton Mountain, Killington Peak, Mount Abraham, Mount Ellen, Camel's Hump, Mount Mansfield, and Jay Peak. But of all the mountains in Vermont, Mansfield and Camel's Hump are the most iconic. Mansfield is the highest at 4,395 feet and looks like the profile of a person's face (lying down) when viewed from the west. Distinctive knobs are known as "Forehead" (the highest point), "Nose," and "Chin." (Some close observers claim they can also distinguish upper and lower lips and an Adam's apple.) The view from the top is spectacular, and includes the White Mountains

to the east, the Adirondack Mountains and Lake Champlain to the west, Montreal to the north, and a sea of peaks all around. Camel's Hump (a genteel version of the name "Camel's Rump" on a 1798 map prepared by Ira Allen, legendary Green Mountain Boy), is the only mountain in the state over 4,000 feet that hasn't been developed in some way. It, too, has a distinctive profile—a crouching lion. Both Mount Mansfield and Camel's Hump (as well as Mount Abraham) have substantial areas of arctic alpine tundra on their bald summits, remnants of the last glacial period some 10,000 years ago. The low-lying species of Bigelow's sedge, alpine bilberry, and mountain sandwort are normally found only in areas a thousand or more miles to the north. These vegetative communities are highly fragile, and walkers must be careful to stay on the trail in these areas and step only on bare rock surfaces. Green Mountain Club "caretakers" are posted on these summits to protect them and to help educate visitors.

Other prominent vegetation along the trail includes vast forests of northern hardwoods, including sugar maple (the state tree), red maple, beech, northern red oak, and yellow and white birch. Of course this is the forest that provides the world-famous fall foliage of stunning reds, oranges, and yellows. Evergreen forests of spruce and fir grow at higher elevations. When first seen by explorer Samuel de Champlain from the lake that now bears his name, he exhorted, "*Voila, les verds monts*" ("Behold, the green mountains"), unknowingly bestowing the contemporary name of the state's dominant geographic feature. As the forest approaches the highest elevations of 4,000 feet, trees become stunted by the short growing season and distorted by the wind and weather, forming the

(ABOVE LEFT) The Long Trail, the first long-distance trail in America, is a 272-mile rollercoaster along the ridgeline of Vermont's Green Mountains.

(ABOVE) An early fall snow highlights the trail through this lovely beech forest; note the white blaze marking the trail.

(LEFT) The trail is frequently cut by delightful mountain streams.

(CENTER) The trail climbs up and over most of the major mountain peaks in Vermont, including colorfully-named Camel's Hump (a genteel version of the original Camel's Rump).

(RIGHT) Early morning hikers might find the surrounding valleys filled with fog.

distinctive krummholz, meaning "crooked wood" in German. Spring wildflowers include trilliums, violets, hepaticas, and spring beauties. Animals include plentiful white-tailed deer at lower elevations, beavers, bobcats, an increasing population of moose (we saw two on the trail), and black bears (we saw one). There is a great debate about whether there are still catamounts (Vermont's version of mountain lions) in the Green Mountains; there continue to be reported "sightings," but scientists insist that they have been extirpated. Notable birds include partridge, wild turkeys, hawks, peregrine falcons, and bald eagles.

You'll encounter lots of interesting features along the trail. Several peaks, including Glastonbury, Stratton, and Belvidere, have fire towers that provide striking 360-degree views. Ski areas share several of the mountains, and a few offer chairlift rides to the top (or bottom) in summer and fall. Stratton Pond and others offer great swimming and are favorites of many hikers. The trail passes through portions of six wilderness areas, all part of the Green Mountain National Forest; in these sections, the trail is more primitive and use levels tend to be low.

Vermont was home to the Abenaki indigenous people long before it was colonized, and it's likely that portions of the Long Trail follow ancient aboriginal travel routes, but there is little physical evidence of the Native American presence. You may be surprised to find artifacts of historical occupation of this land as you walk the trail—occasional rock walls and cellar holes mark the locations of fruitless attempts to farm a land that was both steep and, because of the short growing season, unsuitable for growing crops. By 1850, 80 percent of Vermont had been cleared for timber, ship masts, potash, and sheep farms. Now the state is 80 percent forested. The trail also includes a system of 166 miles of side trails that provide access up to the Long Trail and down to the many other delights of Vermont, including historic villages, B&Bs, artisan cheeses and beer, breakfasts of pancakes and real maple syrup, and, of course, Ben and Jerry's ice cream.

The Long Trail is highly accessible, with many road crossings and its extensive system of side trails, allowing for frequent resupply for thru-hikers and easy access for day use. In fact, all of the trail can be walked in short sections of one to a few days. The trail is serviced with seventy back-country camping areas, many of which include three-sided structures for shelter, and a few primitive lodges; all have water (that must be treated) and privies. These overnight facilities are spaced at 5- to 10-mile intervals. A nominal fee may be required for some shelters where there are caretakers (no charge for GMC members). Shelters and lodges can be crowded, so overnight hikers should carry tents. Many surrounding towns in Vermont have a range of B&Bs and small inns, useful for hikers who don't want to camp. Wayfinding is generally easy as the trail is well marked by white blazes on trees and rocks; side trails are blazed in blue. Walkers are asked to refrain from using the trail until Memorial Day to give forest soils a chance to dry from melting snow. Early summer offers impressive wildflowers, but mosquitoes, blackflies, and ticks as well—wear long pants and a long-sleeved shirt for protection. Fall is glorious with Vermont's renowned colors. The trail is not designed for winter use; backcountry skiers have their own 300-mile Catamount Trail, which runs through the heart of the state. Sturdy, waterproof boots are highly recommended because the trail is often rough and wet. Vermont gets relatively few thunderstorms, but be wary when walking over the highest, exposed portions of the trail.

We advise you not to underestimate the Long Trail, neither the rewards it offers nor the challenges it presents. This is iconic Vermont. Though the Green Mountains aren't especially high, the trail climbs an accumulated 63,000 feet over the course of its length, and it's rough in places. (*Backpacker* magazine deems it "curse-worthy.") Most hikers agree that the northern section is the most challenging, and we concur. We encourage you to walk the Long Trail, or sections of it; just dial down your normal daily mileage expectations. We thank the Green Mountain Club for their heroic work in building and maintaining the Long Trail; the club formed in 1910 with a mission to "make the mountains of Vermont play a larger part in the life of its people." Mission accomplished.

Resources

Website
Green Mountain Club: www.greenmountainclub.org

Guidebooks
Green Mountain Club and Matt Krebs, *Long Trail Guide*, 2017
Green Mountain Club, *End-to-Ender's Guide* (23rd edition), 2022

Map
Green Mountain Club, *Vermont's Long Trail* (5th edition), 2015

The Lost Coast Trail features lots of shorebirds, including pelicans, cormorants, oystercatchers, and several types of gulls.

Lost Coast Trail

Two hundred and thirty miles north of San Francisco lies the remote and solitary "Lost Coast" of California and what *Backpacker* magazine calls "one of the premier ocean-hugging hikes in the world." In studying up for our hike, we learned that Roosevelt elk, one of the largest members of the deer family, had been reintroduced to the area and were thriving and reproducing. Male (bull) elk grow to be 1,000 pounds or more. We hoped we'd be able to get a glimpse of some of these magnificent animals, and on day four of our walk, we saw one of these bulls—up close and personal! That day found us high on the headlands and deep in thick rain forests watered by periodic storms blowing in off the Pacific Ocean. We were watching carefully where we placed our feet in this especially dense stretch of trail when we looked up to see a full-grown bull elk not more than 10 feet in front of us. It was grazing, had vines hanging off its substantial rack of antlers, and was almost perfectly camouflaged. Fortunately, it seemed totally unconcerned with us as we slowly backed away and waited for it to move on before continuing our walk south along the trail. Seeing wild animals on our walks is always a thrill, and the Roosevelt elk we met on the Lost Coast Trail was one of the most thrilling ones ever!

Decades ago, legendary highway US 101 was built along the coast of California. But there's a large area in the extreme northern part of the state that projects out into the ocean, and it was decided that it was not economically feasible to locate the road out and around this obstacle. Instead, the road "shortcuts" this area and goes inland, leaving what is now called the "Lost Coast," a region that remains generally inaccessible and lightly visited. For walkers, this long stretch of beach and headlands offers one of the longest lengths of wild coastline in the lower 48 states. Most of this land is managed by two public agencies, the federal Bureau of Land Management and the California State Parks Department, and this ownership provides ready public access.

LOCATION
California, United States

LENGTH
60 miles

ACCOMMODATIONS
Commercial (e.g., Inns, B&Bs): Some
Huts/Refuges: No
Backpacking/Camping: Yes

BAGGAGE TRANSFER
No

OPTION TO WALK IN SECTIONS
Some

DEGREE OF CHALLENGE
Moderate

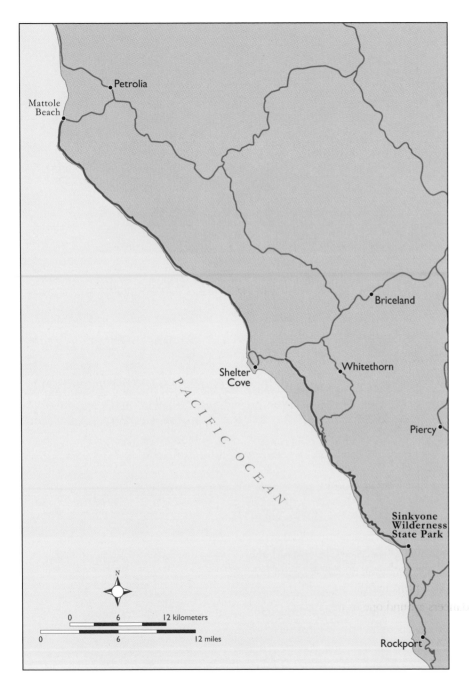

The Lost Coast walk divides naturally into two distinct sections. The northern portion is approximately 30 miles long, traces the edge of the King Range National Conservation Area, and is nearly all directly on wild Pacific Ocean beaches punctuated with massive piles of driftwood, the remains of doomed ships, and other interesting flotsam. Dramatic sea stacks dot the ocean side of the walk, while the inland side is composed of the steep slopes of the unusually high coastal mountains of the King's Range that culminate in 4,088-foot King's Peak. These coastal mountains are cut by numerous streams that spill their water out over the beach and into the Pacific Ocean, providing an important source of fresh water to walkers, interesting canyons to explore, and a series of natural benches that make good campsites. They are also vital components of the life cycle of native coho and chinook salmon, which are born here and eventually return to spawn.

The walk offers close-up views of a wealth of marine life in the form of rich tide pools, pelicans, bald eagles, cormorants, playful sea otters, elephant seals, groups of barking sea lions, and harbor seals that frolic on the waves and form shoreline rookeries. Gray whales can be seen migrating in winter and spring. Look closely for tracks of bears, bobcats, and mountain lions in the morning wet sand. Walkers have made elaborate driftwood structures that serve as good shelters and campsites. Occasional stretches of marine terraces and gentle coastal prairies exist back from the extended beaches and make for easy walking. Fog is common and adds to the wild character of the area. There are a few isolated private cabins along the trail, and hikers must respect these private lands. Each high tide wipes the beach clean of footprints and this—along with the general absence of other walkers—made us sometimes feel like we were the first people to walk these wild beaches.

The northern section of the hike comes to an abrupt end at a small promontory that juts still farther into the ocean and has been developed into the remote community of Shelter Cove. Shelter Cove includes a number of small B&Bs that make a nice respite for walkers after a few nights of camping along the beach; our B&B owner even generously offered to do a load of wash for us. We enjoyed a simple meal and "people-watched" the other visitors to this tiny community.

The southern half of the hike is another 30 miles and is distinctly different, taking hikers through Sinkyone Wilderness State Park. Here, the ocean meets a series of steep cliffs, and hiking is mostly along the striking high headlands that parallel the shoreline. These headlands are covered in a rich old-growth rain forest; trees include coast redwoods, Douglas fir with trunks up to 6 feet in diameter, and large tanoaks. The headlands offer ridgetop vistas out over the ocean, fern-covered canyons, and a few small waterfalls. Occasional streams flow into the Pacific Ocean and sometimes offer access to beautiful pocket beaches, but also make for steep ascents and descents. On sunny days, the ocean lights up in a lovely turquoise, reminiscent of the tropics. The glamour wildlife species of these headlands is the Roosevelt elk. Accessing the southern section of the trail involves a short walk along the road that serves Shelter Cove, and hikers should be very careful of automobile traffic along this narrow, winding road.

Of course the Lost Coast has an important human history as well as natural history. Indigenous people occupied this area as early as 6,000 BCE, and shell middens still exist on several beaches above the high tide line. Abandoned Punta Gorda (Spanish for "massive point") Lighthouse was built in 1912 after the wreck of the *Columbia* killed eighty-seven people. Known as the "Alcatraz of lighthouses" because it was so isolated, it was decommissioned in 1950, and it must have been a lonely station indeed; the lighthouse is on the National Register of Historic Places and is fun to explore. Like many areas of California, the Lost Coast has supported the fishing and timber industries, and if you look closely, you can still see evidence of these and other economic activities: some cattle and sheep ranching, abandoned logging roads, and the harbor at Shelter Cove. The area is also well known as a haven for the hippie generation, and this adds interest; one foggy morning we were surprised to see a group of nude dancers around one of the more isolated driftwood structures.

There are several logistical and safety concerns associated with walking the Lost Coast Trail. Though the area is accessible year-round, the primary walking season is May through September

Streams cut through the unusually high King's Range of coastal mountains, spilling their water out over the beach and into the Pacific Ocean, providing hikers with an important source of fresh water and interesting canyons to explore.

(ABOVE) Periodic natural benches perched above the shoreline offer easy walking compared to the soft sand of the beaches below.

(ABOVE RIGHT) The southern half of the trail is dominated by high headlands covered in rich old-growth rain forests and offering panoramic views of the coastline below.

because there are often strong Pacific storms in the winter and early spring, which bring more than 100 inches of rain annually. Even in summer, temperatures can be chilly, as the area is cooled by the ocean and occasional fog. The primary concern is maintaining personal safety around the ocean. This area of the Pacific Ocean is cold and subject to dangerous currents; we enjoyed wading in the water to refresh our feet, but wouldn't risk swimming. Walkers must bring local tide tables with them and know how to use them (which is not difficult). There are three stretches of beach in the northern half of the hike that can be walked only when the tide is low; these stretches are up to 4 miles long and are inundated by high tide right up to the cliff faces, a potentially deadly scenario. Be sure there is enough time to walk these stretches of beach before the tide comes in; ideally, walk these areas as the tide is receding. Be wary of occasional larger-than-normal waves; "never turn your back on the ocean" is an old saying among people who live along the coast. Dangerous "rogue" or "sneaker" waves can wash ashore and surprise walkers, possibly carrying them out to sea if they're caught unaware. Walking on the beach is a highlight of the northern part of the trail, but this often makes for slow progress, especially with a backpack. Search out the harder sand, usually at the edge of the high tide line, or the area of wet sand, as this will make walking easier. We walked the trail from north to south to keep the prevailing (and often stiff) wind at our backs. The BLM keeps a list of "approved" shuttle services that will pick up and/or drop off hikers at the beginning or ending of the walk. A permit to camp along the northern section of the trail is required from the BLM and can be obtained using the Recreation.gov website. A permit is not needed for the southern section of the trail, but camping is limited to designated sites, and these are first-come, first-served. The Lost Coast Trail begins at Mattole River Beach and ends at Usal Beach; you'll find parking and a

campground at both locations. Drinking water is readily available from occasional streams that flow into the ocean (especially along the northern section of the trail), though it must be treated; these streams can be difficult and dangerous to cross while they're in flood. Hikers are required to carry and use bear canisters to keep food from bears and other wild animals. Walking surfaces are highly variable along the trail, with extensive stretches of sand, loose stones, rocks, and dense rain forests; sturdy boots are recommended, especially through the rain forest. Potential hazards include rattle-snakes, poison oak, and biting insects.

We're partial to coastal walks—both natural and human history seem to be so rich and dynamic where the ocean meets the land. The Lost Coast Trail offers one of the last and best opportunities left in the lower 48 states for an extended walk along a dramatic wilderness coastline. We highly rec-ommend it.

Resources

Websites
Bureau of Land Management: www.blm.gov/visit/lost-coast-trail
King Range National Conservation Area: www.blm.gov/king-range
Sinkyone Wilderness Sate Park: www.parks.ca.gov/sinkyone

Guidebook
Mike White, *Top Trails: Northern California's Redwood Coast*, 2014

Map
California's Lost Coast (3rd edition), 2004

(LEFT) Each high tide wipes the beach clean, making hikers feel like they're the first people to traverse these deserted beaches.

(CENTER) Tide pools and shorelines offer lots of interesting marine life along the walk.

(RIGHT) The northern section of the Lost Coast Trail is nearly all directly on wild Pacific Ocean beaches strewn with driftwood.

Graceful stone pines line upland stretches of the Lycian Way and offer welcome shade.

Lycian Way

We'd finished our walk on the Lycian Way and were spending our last day in a small hotel in the rural fishing village of Adrasan before we traveled that evening to the city of Antalya to begin our journey home. Other guests who had walked several days with us encouraged us to celebrate our walk in the village's traditional Turkish bath, and that sounded like a good idea. Our 2-hour "bath" began with a long session in the steam room, where we sweated toxins. Then we were placed on large marble slabs, where muscular Turkish men first exfoliated and then washed us—very thoroughly and at considerable length— with hot water and rich, soapy lather. This was followed by a facial; local muds were painted on our faces and we were left with pots of tea, waiting for the mud to dry, after which the mud was washed from our faces and the real action began. We were given massages that would best be described as "vigorous." At the end of our massages, we were so relaxed that we each needed help getting up from the table. After heartfelt thanks to the towel-draped men (who spoke no English, but directed us by gestures), we showered to remove the massage oils. At the conclusion of our baths, we felt clean, refreshed, and invigorated—a perfect ending to our adventurous walk in Turkey.

<hr>

Lycia is a large region on the southern coast of Turkey where the Taurus Mountains meet the Mediterranean Sea. The Lycian Way, completed in 1999, offers a 330-mile walking route through the region, taking advantage of an assortment of Greek and Roman roads and aqueducts, mule paths, trading routes, backcountry roads, and forest trails. The route generally follows the coast, running from near the coastal town of Fethiye in the west and approaching the bustling port city of Antalya in the east. As you walk the Lycian Way, you follow in the footsteps of Alexander the Great and his army of 10,000 as they marched east through this area over twenty centuries ago. The *Sunday Times* of England called the Lycian Way one of the world's ten best walks.

LOCATION
Turkey

LENGTH
330 miles

ACCOMMODATIONS
Commercial (e.g., Inns, B&Bs): Some
Huts/Refuges: Some
Backpacking/Camping: Yes

BAGGAGE TRANSFER
No

OPTION TO WALK IN SECTIONS
Some

DEGREE OF CHALLENGE
Moderate–High

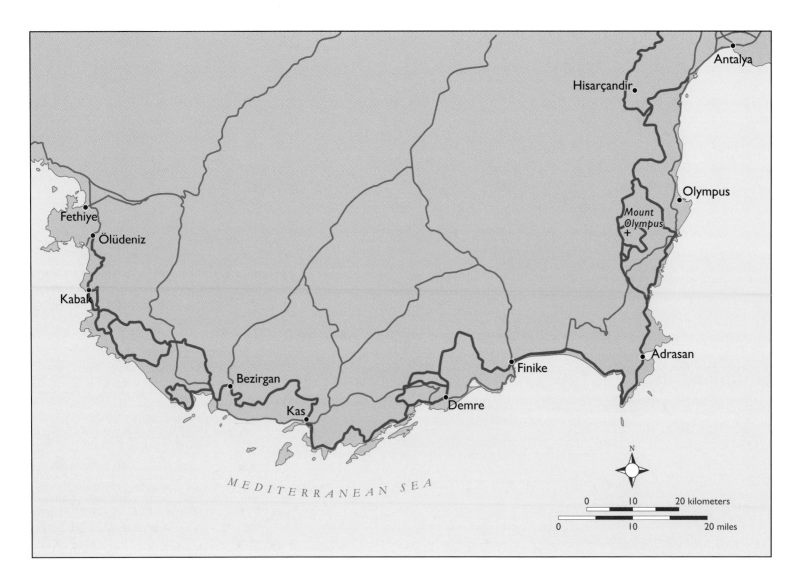

The Lycian region has ancient origins and is culturally diverse (which may be an understatement). The original inhabitants are thought to be Bronze Age people. But in later times, the area was part of the Persian, Greek, Roman, Byzantine, and Ottoman Empires. The region includes a diverse landscape as well, and the Lycian Way accurately reflects this. The trail leads walkers over high mountains, along deserted beaches, over coastal headlands, through forests of pine and cedars,

and into rural villages where fishing and farming have been a way of life for thousands of years. This is a place where East meets West. Modern Turkey is a Muslim country, and every village has a mosque, but the nation is governed in a secular manner. Every village has a statue of Ataturk, who created the contemporary nation of Turkey following World War I, and everywhere Turks proudly fly their distinctive red flag with a single white star.

There were many highlights of our walk. We walked through the ancient and extensive ruins of the port city of Olympus with its temples, theater, and sarcophagi; this was a major center of Lycia and includes inscriptions and a sarcophagus that date to the fourth century BCE. The city was important to all the civilizations that occupied it, including Greeks, Romans, and Byzantines. An image of the city was struck on coins in 167–168 BCE, and some of the buildings are thought to honor Roman emperor Marcus Aurellius. We hiked over Mount Olympus, at 7,763 feet the high point of the trail. We swam in the turquoise waters of the Mediterranean at deserted Pirates' Cove. We had lunch in an open-air restaurant where flatbread was being made by hand and chickens casually strolled under and by the tables. We lingered at iconic Gelidonya Lighthouse, the symbol of the Lycian Way and the southernmost point of Lycia. We walked through the Chimera, where "eternal flames" emanate from the earth and are thought to have burned continuously for 2,500 years. We know now that this phenomenon is related to natural gas deposits in the area, but legend has it that the flames are the

(ABOVE LEFT) We walked through the Chimera, the "eternal flames" that emanate from the earth and are thought to have been burning continuously for 2,500 years; though this phenomenon is related to the natural gas deposits in the area, legend suggests that the flames are the breath of a mythical monster.

(ABOVE) The trail led us through the remains of the ancient port city of Olympus with its temples, theater, and sarcophagi.

(ABOVE) Much of the 330-mile Lycian Way follows the dramatic and beautiful Turquoise Coast of Turkey.

(ABOVE RIGHT) Cyclamen grows wild on the forest floor along the Lycian Way, carpeting it with flowers.

breath of a mythical monster that is part lion, part goat, and part snake, and ancient mariners in this part of the Mediterranean used the flames for navigation. We walked through many coastal villages, most of which are located on river deltas and have extensive greenhouses and orchards where fresh vegetables and fruits—tomatoes, eggplants, oranges, and pomegranates—are grown for shipment to Istanbul and the north. We walked through a grove of cedars—remnants of the ancient "cedars of Lebanon"—where the Bible says, "The righteous shall flourish like the palm tree and grow like a cedar in Lebanon."

Flora and fauna are diverse. There are coastal forests of graceful stone (sometimes called Italian) pines, strawberry trees with their smooth red trunks, palms, carob trees, and the higher-elevation groves of cedars as noted above. Cyclamen, an attractive houseplant in the Western world, grows wild on the forest floor, carpeting it with flowers. Animals include deer, wild goats, badgers, porcupines, foxes, and wild pigs or boars. The wild pigs use their long tusks to defend themselves and to dig for roots—we saw lots of evidence of their digging.

This trail is long, remote, and rough in places—walking the length of the trail is a serious undertaking. A more feasible approach (which we followed and recommend) is to walk selected sections that have support infrastructure. Good options include Ucagiz to Cape Gelidonya and Adrasan to Mount Olympus, each representing about a week of walking. It's increasingly popular to find a small hotel or two in one of the villages in these areas to use as a "base camp" and do a series of daily walks. Best months to walk are April and May and September and October; it's too hot in the summer and too cold in the winter. We found the Turks we met to be friendly and helpful, but not much English is spoken. The sun is hot and stretches of the trail are dry, so be sure to carry water and use plenty of sunblock. The trail is reasonably well marked with a white stripe over a red stripe. Public transportation is available all along the trail. Walkers can find basic commercial accommodations (village houses, pensions, small hotels) in most areas, and wild camping is usually available.

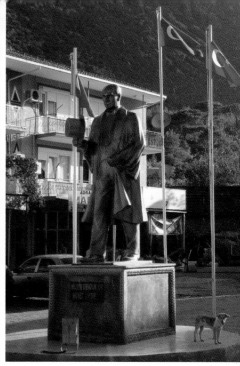

The Lycian Way leads walkers through a land that is diverse to the point of seeming paradoxical at times and places—it ranges from the mountains to the sea, it's old (the landscape and the culture) and new (the trail), its cities are modern and developed and its countryside rural, its culture is born out of both Eastern and Western traditions, its people are deeply religious but its civil affairs are conducted in a deliberately secular manner. We enjoyed this beautiful and seemingly exotic walk and hope you will, too. And don't forget the Turkish bath at the end!

(ABOVE LEFT) Gelidonya Lighthouse is the symbol of the Lycian Way and the southernmost point of Lycia.

(ABOVE) A mosque and a statue of Ataturk, who created the contemporary nation of Turkey following World War I, are in every village, and Turks proudly fly their distinctive red flag with a single white star.

Resources

Website
Cultural Routes Society: https://culturalroutesinturkey.com/the-lycian-way/

Guidebook
Kate Clow. *The Lycian Way*, 2014

App
Lycian Way by Cultural Routes Society

The ruins of the fourteenth-century Chateau des Lascaris rise above the medieval village of La Brigue; the round donjon tower offered residents safety from possible sieges.

Maritime Alps

Football (American soccer) fans around the world know Lionel Messi as one of the greatest of all time, captaining the Argentina National Team and playing at the highest level of European professional football. We had fun watching a pint-size, Messi-jersey-wearing eight-year-old French boy practicing his moves in the public square of the medieval town of Sainte-Agnes. (And this Messi wannabe was pretty good!) You could just tell that he was counting down the seconds and making the game-winning shot for a World Cup victory. In many ways, things are pretty much the same around the world, aren't they? In fact, the child playing football reminded us of our own children. This scene could have played out anywhere in the world, but the pleasing blend of this football hero in the making and the medieval backdrop of the town was somehow endearing. Walking allows you to notice these kinds of details and offers insights into culture. This was a nice moment for us.

———— ≈ ————

The Alps are the defining mountain range of Europe and one of the most recognizable in the world, stretching 750 miles in a broad arc across the continent and traversing eight countries. These mountains were formed over tens of millions of years, and they affect the very climate and natural history of this vast area of geography. The Alps even figure in the continent's celebrated history, as when Hannibal and Napoleon famously marched their armies across the range, changing the political map of Europe in the process. At nearly 16,000 feet, Mont Blanc stands as the continent's highest peak, though the Matterhorn may be the most recognizable. (See the Tour du Mont Blanc and the Walker's Haute Route later in this book for other long-distance walks in the Alps.)

The southern range of these mountains—often called the Maritime Alps—dances along the border of France and Italy and embraces the small sovereign city-state of Monaco as the mountains dip gracefully into the Mediterranean Sea. This southern, more gentle version of the Alps offers delightful walks of a week to ten days as trails wander over passes and through a series of historic "perched" villages (seemingly balanced on the steep slopes), ultimately reaching the seaside resorts

LOCATION
France

LENGTH
65 miles

ACCOMMODATIONS
Commercial (e.g., Inns, B&Bs):
Yes
Huts/Refuges: Some
Backpacking/Camping:
Limited

BAGGAGE TRANSFER
Yes

OPTION TO WALK IN SECTIONS
Most

DEGREE OF CHALLENGE
Moderate

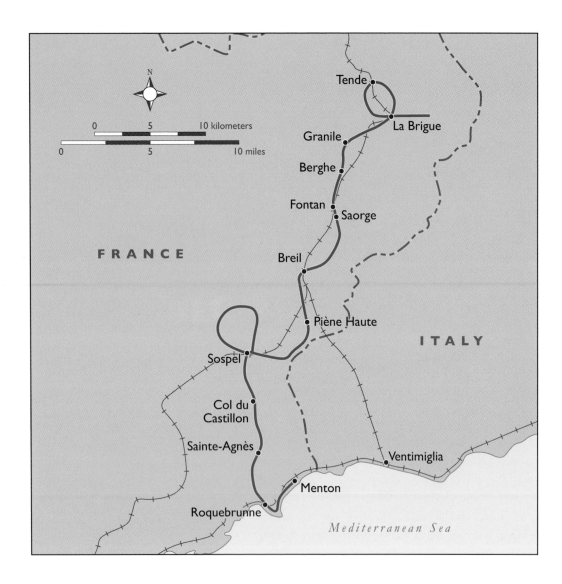

of the famous Cote d'Azur, including glitzy Nice and its more staid neighbor, Menton. The seaside resorts bustle with excitement, but the larger, sparsely populated uplands—reaching heights of over 10,000 feet—remain delightfully rural and rich in history and nature. This is a diverse region of Europe that demands exploration on foot.

The Maritime Alps are rich in both natural and cultural history. The especially large range of elevations across the region results in highly variable temperatures, plants, and animals. However, the Mediterranean climate binds the region together, with its precipitation falling mostly in the winter; summers are dry. And, of course, there's lots of sunshine—an average of 300 days a year! This mild, sunny climate, especially along the Mediterranean coast (or the Cote d'Azur, or French Riviera as it's often called) has attracted tourists from throughout Europe and around the world for centuries. The combination of beach-going on the seashore and active sports in the mountains is a strong draw.

The cultural history of the area can be traced back to Roman times, when the region was established as a military district by Augustus in 14 BCE. Since then, political boundaries have shifted regularly, as they often did in much of Europe. Important dates and events include the Napoleonic Wars in the early nineteenth century and the Treaty of Paris in 1947. Most hikers in the Maritime Alps spend the majority of their miles on the French side of the mountains, but Italy is often just a short distance away. Accordingly, Italian influences in language, food, and architecture are often obvious, enriching the culture.

Menton, with its historic homes and long promenade along the shore of the Mediterranean, is known as the "Pearl of France."

As if the mountains and seashore weren't enough, the hike through the Maritime Alps offers a string of medieval villages, many of them clinging to the steep hillsides; they're lovely to look at, delightful to stroll through, and make ready accommodations for long-distance walkers. We chose to start our walk in La Brigue, an ancient French town annexed from Italy to France as part of the Treaty of Paris. La Brigue is a typical French medieval mountain settlement, offering colorful buildings made from local stone, arcades, vaulted passages, and winding cobblestone streets to explore. The fourteenth-century Chateau des Lascaris is just above the village and is in ruins, though the impressive donjon (or "keep") tower—the fortified area to which occupants could escape during a siege—remains. Consider staying in La Brigue for an extra night, as there are good day-hiking opportunities to nearby towns and attractions, including an out-and-back walk to Notre Dame des Fontaines and a longer loop that includes the historic village of Tende.

Another favorite village is Sospel, dating back to the fifth century, when it served as an important staging post on the royal road connecting Nice and Turin; the town sits at the entrance to

(ABOVE) Some of the medieval churches encountered in the Maritime Alps may appear simple on the outside, but the interiors are works of art.

(ABOVE RIGHT) The large and handsome bridge at Sospel required medieval travelers to pay a toll.

the large Roya Valley and is part of the extensive Mercantour National Park. The large and handsome toll bridge constructed over the Bevera River is a distinctive feature; though it was bombed during World War II, it was reconstructed using the same stone, and the tower in the center of the bridge, originally used as a tollhouse, is now occupied by the local tourist office. The current community includes a medieval old town and a more recent area along the river-front. From the bridge, there are pleasing views of houses along the riverbanks, but look closely because some have been painted using a very realistic trompe l'oeil style, a technique used to create the optical illusion that suggests items exist in three dimensions. Also called "forced perspective," some very real-seeming doors and windows are actually illusions. Rue de la République leads to the Chapel des Penitents Blancs, also known as the Chapel Sainte Croix. This sixteenth-century building doesn't appear remarkable on the outside, but its interior features numerous paintings and frescoes. The streets of the old town include many attractive medieval houses and open into small squares, some with interesting fountains. The baroque-style Cathedral of St. Michael was constructed in the seventeenth and eighteenth centuries and celebrates survival of local residents during the Black Death.

Sainte-Agnès is a quintessential example of a perched medieval village, built into the steep hillsides of the Maritime Alps. Its location at 2,500 feet above sea level offers striking views of the Mediterranean coastline and the sea beyond. The town has many of the charming features of medieval villages, such as cobblestone streets and arched pathways, but these have been tucked into extensive terracing constructed into the steep hillside. The village lends itself nicely to tourism, with many historic buildings converted into small hotels, restaurants/cafes, and shops. Notable buildings and

The Maritime Alps mark the southern extent of the 750-mile Alps mountains.

(ABOVE) Many of the towns in the Maritime Alps are "perched" on the steep slopes that characterize the landscape.

(ABOVE RIGHT) Mountain trails sometimes take walkers through lovely olive groves.

related sites include the baroque Church of Notre Dame des Neiges (Our Lady of the Snow), Fort Sainte-Agnes Museum (housed in a military bunker that was part of the Maginot Line defensive system of World War II), and the ruins of a feudal castle above the village that has a lovely medieval garden with dramatic views over the Mediterranean Sea. The town has been included on the list of "The Most Beautiful Villages in France."

Ultimately, our hiking route through the Maritime Alps led us down to the stately seaside city of Menton, nicknamed the "Pearl of France." Menton has attracted human occupation since the Paleolithic period; remains of prehuman ancestors, including the famous Grimaldi Man, have been found in cave sites in the Menton region. Because of its especially mild weather and abundant sunshine, the town became an important destination for those suffering from tuberculosis in the nineteenth century, and its favorable climate and striking beauty have made it an especially vital tourist attraction. The climate supports citrus fruits, including clementines, oranges, tangerines, and lemons (the latter has been adopted as one of the town's symbols). Citrus groves cling to the slopes overlooking the town. Writers extoll Menton as "the best kept secret in France" and as having "the best of

Trails along the famed Cote d'Azur lure walkers to explore this dramatic coastline.

everything": a warm year-round climate, grand mansions with beautiful gardens, excellent French and Italian food, sandy beaches that spill into the aqua-blue Mediterranean, a graceful promenade, and a lively historic old town. Menton is a small city, but it has a village feel to it, and it makes a lovely end to this classic hike through the Maritime Alps. We strongly recommend lingering in the town for a couple of days, enjoying the ambience while celebrating your walk.

The Maritime Alps offer lovely walks of a week to ten days wandering through these gentle mountains, visiting historic towns, and appreciating the natural and cultural history of this distinctive region. Trails are generally well marked and maintained. While there are occasional climbs to scenic mountain passes, the route from the mountains to the sea is, by definition, mostly downhill!

Resources

Guidebook
Gillian Price, *Walks and Treks in the Maritime Alps*, 2016

The Milford Track is famously known as "the finest walk in the world."

Milford Track

We'd been warned about kea birds, large parrots known for their intelligence and curiosity. If you leave your pack unattended, they'll find a way in, looking mostly for food but known to carry away anything of interest, including small cameras and even one unfortunate walker's passport. But we weren't prepared when several birds kicked open the screen door of our cabin, one bird holding the door open while the others prepared to plunder our possessions. Regaining our composure and territorial instincts, we easily shooed them away. This organized raid was a clear demonstration of the social nature of these birds, often called "the clown of the mountains." New Zealanders simply call them "cheeky." Adult keas are olive green and have a large, sharply curved beak, stand nearly 20 inches tall, and weigh more than 2 pounds. They are one of only a few alpine parrots and are endemic (naturally found nowhere else) to the South Island of New Zealand. Their name is derived from the language of the indigenous Maori people and probably refers to the sharp screech the birds utter. Keas were thought to attack sheep, and the kea population was sharply reduced by local ranchers, but the birds are now protected in parks and reserves.

~

The Milford Track has a long history and glowing reputation in the walking world. Developed in 1888, it was called by some "the eighth wonder of the world," and a 1908 article in the *London Spectator* called the track "the finest walk in the world," a moniker that has stuck. The trail has its origins as a travel route used by the native Maori people for gathering and transporting valuable greenstone. The Milford Track is one of New Zealand's ten "Great Walks."

The trail is 33 miles long, traversing part of Fjordlands National Park, a major reserve in the southwest quadrant of the South Island of New Zealand; the park is part of the larger Te Wahipounamu World Heritage Area. The track follows two large, glacially carved valleys that are

LOCATION
New Zealand

LENGTH
33 miles

ACCOMMODATIONS
Commercial (e.g., Inns, B&Bs): Yes
Huts/Refuges: Yes
Backpacking/Camping: No

BAGGAGE TRANSFER
No

OPTION TO WALK IN SECTIONS
No

DEGREE OF CHALLENGE
Low–Moderate

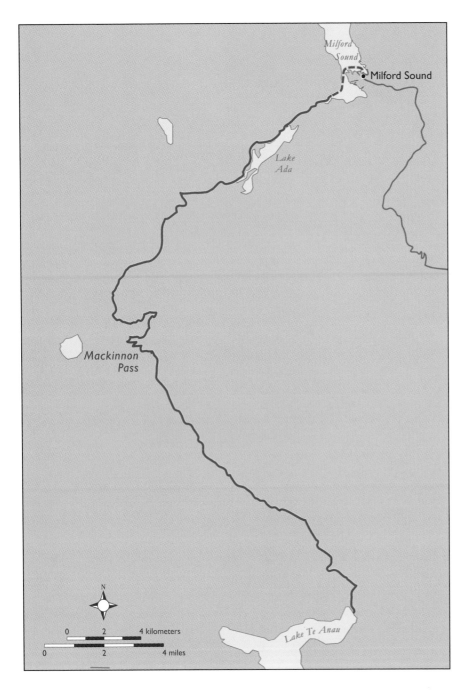

connected by a climb over dramatic, nearly 3,800-foot Mackinnon Pass, which offers impressive views. The Milford Track includes many distinguishing features, including biologically rich and strikingly beautiful rain forests, several suspension bridges that cross the lovely emerald Clinton and Arthur Rivers, countless water-falls and cascades, steep mountains topped with glaciers, ice fields and permanent snowfields, alpine wildflowers, pristine lakes, small glacially formed mountain ponds called tarns, and thick coatings of moss on nearly every-thing. Of course it takes rain to support rain forests, and the area is famous as one the wettest places in the world, with an impressive average of nearly 270 inches of pre-cipitation annually; locals refer to the rain as "liquid sun-shine." There are exotic (to us) plants, and the area's tree ferns are a highlight. Tree ferns can grow to 60 feet high and have very large fronds; unlike conventional trees, the trunks are not woody but are composed of a mass of fibrous roots. There are an estimated 1,000 species of tree ferns in the world, many found only in New Zea-land. A highlight for most walkers is Sutherland Falls, a 1,900-foot cascade, fourth highest in the world, reached on a 45-minute side trail.

Walkers emerge from the Milford Track at Sand Fly Point (more about that in a moment) near Milford Sound, a 12-mile-long fjord, and most stay overnight in the town of Milford for a boat trip on the sound, which we highly recommend. Distinctive Mitre Peak rises over a mile above the water, there are numerous cascades and waterfalls that drop into the sound, and boaters are likely to see fur seals, dolphins, and possibly the rare Fjordland crested penguin. The walk of the Milford Track is typi-cally done over four days and three nights, plus a fourth night in the town of Milford for the cruise on Milford Sound.

The Milford Track is not a highly demanding walk. The primary challenges are the climb over Mackinnon Pass, the rain, and sand flies (and, of course, defending yourself from keas!). The climb over the pass is not overly demanding, as it's moderately graded and well maintained; it just requires resolve. Most of the rest of the walking is relatively flat, following the beautiful Clinton and Arthur Rivers. The rain can be bothersome, but less so if you're prepared with good-quality, breathable rainwear. Encountering some rain can be advantageous, as it produces dozens of ephemeral cascades and waterfalls. Some walkers encounter sand flies, a biting insect that can be pesky. Captain Cook visited Milford Sound in 1773 and described sand flies as "most mischievous animals that cause a swelling not possible to refrain from scratching." They didn't bother us.

(ABOVE LEFT) The walk up and over 3,880-foot Mackinnon Pass offers dramatic views into the Clinton and Arthur River Valleys.

(ABOVE) The clear turquoise waters of the Milford Track's rivers and streams are a constant companion of walkers.

The trail is walker friendly with a series of well-developed huts (camping is not allowed). "Freedom walkers" (independent travelers also known as "trampers" in New Zealand) use the well-equipped public self-service huts. Huts sleep forty in large, bunkhouse-style rooms, and there are communal sitting areas and modern kitchen facilities. Commercial groups ("pamper-trampers") use a series of private huts that are more like lodges or guesthouses, though most guest rooms are semi-private. These serve breakfast and dinner (complete with New Zealand wine) and provide supplies for pack lunches; they also offer hot showers and communal lounges. Companies that conduct organized tours use local guides and rent equipment, a convenience for the walker who does not have the proper rain gear, and commercial hikers walk with only a daypack. Private huts have large, heated drying rooms where wet clothes and packs can be dried overnight, but be careful drying wet leather boots in this manner, as they may shrink substantially. Both types of huts offer good opportunities to meet other walkers from all over the world.

A permit is needed to walk the track, and these must be secured well in advance, especially during the Great Walks season from late October through April, and the walk must be conducted

(ABOVE) The Clinton and Arthur River Valleys include extensive and biologically rich rain forests, with tree ferns that grow up to 60 feet high.

(ABOVE RIGHT) A playful kea bird (a species of parrot) inspects a hiker's gear.

from south to north (to minimize encounters among walking groups). For commercial groups, the tour companies arrange for permits, but freedom walkers must arrange for a permit from the New Zealand Department of Conservation. Commercial trips are conducted only during the Great Walks season, but freedom walkers may hike throughout the year. However, walking the trail during the off-season can be very challenging—even dangerous—due to poor weather. Access to the Milford Track is generally through Queensland, which has developed a reputation as the adventure capital of New Zealand, offering bungee-jumping, river rafting, skydiving, and parasailing. But walking the Milford Track may be the best adventure of all.

Resources

Website
New Zealand Great Walks: www.doc.govt.nz/parks-and-recreation/things-to-do/walking-and-tramping/great-walks/

Guidebook
Alexander Stewart, *New Zealand—The Great Walks* (2nd edition), 2009

Map
Sergio Mazitto, *Fjordland National Park: Trekking, Hiking, Walking—Complete Topographic Map Atlas—Milford Sound, Routeburn Track*, 2018

Hundreds of inches of annual precipitation per year result in impressive waterfalls all along the trail.

Hikers enjoy the fruits of their labor by soaking in the view of the Great Smoky Mountains from the summit of Mount LeConte.

Mount LeConte

We chose the Alum Cave Trail the first time we hiked Mount LeConte; this trail is the shortest route to the top, a good choice on a cool day. As usual after an uphill trek, we arrived at our destination in need of rest and refreshment. We wandered into the LeConte Lodge's main building and were delighted to find we had our choice of seating, both inside and outside. We wisely chose the comfortable rocking chairs in the sun on the building's back porch and opted for the lodge's famous "bottomless" hot chocolate. Soon we felt invigorated. Was it the particularly nice view of the Great Smoky Mountains that we found so refreshing? The relaxing chairs? The multiple refills? Whatever the source of our newfound energy, our decision to stop at LeConte Lodge and visit the dining hall before walking the short distance to the summit of the mountain was a good one, and we heartily recommend it. And when they say "bottomless" hot chocolate, they aren't kidding.

Great Smoky Mountains National Park is a land of superlatives. As part of the great Appalachian Mountain Range, the Smokies are among the oldest mountains on earth. Thought to have once been as high as the present-day Alps and Rockies, natural forces eroded, sculpted, and rounded them into the more gentle landscape we see today. The park is the most biodiverse of all the US national parks. More than 10,000 species have been documented, and scientists believe that as many as 100,000 species may live here; this biodiversity has earned the area its World Heritage Site recognition. Visitation each year is nearly double that of any other US national park.

The park's more than 500,000 acres lie along the spine of the Great Smoky Mountains, half in North Carolina and half in Tennessee, and include dramatic mountain vistas, rocky streams (locals call them "prongs"), many impressive waterfalls, old-growth forests, a remarkable array of flowering plants, iconic wildlife, and remnants of early American settlements. The park's characteristic "smoke" is actually fog or mist derived from rain and evaporation.

LOCATION
North Carolina and Tennessee, United States

LENGTH
Variable

ACCOMMODATIONS
Commercial (e.g., Inns, B&Bs): Yes
Huts/Refuges: No
Backpacking/Camping: Yes

BAGGAGE TRANSFER
No

OPTION TO WALK IN SECTIONS
No

DEGREE OF CHALLENGE
Moderate

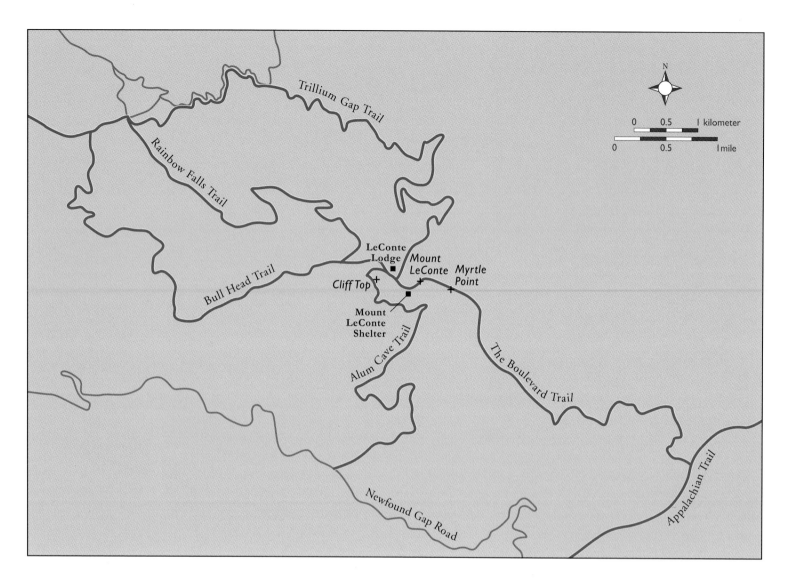

Prominent types of vegetation include old-growth forests, with many trees that predate European settlement. Among the park's extensive collection of flowering plants, masses of showy mountain laurel and rhododendron draw visitors from around the world. Also interesting are the park's "balds," treeless areas of unknown origin on a number of mountain summits. Of course, this park's wide range of habitats means that many animals thrive here, including more than sixty species of

mammals. Iconic examples are black bears, white-tailed deer, red and gray foxes, and elk. The park also has more than 200 species of birds, 39 species of reptiles, and 50 species of fish.

For centuries before there was a national park, the Cherokee people lived in this area in a sophisticated society that hunted and gathered in the forests. Under the Indian Removal Act of 1830, more than 15,000 Cherokee were marched out of their homelands for resettlement in Oklahoma to make way for gold mining and early American settlement. About 4,000 perished on this arduous, six-month journey, the infamous Trail of Tears.

Frontier people began settling the area in the eighteenth and early nineteenth centuries, but the Civil War severely disrupted life in this region. The early twentieth century saw clear-cutting of large areas of virgin forests, leading to calls for preservation of the area. The park was finally established in 1934.

With an impressive 800-plus miles of trails that feature many of the park's finest attributes, including 71 miles of the iconic Appalachian Trail, this is a hiker's park. Get off the crowded roads and into the backcountry, where you'll find the real Great Smoky Mountains. And there's no better destination than Mount LeConte. At 6,593 feet, it's only the park's third-highest peak, but it's iconic. When the federal government sent a party to the area in the 1920s to consider establishing a national park, local supporters took them to Mount LeConte, confident in the mountain's ability to impress. It worked.

The mountain has another appeal as well. Several trails lead to its summit, offering hikers options and a diversity of experiences, including a chance to become familiar with the flora and fauna that make the Smokies unique. Having trail options sets up a tough choice, and one solution is to climb on one trail and descend on another to appreciate the many charms of hiking in the park

(ABOVE LEFT) There are several hiking options to reach the summit of Mount LeConte, all with their own attractions.

(ABOVE) "Foot logs" help hikers cross the many streams that lace Great Smoky Mountains National Park.

Masses of rhododendrons draw visitors from all over the world to the Smoky Mountains.

Guests at LeConte Lodge enjoy hearty family-style meals with like-minded visitors in the lodge's dining room.

(though you may need to use a commercial shuttle service or two cars, since you might be using separate trailheads). Of course, another choice is do this hike more than once, and we endorse this plan.

The Alum Cave Trail is the shortest route to and from the summit—about 11 miles (round-trip) and climbing about 3,000 feet—and is steep and fairly strenuous, but it offers several interesting features, including its namesake cave-like recess (it's really a large overhanging rock ledge) and creek, Arch Rock, Alum Cave Bluff, views from aptly named Inspiration Point, and a narrow cleft that climbs a steep slope and has steel cables for handholds, much like *via ferrata*-style climbing in Europe. Portions of the trail feature large (ancient) red spruce and tulip trees, and there are "foot logs" over many stream crossings (this type of bridge is common in the park and typically consists of a sizable sawn log—flat side up!—and a handrail). Look for ravens and peregrine falcons in the Alum Cave area, and prepare yourself for lots of other hikers enjoying themselves along this trail, especially on the lower section. Some Mount LeConte hikers go out-and-back on this trail, while some prefer it for descent only because of its steepness.

Another option is the 7.8-mile (one-way) Boulevard Trail that ascends 3,000 feet over its route to the summit of Mount LeConte and is especially diverse. It starts with a 2.7-mile climb on a section of the Appalachian Trail (look for the white blazes that mark this trail over its 2,200-mile distance); the Boulevard Trail then branches off and undulates along a narrow ridge (the namesake "boulevard") with steep forested slopes on both sides. Cross the remains of a giant landslide (fixed steel cables help hikers through this section) and then finish the hike with a challenging climb to reach the summit area. Note the red spruce and balsam fir along the way, and enjoy the impressive views.

The Rainbow Falls Trail and the Bull Head Trail leave from the same trailhead and make a convenient loop hike that includes Mount LeConte; the trail is 13.6 miles (round-trip) with 3,800 feet of elevation gain. Start your hike on the Rainbow Falls Trail, climbing to the falls over the trail's first 2.7 miles; entertaining LeConte Creek will keep you company most of the way as you cross and recross it on foot logs. Rainbow Falls spills 80 feet over a hanging ledge; try to resist climbing on the rocks around the falls, which can be hazardous. You'll share this trail with lots of other hikers, but you'll leave most of them behind as you continue on the Rainbow Falls Trail to eventually join the Bull Head Trail, which passes through a long tunnel of mountain laurel and rhododendron and ultimately leads to the summit area of Mount LeConte. Return to the trailhead on the Bull Head Trail, enjoying the spring and summer wildflowers, the Bull Head (a heath-covered bald that resembles the shape of a bull's head), and the Pulpit, a (very) large stone cairn built by the Civilian Conservation Corps in the 1930s to enable views over the bordering, tall rhododendrons. Note that both of these trails tend to be rocky.

Trillium Gap Trail is another good option to get to the summit of Mount LeConte; it's about 6.7 miles (one-way) to (or from) the summit area; the elevation change is 3,400 feet. This is the trail that guides/wranglers use to lead a string of llamas up and down the mountain to resupply LeConte Lodge several times a week, and seeing the llamas is a memorable experience for many hikers. The trail features lovely Grotto Falls and memorable Trillium Gap (a "beech gap" that's characteristic of the region); here you'll find dense grass and stands of graceful American beech trees. An early wildflower, spring beauty, carpets the forest floor and suggests freshly fallen snow. The upper stretches of the trail are especially verdant, covered with mosses, lichens, ferns, wildflowers, shrubs, and trees, but the trail itself is rocky.

Note that all of these trail options lead to the summit area, but the true summit of the mountain is Cliff Top—a short hike from the summit area—and nearby Myrtle Point offers the finest views from the summit area.

The other big advantage of climbing Mount LeConte is the charming, rustic lodge near the top; it's unusual in US national parks to find backcountry lodging. Jack Huff, a Gatlinburg mountaineer and founder of the lodge, began building the retreat in 1926. Eight years later, Jack and Pauline Huff were married there at a sunrise service; this started a tradition, and the site still hosts weddings on the mountain. LeConte Lodge has no road access and is hike-in only. Guests stay in hand-built, rough-hewn log cabins with propane heat, kerosene lanterns, clean linens, and warm Hudson Bay wool blankets, with a washbasin and soap for bathing. Hearty meals are served family style in the dining room, where you share your hiking adventures with people from all over the nation and even the world. Some would call the lodge rustic, and we thought it charming. After supper, most guests do the short climb to Cliff Top for sunset; fewer guests hike to Myrtle Point for sunrise. The summit area also includes the Mount LeConte Shelter for those who wish to camp.

Treat yourself with this extraordinary hiking opportunity and take two to three days for this trip. Though the distances aren't great, the hiking is challenging; besides, the lodge offers a special kind of experience available in few other national parks. Relax and enjoy both the natural and cultural history of Great Smoky Mountains National Park by hiking Mount LeConte. (For more hikes in the US national parks, see our book *Walks of a Lifetime in America's National Parks*.)

Resources

Websites
Great Smoky Mountains National Park: www.nps.gov/grsm
LeConte Lodge (official concessionaire): www.lecontelodge.com

Map
National Geographic Trails Illustrated Map 229, *Great Smoky Mountains*, 2021

Simple but well-located cabins offer overnight accommodations for guests at LeConte Lodge.

Lots of annual precipitation and steep mountain slopes combine to form waterfalls throughout Great Smoky Mountains National Park.

The Presidential Traverse snakes along the ridgeline of New Hampshire's dramatic White Mountains.

National Scenic Trails Samplers

The first long-distance trail we walked—Vermont's aptly named Long Trail—was also America's first long-distance trail, wandering 272 miles along the ridgeline of the state's Green Mountains, from Massachusetts to Canada. We walked the trail in sections—a combination of day hikes and a few short backpacking trips—using the Long Trail's intersections with roads as trailheads. We were so obsessed with walking every step of the way that we made a point of walking across the road between trail sections. We laugh at this now. While it can be profoundly gratifying to walk the full complement of a long-distance trail, it's okay to walk sections of these trails as well; in fact, it can be liberating. This is particularly true for the nation's especially long National Scenic Trails; for example, the North Country National Scenic Trail is 4,600 miles! We encourage you to consider walking portions of these trails, and offer a couple of attractive and representative examples below.

The US National Trails System includes an astounding 88,600 miles of trails (longer than the Interstate Highway System!). These trails crisscross much of the diverse and sublime landscapes of North America and are a model for the world. The flagships of this system are the eleven National Scenic Trails, the best known of which are the Appalachian National Scenic Trail (AT), Pacific Crest National Scenic Trail (PCT), and Continental Divide National Scenic Trail (CDT); these three are sometimes called the "Triple Crown" trails. Known affectionately as the "footpath for the people," the AT was proposed in 1921 by landscape architect Benton MacKaye and completed in 1937 and runs approximately 2,200 miles between Springer Mountain, Georgia, and Mount Katahdin, Maine. The trail traverses wooded, pastoral, wild, and culturally important lands throughout the Appalachian Mountains. The PCT was completed in 1993 and traverses some of the most outstanding and beautiful scenery in the United States over its 2,650-mile length, connecting California's border with Mexico and Washington State's border with Canada. The CDT travels 3,100 miles as it follows

LOCATION
United States

LENGTH
Variable

ACCOMMODATIONS
Commercial (e.g., Inns, B&Bs): Some
Huts/Refuges: Some
Backpacking/Camping: Some

BAGGAGE TRANSFER
No

OPTION TO WALK IN SECTIONS
Some

DEGREE OF CHALLENGE
Variable

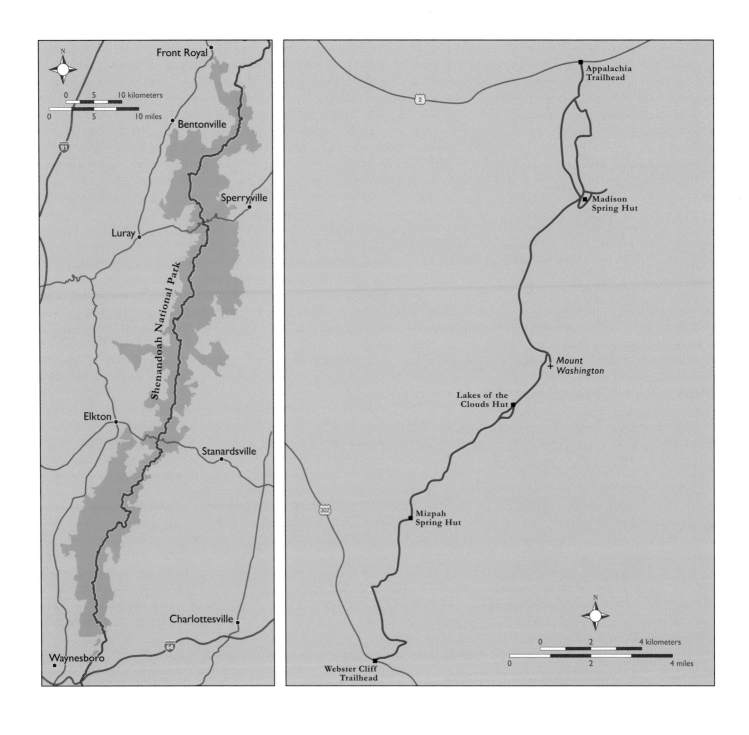

the spine of the continent, defining the nation's two great watersheds, the Atlantic and the Pacific, and connecting the United States with Mexico and Canada.

Unfortunately, most of us just don't have the time, inclination, or maybe the ability to do these months-long hikes. But here's the good news: We can hike these trails vicariously by enjoying the books of those who have done so, and even watching the Hollywood films that celebrate these walks, such as *A Walk in the Woods*, Bill Bryson's hilarious story of his walk along the AT, and Cheryl Strayed's story of redemption in *Wild: From Lost to Found on the Pacific Crest Trail*. (Interestingly, neither Bryson nor Strayed walked the full distance of their chosen trails.) All of the National Scenic Trails have sections—sometimes even their most glorious parts—that can be hiked in a few days to a few weeks; there are even some great day hikes that are accessible along these trails. In this chapter, we suggest seeking out and walking some of the outstanding sections of these trails, and illustrate this suggestion with two sections of the AT that we've had the pleasure of walking.

There's no denying the deep sense of satisfaction of walking the full length of a long-distance trail: The trails in this book are just some of the dozens of long-distance trails we've been privileged to walk, most of them in their entirety. However, we've chosen not to tackle the Triple Crown trails, opting instead to walk a greater diversity of trails around the world, and have found this highly rewarding as well. There's a saying in the walking community: "Walk your own walk," and we think this is good advice. As important parts of our walking lives, we've hiked multiple sections of the Triple Crown trails. For example, we've walked the Presidential Traverse in the White Mountains of New Hampshire (a section that many AT hikers would agree may be the most dramatic and strikingly beautiful), the 100-mile southernmost section of Vermont's Long Trail that doubles as the AT,

(ABOVE LEFT) Large cairns mark the trail and help guide hikers when clouds descend over the mountaintops.

(ABOVE) Aptly named Lake of the Clouds Hut welcomes hikers with shelter, meals, and camaraderie with other hikers.

Waterfalls are common in the lower-elevation forests along the Presidential Traverse.

the lovely 101-mile section of the AT that rambles though Shenandoah National Park in Virginia, and much of the 71-mile section that tracks through Great Smoky Mountains National Park. We thoroughly enjoyed these walks, and they gave us a good sense of the AT. In this chapter, we briefly describe the Presidential Traverse and the section of the AT through Shenandoah in an effort to stimulate your thinking about sampling our remarkable National Trails System, particularly the National Scenic Trails.

Presidential Traverse

In contemporary language, this is an "epic" hike, a 20-or-so-mile route along the ridgeline of New Hampshire's renowned White Mountains. Using a series of trails—most of them part of the AT— the hike includes the summits of seven 4,000-foot peaks, all named for American presidents: Madison, Adams, Jefferson, Washington, Monroe, Eisenhower, and Pierce. At 6,288 feet, Washington is the highest peak in New England. The mountain was called Agiocochook (Home of the Great Spirit) by some Native American tribes in the region.

Much of the Presidential Traverse, from Crawford Notch to Mount Washington, follows the historic Crawford Path, the oldest continuously maintained trail in America. In 1819, Abel Crawford and his son, Ethan, cleared a path to tree line, and the trail was eventually extended to the summit of Mount Washington. In fact, many of the trails in the White Mountains were developed more than a hundred years before designation of the AT. In deference to local pride over this history, the trails generally carry their historic names in addition to being signed as the AT.

The grand system of huts operated by the Appalachian Mountain Club (the oldest conservation group in the nation) are a highlight of this hike. Three huts serve the Presidential Traverse: Mitzpah Spring, Lake of the Clouds, and Madison Spring, and they're located a day's hike apart; all offer comfortable bunks, family-style meals, and even occasional home-grown entertainment. Be aware that the huts are popular and reservations, especially for weekends, must be made well in advance. Because the huts are expensive to maintain (most supplies are toted up to the huts on the backs of the "croo," the young men and women who staff the huts), the cost to hikers is relatively high. Consider joining the AMC to support the organization that has done so much for walkers for so long (and to take advantage of discounted rates at the huts!). We walked the Presidential Traverse in three days, using the AMC huts for overnights.

Despite its relatively short length, the Presidential Traverse is a challenging hike, including nearly 9,000 feet of elevation gain. The trail can be rough in places, especially above tree line, so the going is slow; we recommend sturdy hiking boots and trekking poles. But weather is the most important consideration, as dramatic changes in weather can develop quickly, and hikers are often fully exposed when well above tree line. Too many people have died from exposure in the White Mountains; check the weather forecast closely before attempting the Presidential Traverse, and pack rain pants and coats and warm clothes no matter the forecast.

Shenandoah National Park

By the time the first national parks were being established on the vast public domain lands of the West, most of the land in the eastern United States was already developed or in private ownership. That's one of the things that has made national parks in the East so challenging to establish, but so valuable as well: They're accessible to so many people. Lovely Shenandoah National Park is a prime example, located just 75 miles from the Washington, DC, area. This long and narrow park runs along the spine of the Blue Ridge Mountains of Virginia (the front range of the ancient Appalachian Mountains) for more than 100 miles, with the historic Shenandoah River and its peaceful valley on the west and the gentle, pleasing hills of the Virginia Piedmont on the east. Most visitors to Shenandoah know this park for its Skyline Drive, the scenic, winding road that runs its length, offering spectacular views from its dozens of overlooks. Less well-known are the more than 500 miles of trails that show off the behind-the-scenes version of the park to those who are willing to explore it on foot. An added bonus is that 101 miles of these trails are part of the AT—one of the most consistently beautiful sections of this Triple Crown trail.

The AT through Shenandoah National Park features showy mountain laurel that blooms in spring.

(ABOVE) AT thru-hikers in Shenandoah gladly shed their packs as they resupply at this store.

(ABOVE RIGHT) AT hikers in Shenandoah National Park enjoy splendid views of the surrounding mountains.

Hiking options include following the trail on a backpacking trip or sampling it over a series of day hikes; we've done some of both. For the former, you'll need a permit from the National Park Service to camp along the trail; for your convenience, there's a series of shelters scattered along the AT—these are rough, three-sided structures that offer protection from the weather and can be a good alternative to carrying a tent.

We've also day-hiked several trails that are part of the AT, and recommend them. For example, at just over 4,000 feet, Hawksbill Mountain is the highest in the park and demands to be summited. This is only a modest climb of less than 1,000 feet distributed over a 2.9-mile circuit. Start at the trailhead on the northern end of the Hawksbill Gap Parking Area (Mile 45.6) and take a short spur trail to join the AT. Note the white blazes on trees and rocks that mark the trail's 2,200-mile length. You're walking on a particularly lovely stretch through a mature forest with an abundance of lichen-covered boulders, ferns, two large talus slopes, and lots of mountain laurel (blooms are usually at their peak in June). The summit of the mountain offers striking views, including Stony Man to the north and a shelter named for legendary Virginia senator Harry F. Byrd Sr. Be sure to look for peregrine falcons, as park staff and partners have worked hard to restore these iconic birds to the park. Complete the loop by walking downhill (steeply in places) on the Lower Hawksbill Trail.

The park's famous Rapidan Camp is another good day hike that highlights an especially appealing section of the AT. In the late 1920s, President Herbert Hoover established Rapidan Camp at one of the prettiest sites in what would become Shenandoah National Park. The camp includes three buildings that have been nicely preserved; the back of Brown House, where Hoover maintained his office, has the best views, and the back deck beckons hikers to sit a spell (we ate our pack lunch there). Visit this magical place and the surrounding countryside on a grand 7.4-mile loop that incorporates portions of Rapidan Camp Trail, Laurel Prong Trail, and Hazeltop Loop. Start at Mile 53 on Skyline Drive and follow Mill Prong (locals often call streams "prongs") to Rapidan Camp, then follow Laurel Prong to the AT, where you'll walk along on an especially pleasant section of this epic trail back to the trailhead where you started.

The park has five developed campgrounds and three sets of lodges/cabins to use as base camps for day hiking. Note the many AT crossings as you travel Skyline Drive, and consider walking a few steps, or a few miles, on the world-famous long-distance trail.

The Presidential Traverse and Shenandoah National Park are just two examples of how hikers can sample representative sections of the most iconic long-distance trails in the United States. Several of the hikes featured in this book are other good examples: the John Muir Trail shares 160 glorious miles with the PCT, the Tahoe Rim Trail includes 49 miles of the PCT through the dramatic Desolation Wilderness, the Colorado Trail shares 315 miles with the CDT (235 miles on the Collegiate East option and 80 miles on the Collegiate West option), the Long Trail and the AT share 100 miles in southern Vermont, the Ocala Trail travels 72 miles on the Florida National Scenic Trail, a portion of the Superior Hiking Trail is part of the North Country National Scenic Trail, and the Chesapeake and Ohio (C&O) Canal Towpath is part of the Potomac Heritage National Scenic Trail. Moreover, we encourage you to be creative: Study maps of the national scenic trails and find good options for shorter hikes, and Google "best sections of the (name of) National Scenic Trail" to find lots of recommendations that include both day and multi-day hikes. What a great way to celebrate and appreciate this country's national trails.

White blazes mark the AT on its epic 2,200-mile journey along the Appalachian Mountains.

Resources

Websites

US National Trails System: www.nps.gov/subjects/nationaltrail system
Shenandoah National Park: www.nps.gov/shen
Appalachian Trail Conservancy: www.appalachiantrail.org
Appalachian Mountain Club Huts: www.outdoors.org

The 72-mile Ocala Trail traverses its namesake national forest, the first one in the eastern United States, signed into law by President Theodore Roosevelt in 1908; the trail is the birthplace of the nearly 1,500-mile Florida National Scenic Trail.

Ocala Trail

We meet the most interesting people on our walks. Take Ken, for instance, a "trail angel." We had decided to walk the Ocala Trail in Florida, and we needed some help with rides. Folks at the offices of the Florida Trail Association (the Ocala Trail is part of the much longer Florida National Scenic Trail) suggested Ken, a volunteer who helps Ocala Trail walkers with logistics. So we contacted him, meeting for breakfast the first morning of our walk. Ken was well over 80 years old but looked decades younger, and a few months earlier had led a two-week backpacking trip across Florida for other octogenarian walkers. Ken has worked on the Florida National Scenic Trail for forty years and told us great stories about the area as he shuttled us to one end of a trail section. We needed another ride a few days later, but Ken wasn't available, so he recommended we ask Pat, owner of a hunting and fishing shop near the trail. Pat was retired from the US Army, where he had been an MP, and his size alone must have made him effective as a law-enforcement official. Born and raised in the Ocala area, Pat retired there to open his shop, and when he talked about the area, it was clear that he loved this place and wanted to share it with others. Pat was pleased to give us a ride one morning, and his courtly manners were a charming artifact of his Southern roots. He cheerily told us lots of stories about fishing and "'gators," but when we asked him about snakes, his demeanor changed: "I'm a big ole' boy myself, but I'm scared to death of snakes!" All trails have angels, and Ken and Pat are good examples on the beautiful Ocala Trail. We paid our new friends a nominal fee to cover their gas—that's all they would take—and left with an appreciation for both the trail and the community of walkers who are pleased to help one another (and an increased determination to be trail angels ourselves when possible).

───── ≈ ─────

The Ocala Trail runs the length of the historic and ecologically important Ocala National Forest in north-central Florida. This is the southernmost national forest in the continental United States,

LOCATION
Florida, United States

LENGTH
72 miles

ACCOMMODATIONS
Commercial (e.g., Inns, B&Bs): Some
Huts/Refuges: No
Backpacking/Camping: Yes

BAGGAGE TRANSFER
No

OPTION TO WALK IN SECTIONS
Yes

DEGREE OF CHALLENGE
Low

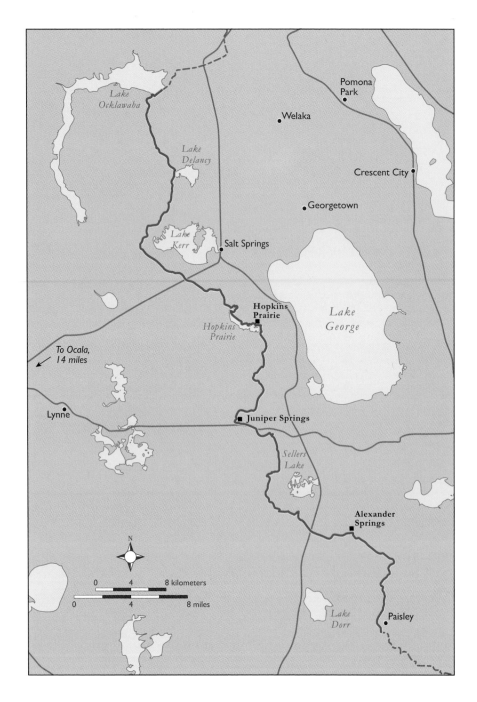

covering nearly 400,000 acres. It was the first national forest in the eastern United States, signed into law by "conservation" president Teddy Roosevelt in 1908. The Depression-era Civilian Conservation Corps developed many of the forest's recreation facilities in the 1930s, and they resonate the CCC sensibility and aesthetic. Locally, the Ocala National Forest is simply known as "the forest." The Ocala Trail bisects this land on a north–south axis for 72 miles. It offers mostly dry, level walking through pine and hardwood forests, along the edges of ponds and prairies (large wet meadows), and across narrow sections of hardwood swamps. The trail is the birthplace of the nearly 1,500-mile Florida National Scenic Trail that connects the Gulf Islands near Pensacola to just north of Everglades National Park. Many hikers consider the Ocala Trail to be the "crown jewel" of the Florida Trail; the southern section of the Ocala Trail at Clearwater Lake is where Florida Trail Association founder Jim Kern and several hikers painted the first hopeful blaze in 1966. The Ocala Trail is now a prime destination for backpackers who want to spend a week on the Florida Trail.

This is an area rich in natural history. Much of Florida is only a few feet above sea level, and the underlying bedrock is primarily limestone, a sedimentary rock composed mainly of the consolidated skeletal remains of marine organisms. Rainwater percolates quickly through this thick (up to 2 miles) layer of limestone, forming the Floridan Aquifer, a source of fresh water vital to both humans and wildlife. In places, water has dissolved the limestone and formed large basins, and springs discharge this fresh water to the surface. The Ocala Trail passes by or near several of these impressive water features, including Alexander Springs, Juniper Springs, and Salt Springs, and these areas demand a visit.

Much of the trail passes through the largest forest of sand pines left in the world. These are short-lived trees (living about forty years) that grow to about 8 inches in diameter. They form a dense canopy with a shrubby understory, and this endangered ecosystem is commonly called the "Big Scrub." Other important ecosystems include slightly higher-elevation "islands" of longleaf pines (this ecosystem is also endangered), lower swamp forests of impressive bald cypress with their buttresses and "knees," and stands of low-growing oaks with extensive and striking understories of saw palmettos.

There are many opportunities to watch interesting wildlife. You can count on seeing alligators in the area's ponds, rivers, and wetlands, and it's not unusual to see black bears; deer and wild turkeys are common. There are many species of birds, including eagles and endangered Florida scrub-jays (found in family groupings) and red-cockaded woodpeckers. These woodpeckers make their nests by boring out a cavity in pine trees, usually with a distinctive small round opening about 20 feet off the ground. To protect their eggs from snakes, they disturb the bark in a circle around the tree below the opening of the nest so that sap runs down the tree, hardens, and makes a barrier too difficult for snakes to cross. One morning we started our walk early at Rodman Reservoir at the northern end of the trail. In the mist and at close range, we saw three sandhill cranes that were "vacationing" in this area for the winter. They made their distinctive call and took to flight, displaying their impressive size and providing us with an unforgettable moment. We also enjoyed watching several bald eagles rise and swoop at Hopkins Prairie.

The Ocala Trail crosses the Juniper Prairie Wilderness, portions of which had burned in wildfires. Since wilderness areas are supposed to be as natural as possible, the US Forest Service allows lightning-caused fires to burn when this can be done safely, replicating nature in this fire-dependent

(ABOVE LEFT) The Ocala Trail offers mostly dry, level walking through pine and hardwood forests and along the edges of ponds and prairies (large wet meadows).

(ABOVE) Large stands of low-growing oaks with extensive and striking understories of saw palmettos are common along the Ocala Trail.

(ABOVE) We enjoyed seeing and hearing sandhill cranes that "vacation" along the trail for the winter.

(ABOVE RIGHT) The Ocala Trail is dotted with shallow lakes that attract wildlife, including alligators.

ecosystem; on our first two days of walking, we saw smoke in the distance from wildfires in other parts of the forest. The Yearling Trail, a short side trail in the Juniper Prairie Wilderness, leads to the area that was the inspiration for Marjorie Kinnan Rawlings's Pulitzer Prize–winning novel, *Cross Creek*, later made into the movie *The Yearling*.

We finished walking the Ocala Trail with an extra day to spare, and our trail angel friend Ken suggested we join an organized walk conducted by the Florida Trail Association on a portion of the nearby Cross Florida Greenway. This 110-mile corridor was originally intended to be the Cross Florida Barge Canal, a shipping route connecting the Gulf of Mexico with the Atlantic Ocean, a plan that was eventually scrapped in the 1960s because of its massive environmental implications. Now the corridor is being developed into three trails serving walkers, bicyclists, and equestrians. We walked with a group of about eighty Florida Trail Association members; we were welcomed and enjoyed swapping trail stories, and we also appreciated the organizational process necessary to manage such a large group! The highlight was walking over the "land bridge" that spans I-75. Here, an overpass has been constructed for walkers and equestrians only—it's covered in sandy soil and landscaped so well with local plants that you find it hard to believe an interstate highway lies just below the vegetative barrier. It presents an odd appearance to the drivers below, too, as they see an overpass covered with trees and bushes.

The Ocala Trail is well marked with orange blazes, and the Florida Trail Association publishes a good guidebook that covers the entire Florida National Scenic Trail. The US Forest Service is also a good source of information and maintains a visitor center at Silver Springs. The nearby town

(ABOVE LEFT) Wide, shallow rivers bisect the Ocala National Forest.

(ABOVE) Stately oaks covered in Spanish moss grace upland regions along the Ocala Trail.

of Ocala makes a good "base camp," and a number of road crossings allow the trail to be walked in a series of day hikes. The trail can be walked any time of the year, though the best months are between October and April—it can get pretty hot and humid in the summer. We did our walk in January during an unusual cold snap. A few mornings, it was well below freezing, but bright sunshine warmed temperatures into the 50s each day, great conditions for hiking. Walkers should be wary of deer hunters between November and January—these months are the only time primitive camping may be restricted, and wearing bright orange shirts or vests is recommended during hunting seasons. Backpackers are required to use a bear bag or bear canister to keep food away from wild animals.

The Ocala Trail offers walkers an up-close and personal view of some of the most exotic and endangered ecosystems in the southeastern United States. It's a good option for a walk during the winter months when most other long-distance trails in the United States are snowed under. If you decide to walk it, we hope you meet interesting trail angels, too.

Resources

Websites
Florida Trail Association: www.floridatrail.org
US Forest Service, Ocala National Forest: www.fs.usda.gov/ocala

Guidebooks
Sandra Field and John Keatley, *The Florida Trail Guide*, 2013
Dan Mock, *The Florida Trail Data Book, 2021-2022* (available from the Florida Trail Association)

The Ohio and Erie Canal Towpath Trail
follows the historic canal for 90 miles; the
towpath, used by mules to pull canal boats
in the nineteenth century, now offers an ideal
walking path.

Ohio and Erie Canal Towpath Trail

Our walks have taken us through many national parks in Europe and other densely populated regions of the world, and we've been struck by how different they are from our familiar US national parks. National parks like Yellowstone and Grand Canyon are huge areas that are primarily public lands where few or no people live. But this isn't feasible where population densities are high, so national parks in other areas of the world are often smaller, include private lands, and accommodate lots of residents, sometimes whole towns. So we were especially looking forward to our long walk on the Ohio and Erie Canal Towpath Trail because it has a 20-mile segment that runs through Cuyahoga Valley National Park. This is a new kind of national park in the United States, located in the urbanized area bounded by Cleveland and Akron, Ohio. Cuyahoga Valley is a relatively small national park (33,000 acres compared to Yellowstone's 2.2 million acres), and limited lands purchased and managed by the National Park Service are mixed with private lands where towns and private landowners are encouraged to conserve the natural and cultural integrity of their properties. How well is this working, we wondered? We came away impressed with the way the valley's key natural and cultural resources—lush farmlands, rolling hills covered in forests, a historic river, an abundance of waterfalls, narrow ravines, important wildlife habitat, and wetlands—are being protected and appreciated by local residents. Moreover, this new model of national park brings parks to people who live in and around urban areas. Walk the 20 miles of the Ohio and Erie Canal Towpath Trail in Cuyahoga Valley National Park, but consider walking more of this remarkable towpath trail that extends for 90 miles (eventually 101 miles) south of Cleveland.

LOCATION
Ohio, United States

LENGTH
90+ miles

ACCOMMODATIONS
Commercial (e.g., Inns, B&Bs):
Yes
Huts/Refuges: No
Backpacking/Camping: Some

BAGGAGE TRANSFER
No

OPTION TO WALK IN SECTIONS
All

DEGREE OF CHALLENGE
Low

───────≈───────

Portions of a handful of America's historic canals have been preserved and make great long-distance walking trails. Artifacts of the nineteenth century, these waterways carried specially designed

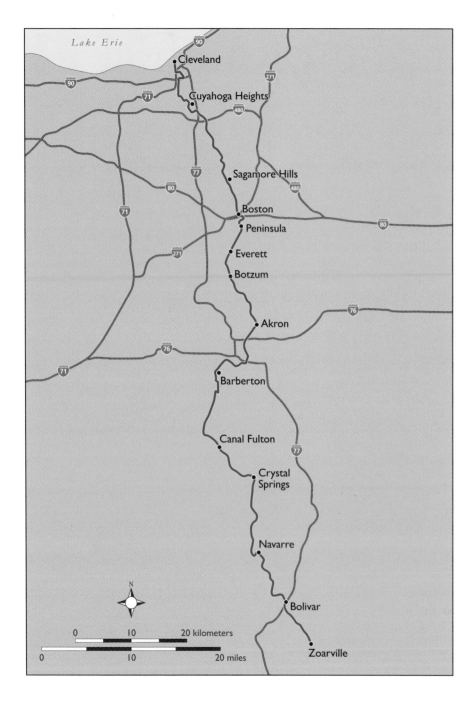

canal boats—long and narrow—loaded with passengers and cargo. Beside each canal was a towpath where mules pulled the boats, and these towpaths became ideal trails—mostly flat and well groomed and traversing a great variety of landscapes. (See the chapter on the Chesapeake and Ohio [C&O] Canal Towpath for another good example of a canal-based long-distance walking trail.)

Canals were important manifestations of the nation's Industrial Revolution, large-scale manipulations of the landscape designed to advance commerce and regional economies. And that's what happened in northeastern Ohio in the early nineteenth century. Ohio gained statehood in 1803, but was sparsely populated and geographically isolated because of its poor accessibility to the rest of the nation and the sea. Agricultural products could serve only local markets, and there was little capacity for manufacturing. Talk of a canal linking Lake Erie to the Ohio River (and on to the Mississippi River, New Orleans, and the Gulf of Mexico) can be traced as far back as George Washington and Thomas Jefferson, and the state of Ohio acted on this impulse in 1825 when construction of the Ohio and Erie Canal began. The canal was completed in 1832 and totaled an impressive 308 miles (including several relatively short feeder canals connecting local communities); 152 locks raised and lowered the water level as needed to permit navigation.

The canal proved a good investment as this region of Ohio flourished; in the 1840s, Ohio became the third most prosperous state in the union. Linking the Ohio River with Lake Erie completed a network of water-based transportation routes that ran from New York City and the Atlantic Ocean, through the Great Lakes, and on to the Gulf of Mexico. New towns popped up along the canal and existing communities thrived, helping fuel the

nation's westward expansion. Moreover, the national economy expanded as well; raw materials and products from Ohio could be shipped to the East Coast region, supplying its cities and industries, and this diminished the need for trade with Europe. America's canals are sometimes called "routes of prosperity."

However, the nation's railroad system expanded rapidly in the second half of the nineteenth century, carrying freight and passengers faster and more economically than canal barges, and all of the country's canals rapidly declined. The Ohio and Erie Canal lost most of its transportation traffic, though its waters still generated power and were a source of water for industry. But in 1913, Ohio experienced the Great Flood, which destroyed much of the Ohio and Erie Canal's remaining operational capacity.

This extended walk along the route of the Ohio and Erie Canal tells the story of how canals contributed to America's nineteenth-century Industrial Revolution. But it also tells the transcendent story of the nation's more recent environmental revolution. The area's Cuyahoga River played a paradoxical role in helping foster the modern conservation movement. In June 1969, ongoing industrial activities along the river caused oil and other contaminants and debris to collect at a railroad trestle,

A faithful reproduction of the stern of one of the historic canal boats is on display at Cuyahoga Valley National Park's Hale Farm and Village.

where the river caught fire, horrifying the nation! This and related events throughout the country convinced people that more environmental protection was desperately needed, resulting in a suite of federal legislation, such as the landmark Environmental Protection Act of 1970 and the Clean Water Act of 1972. Now, the river has a strong record of improving water quality, so much so that a great variety of water-related birds—great blue herons, great egrets, loons, ospreys, belted kingfishers, and even bald eagles—are now seen by many walkers along the towpath.

Today, the canal is still used for transportation, but of a very different kind—local residents and visitors enjoy walking, running, and biking on the towpath. In fact, much of the remaining Ohio and Erie Canal has been preserved thanks to the National Park Service, local governments up and down the canal, and lots of grassroots organizations. Effective advocacy led to the area being designated the Ohio and Erie Canalway National Heritage Area in 1996, and Congress designated a portion of the canal and surrounding lands as part of Cuyahoga Valley National Park in 2000, now one of the most heavily visited units of the National Park System. (For other great walks in the US national parks, see our book *Walks of a Lifetime in America's National Parks*.)

For those who want a long walk steeped in history and beauty, the full Towpath Trail runs for 90 miles in northeastern Ohio, from Cleveland's Scranton Flats south to Zoarville. Plans are in the works to extend the trail to New Philadelphia, increasing the length to 101 miles. The trail passes through diverse urban and rural landscapes, and visitors enjoy a series of canal locks, restored historic buildings, lovely villages, and lots of parklands. The constants are the canal (constructed of sandstone and often still filled with water), the accompanying towpath surfaced with firmly packed crushed stone and occasional paving, a few bridges and boardwalks, and strategically placed interpretive signs and exhibits along the way. Many road crossings and trailheads provide convenient access to the trail.

There are lots of highlights along the route. The floating bridge over Summit Lake (south of downtown Akron) has been described as "stunning," and the two suspension bridges that take the trail over busy intersections in Cleveland as "world class." Enjoy the Old Portage and Cascade Locks, where you can see five of the fifteen "staircase" locks that were once used to lift boats up a very steep escarpment. At the town of Canal Fulton, find the *St. Helena III,* a working replica of a canal-era freight barge that offers excursions on the canal. The charming village of Peninsula, once

The historic Towpath Trail winds through the woods of Cuyahoga Valley in northeastern Ohio.

a hub of canal activity, now offers visitor-friendly restaurants, galleries and antiques shops, and historic homes. Take a short side trip to the Congressman Ralph Regula Canalway Center in Massillon to learn more about the canal and this local champion of the canal and Towpath Trail. The Richard Howe House, historic home of the resident engineer for construction of the canal, adds an interesting dimension to the history of the canal. Near the south end of the trail are the Fort Laurens State Memorial (Ohio's only Revolutionary War–era fort), extensive parklands, and the German community of Zoar with its lovely gardens.

Is a walk of 90 miles not long enough for you? You're in luck, because the Towpath Trail is a component of the Ohio to Erie Trail, a growing 320-mile network of trails that will eventually span Ohio from the shores of Lake Erie in Cleveland to the Ohio River in Cincinnati.

Out-of-town visitors to northeast Ohio may want to consider walking a shorter section of the trail, and we recommend the 20-mile stretch of the canal preserved as part of Cuyahoga Valley National Park. This is an especially pleasing walk, as much of the canal and associated towpath are well preserved, and most of the surrounding land is in its natural condition. The park is in a transition zone between the Allegheny Plateau and the Central Lowlands; consequently, it includes a variety of land types, including wetlands, floodplains, and uplands in various stages of natural and human-caused succession. The result is an unusually rich variety of plants and animals.

The human history of the park is also interesting. People have lived in this area for nearly 12,000 years, leaving hundreds of archaeological sites scattered throughout the valley. The Cuyahoga River

(ABOVE) Canada geese are among the many waterfowl that now thrive in the Cuyahoga Valley.

(ABOVE RIGHT) The Towpath Trail traverses diverse landscapes, including wetlands where boardwalks and bridges offer the opportunity to explore.

(and its surrounding valley) was an important transportation route and thus considered neutral territory among the area's many indigenous people. Prehistoric artifacts suggest that these people traveled and traded widely. European settlers moved to the area in the nineteenth century to take advantage of the agricultural potential.

We especially enjoyed walking this 20-mile stretch of the trail in two easy days, sharing it in places with bikers, and we used a local B&B for our overnight and the Cuyahoga Valley Scenic Railroad to return to our starting point. The local villages of Boston and Peninsula (both canal boat building centers) and the park's Canal Exploration Center at Lock 38 (which has been restored to its 1905 condition) serve Towpath Trail walkers. Along the path there are occasional benches, picnic areas, interpretive signs, and a number of road crossings with vehicle parking that can be used as trailheads. Generally, the trail is located between the canal and the river. On its journey through the park, the trail includes access to many canal-related structures, including locks, aqueducts, feeder canals, weirs, sluices, and gates, offering lots of opportunities to learn the fascinating story of canal construction and operation. The segment of the Towpath Trail that runs through the park also immerses walkers in the natural history of the valley, passing through forests, fields, and wetlands. We highly recommend the mile-long side trail at Boston to 63-foot Brandywine Falls.

The logistics of walking the Towpath Trail are pretty straightforward, with trailheads at many crossroads, several town parks, and plenty of commercial services such as accommodations (including camping) and restaurants. The smartphone-friendly Towpath Trail map can be downloaded from the Ohio and Erie Canalway website. The Cuyahoga Valley Scenic Railroad parallels the river

The Cuyahoga Valley Scenic Railroad offers walkers the opportunity to ride back to the start of their hike.

on its route linking downtown Akron to the park's northern border and makes regular stops in the town of Peninsula.

Resources

Websites

Ohio and Erie Canalway: www.ohioanderiecanalway.com
Ohio and Erie Canal Coalition: www.ohioanderiecanal.org
Cuyahoga Valley National Park: www.nps.gov/cuva

Expanses of boardwalks have been constructed along portions of the Overland Track to help protect the notable button grass that grows on the area's moorlands.

Overland Track

We usually do our walks as independent travelers because planning the trips can be both an educational and entertaining part of the walking experience. But we joined an organized group to walk the Overland Track, partly because it was too late for us to get the required permit (the company we booked with had reserved a block of permits) and partly to see firsthand the system of sustainable huts that had been built recently to accommodate organized groups. We were pleased to find a system of simple, comfortable, "green" huts located a day's walk from one another and sited at inconspicuous locations just off the main trail. These traditional "bush huts" were small and constructed largely of local materials. A woodstove provided heat and hot water, and the water supply was collected off the roof, stored in tanks, and pumped by walkers. Lights and cooking stoves were powered by propane. There were two Tasmanian guides for our fourteen-person group, and they spent a good deal of time making sure we understood and appreciated the remarkable landscape through which we were walking. They also prepared our meals using local foods to the extent possible (including Tasmanian wines). Our group was composed of eight Australians, four Brits, and two Americans, and we all seemed to enjoy each other's company. So what's the verdict on our experiment with organized groups on the Overland Track? We enjoyed comfortable, environmentally sensitive huts, good company, informed guides, and distinctive local foods—what's not to like?

———— ≈ ————

The Overland Track is a multi-day route through Cradle Mountain-Lake St. Claire National Park in the heart of Tasmania (what the locals call "Tassie"), a large island off the southeast coast of Australia. It's regarded by the walking community as one of the finest treks in Australia and is walked by thousands of people annually. (Aussies call this type of hiking "bushwalking," but that makes it sound harder than it really is.) The route traverses the highest mountains in Tasmania and offers a stunning

LOCATION
Australia

LENGTH
51+ miles

ACCOMMODATIONS
Commercial (e.g., Inns, B&Bs): No
Huts/Refuges: Yes
Backpacking/Camping: Some

BAGGAGE TRANSFER
No

OPTION TO WALK IN SECTIONS
No

DEGREE OF CHALLENGE
Moderate

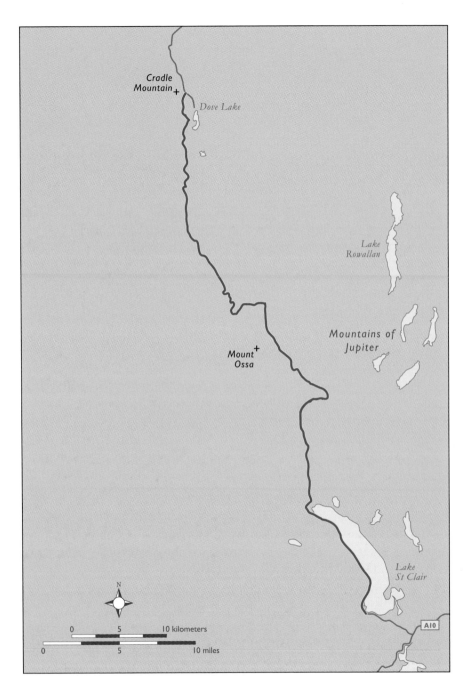

and diverse array of natural history that includes the mountains themselves, alpine lakes, rain forests, waterfalls, wild rivers, and some of the most distinctive plants and animals in the world. For these reasons, the trail and its surrounding lands are part of the Tasmanian Wilderness World Heritage Area, a place of outstanding natural and cultural value to all people of the world.

The walk begins by ascending distinctively shaped Cradle Mountain; the summit reaches 5,070 feet, though walkers don't climb all the way to the top. The geology of the Tasmanian mountains is revealed in the glacially carved Carter and Dove Lakes at the foot of the peak. Other classic signs of glaciation include the generally U-shaped valleys (as opposed to V-shaped valleys carved by rivers), cirques (roughly semicircular basins on the side of mountains where rock has been eroded), moraines (mounds of sand and gravel deposited along the sides and foot of glaciers), and erratics (large rocks carried by glaciers and deposited elsewhere). The twin peaks of Cradle Mountain and many of the other high mountains are what geologists call "nunataks," peaks that rose above the glaciers and were largely unaffected by them. The tops of these mountains remain fluted and craggy, while the lower elevations have been smoothed by glacial action.

While the geology is interesting, it's the flora and fauna of Tasmania and the Overland Track that make it world famous, and justly so. The isolation of the island over a very long period of time has given rise to distinctive plants and animals. Once part of the ancient supercontinent that geologists call Gondwana, which encompassed mainland Australia and parts of Africa and South America, the island of Tasmania has been physically isolated for the last 80 million years, allowing for divergent forms of evolution. The island contains a remarkable thirty-one species of marsupials, a class of mammals in which

newborns are carried by females in an exterior pouch (called the marsupium). Animals you are likely to encounter along the track include wombats (watch for their curious cube-shaped droppings), echidnas, wallabies, possums, and platypuses. Tasmanian devils, made famous in children's cartoons, are present, but they are declining due to a mysterious disease and are not often seen. There are also three species of venomous snakes (whip snake, copperhead, and tiger snake), and some walkers prefer to wear gaiters because of this. Distinctive birds include the yellow-tailed black cockatoo (a large parrot), the yellow wattlebird (whose call sounds like someone having a pronounced belch), the black currawong (large black birds whose sharp metallic calls are synonymous with the Tasmanian wilderness), and several species of honeyeaters. Notable vegetation includes large moorlands of distinctive button grass, silver banksia, cushion plants, and forests of myrtle, eucalyptus, leatherwood, King Billy pines, and pencil pines.

The track has an interesting cultural history as well. Evidence, such as quarries, stone artifacts, campsites, shelters, and fire sites, suggests that aboriginal people have lived in Tasmania for more than 30,000 years and may have used portions of what is now the Overland Track as a travel route. More recent history is focused on protection of the area and development of the current-day Overland Track. Austrian immigrant Gustav Weindorfer built a chalet called Waldheim at the foot of Cradle Mountain in the early 1900s and encouraged Australians to visit the area; he worked hard to ensure the area was protected as a national park. The Overland Track, managed by the Tasmanian Parks and Wildlife Service (see the website below for instructions on how to obtain a mandatory

(ABOVE LEFT) Walkers climb distinctively shaped Cradle Mountain at the beginning of the Overland Track; the mountain is what geologists call a "nunatak," a peak that rose above the glaciers and was largely unaffected by them.

(ABOVE) Remarkable tree ferns line portions of the trail.

Most walkers spend the night in a system of clean, comfortable public huts spaced along the trail.

permit), officially begins at Waldheim, though the current structure is a reproduction. Trapper Bert Nicholls blazed the track in 1930, and the first thru-hike was completed the following year.

About halfway along the track, a side trail leads to the top of 5,305-foot Mount Ossa, the highest peak in Tasmania. If the weather is good, we recommend this diversion; from the top you can see nearly half of Tasmania. The walk ends at Lake St. Clair, the deepest lake in Australia and the best place to see platypuses. The track runs along the lakeshore, but most walkers complete the journey with a leisurely ferry ride across the lake instead. We recommend staying on the trail for another day to make time for these bonus miles.

The Overland Track is not a difficult hike if the weather cooperates, and it certainly did for us. We experienced sunshine and some of the clearest air we've ever encountered—views were almost surreal because of their startling crispness. However, the rain forests along portions of the track suggest that stormy weather is not unusual, and walkers should be prepared with waterproof outerwear and warm clothes. The track is well marked, is generally walked from north to south (to reduce encounters among hiking groups and enhance the sense of solitude), and includes a system of self-service huts, some of them historic (these huts are in addition to the private huts described at the beginning of this chapter). Walkers planning to use the self-service facilities should still carry a tent because bunks in the huts are first-come, first-served; camping spots are provided nearby. The huts offer rainwater tanks (though this water must be treated before drinking), but no other supplies are available along the trail. The classic walk is six days and covers 51 miles, but consider adding another couple of days of walking to allow visits to some of the worthwhile attractions off the main track. Walking is easy along the expanses of boardwalk (locally called "duckboard") that facilitate traversing wet areas and protect low-lying vegetation. The prime walking season is October 1 through May 31, when the track is usually at capacity. Access to Tasmania is by plane serving several small cities and by ferry from mainland Australia.

It was obvious that the Australians we walked the track with considered their trip a pilgrimage of sorts—a place every Australian should see and experience. Based on our walk, we'd extend that sentiment to the world more broadly. Walk this trail—you'll be glad you did.

Resources

Website
Overland Track/Parks and Wildlife Service Tasmania: https://parks.tas.gov.au/explore-our-parks/cradle-mountain/overland-track

Guidebook
Warwick Sprawson, *Hiking the Overland Track*, 2020

(ABOVE LEFT) We strongly recommend the side trail to the top of 5,305-foot Mount Ossa, the highest peak in Tasmania.

(ABOVE) We enjoyed the remarkable air quality along the trail, perhaps the clearest air we've ever encountered.

Paria River Canyon is one of the major slot canyons in the vast Colorado Plateau in the southwest quadrant of the United States; slot canyons are formed by rivers that cut deeply into comparatively soft sandstone bedrock, carving narrow, sinuous, steep-walled canyons.

Paria River Canyon

It was the middle of March, not the conventional time for visiting the dramatic Paria River Canyon in the glorious Southwest of the United States. But travel brought us to the region, and this walk was too good to pass up. We watched the weather forecast closely, and it was sure to be clear (no chance of rain—the most important consideration), but cold. Sure enough, there was a skim of ice on the river as we started the first day of our walk along the Paria River. Soon the canyon walls narrowed and we reached a point where we had to cross the river. This was not a serious matter because the river was no more than knee deep and about 20 feet wide. But we were skittish about getting our feet wet, so we worked hard to find the shallowest crossing, scouting out a few strategically placed rocks in the water, and made our move. Of course our feet got wet anyway, and by the end of our four-day walk we laughed at our initial attempt to keep dry. Over the course of the trek, we crossed the river nearly 500 times, walking some of the narrowest stretches of the canyon right down the middle of the river! Fortunately, wet feet turned out not to be cold feet because walking kept us warm.

─────── ≈ ───────

The Paria River Canyon is a geologic marvel. It's one of the major "slot" canyons in the vast Colorado River Plateau in the southwest quadrant of the United States. Slot canyons are formed by rivers that cut deeply into comparatively soft sandstone bedrock, forming narrow, sinuous, steep-walled landforms. The Paria River Canyon has been called "the premier narrows hike on the Colorado Plateau" and "one of world's best canyon walks." We're convinced. Long portions of the canyon are only a few yards wide, and sidewalls rise vertically for 1,000 feet or more. The river is a tributary of the legendary Colorado River (see the Kaibab Trail description in an earlier chapter of this book for an account of this classic Grand Canyon walk), starting in southern Utah and reaching the Colorado River at historic Lee's Ferry, Arizona, where all raft trips of the Colorado River through the

LOCATION
Utah and Arizona, United States

LENGTH
38 miles

ACCOMMODATIONS
Commercial (e.g., Inns, B&Bs): No
Huts/Refuges: No
Backpacking/Camping: Yes

BAGGAGE TRANSFER
No

OPTION TO WALK IN SECTIONS
Some

DEGREE OF CHALLENGE
Moderate

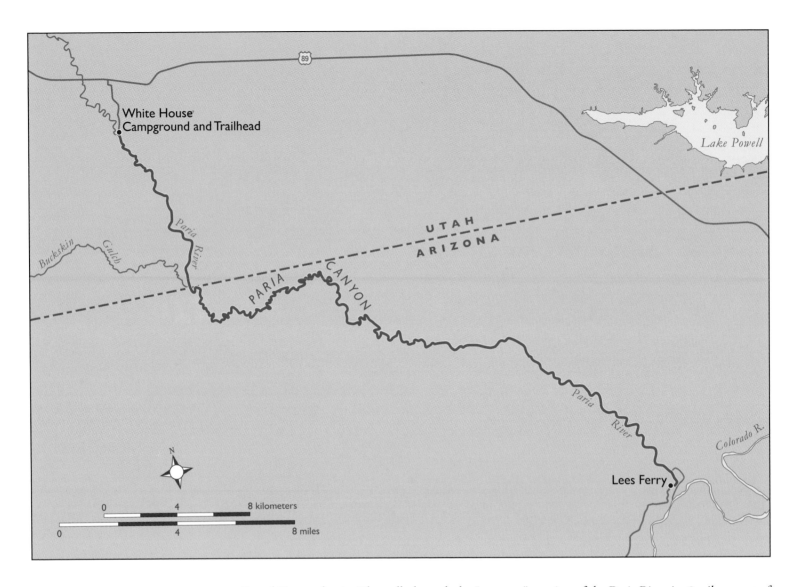

Grand Canyon begin. The walk through the "narrows" portion of the Paria River is 38 miles, most of this within the 112,500-acre Paria Canyon–Vermillion Cliffs Wilderness.

The Paria River Canyon walk is more than geology, but that's where we should begin. *Paria* means "muddy water" in the Paiute language, and this hints at the canyon's origin, including its geology and hydrology. The water is perpetually clouded with the tons of sediment it has eroded over

the eons, and the granular character of the river's water helps it cut through the comparatively soft sandstone bedrock. This erosive action is magnified by the simultaneous geologic uplift of the entire Colorado Plateau region. In this process, the Paria River has cut through and exposed seven major geologic formations (e.g., former sand dunes and sea bottoms) spanning 85 million years of geologic time, and all of this can be clearly read in the range of colors and forms on the canyon walls.

Water is vital to the arid Southwest, and the Paria River is an integral component of the vast Colorado River drainage. The gauging station that measures water levels at the confluence of the Paria and Colorado Rivers has been called one of the most important in the United States because it's the first on the Colorado River below the mighty Glen Canyon Dam.

The first few miles of the hike are relatively open, and the surrounding landscape features a variety of "hoodoos"—domes, spires, and other formations carved out of the reddish sandstone. Then the walls close in sharply for the next 20 miles, with sun and shadow casting unusual plays of light and dark on the canyon's fluted, polished walls. In this deeply entrenched area, the sun reaches the riverbed for only a few hours a day. A number of side canyons flow into the Paria River, including dramatic Buckskin Gulch and Wrather Canyon. We recommend exploring both, the former an exceptionally narrow slot canyon featuring deep pools of cold water, and the latter offering a short hike to Wrather Arch, one of the largest natural stone arches in the world. Plan to linger a little at the

(ABOVE RIGHT) Hanging gardens of maidenhair ferns and monkey flowers mark the location of seeps and springs that offer hikers fresh water.

(ABOVE) Hikers camp on sandy benches just above the river; in summer, cottonwood trees provide welcome shade.

Long portions of Paria River Canyon are only a few yards wide, and sidewalls rise vertically for 1,000 feet or more.

confluence of the Paria and Buckskin Gulch, one of the most magical areas in the Southwest, and be sure to notice the many hanging gardens of maidenhair fern and monkey flowers in the numerous seeps in the canyon walls. The last portion of the canyon—about 10 miles—widens substantially, and the route climbs away from the river, crosses open desert, and requires some scrambling. Here, you leave the wilderness portion of the hike and find several abandoned ranches, mines, and petroglyph panels. This area also has petrified wood and dinosaur bones and tracks. When you reach Lonely Dell Ranch, turn around and look back at the canyon's geologic formations rising 2,800 feet above the river.

Paria Canyon harbors many interesting plants and animals. Large cottonwood trees offer shade and often mark good campsites. A number of animals make their home in Paria Canyon, or at least pass through looking for food and shelter. These include pronghorn, coyotes, bobcats, mountain lions, desert bighorn sheep, mule deer, foxes, porcupines, beavers, cottontails, and ground squirrels, though walkers rarely see many of these animals. Birds include California condors (reintroduced to this area in 1996), bald and golden eagles, peregrine falcons, red-tailed and Cooper's hawks, great blue herons, great horned owls, and hummingbirds. Listen for the call of canyon wrens—a melodious series of descending notes characteristic of the canyon country of the Southwest. There are also rattlesnakes, black widow spiders, and scorpions—be sure to shake out your boots in the morning.

Of course the Paria River Canyon has an interesting historical and cultural component as well. It's thought that Native Americans used the area for at least 10,000 years, but primarily as a travel route. Walkers can find a number of ancient rock art panels—groups of images and symbols carved into (petroglyphs) and painted onto (pictographs) flat rock surfaces. And Lee's Ferry was an important Colorado River crossing for early settlers who tried (in vain) to develop ranching and mining in this arid land.

This is world-class walk. From a purely physical standpoint, it's not overly difficult in that there is very little elevation change. But it's not without some important safety considerations. This is a wilderness backpacking trip—once you enter the canyon, there is no way out except returning to the start or continuing to the end. You will be walking a route, not a maintained trail. For the most part, it will not be difficult to find your way (just follow the river downstream), but you will have to pick the places you want to cross the river. By far, the most important consideration is avoiding periodic flash floods that can occur, primarily in July, August, and early September. We noticed flood debris—logs, brush, and so forth—lodged between the canyon walls at heights of 50 feet or more above the riverbed! Avoid this walk (and other slot canyons) if there is the threat of thunderstorms anywhere in the vicinity—flash floods can be caused by heavy rain anywhere in the extended watershed, not just in the Paria River Canyon narrows. Another potential hazard is deep mud and even occasional pockets of quicksand. Finally, there is no water available in the last 10 miles of the hike—be sure to stock up on water before you reach this point.

There are four trailheads that serve the hike—Buckskin Gulch, Wire Pass, White House, and Lee's Ferry. The first two require hiking all or most of challenging Buckskin Gulch to reach the river, so we recommend White House, which is located directly adjacent to the Paria River. (Buckskin Gulch can be a fabulous hike, but it's long and slow, and there is no camping until you reach

(ABOVE LEFT) Watch for ancient rock art panels—images and symbols carved and painted on flat rock surfaces.

(ABOVE) The 38-mile walk through the narrow canyon requires crossing the shallow Paria River many times, and walking right down the middle of the river occasionally; the going can be slow, but the scenery is stunning.

Remarkable Paria River Canyon runs for 38 miles, most of it through the 112,500-acre Paria Canyon–Vermillion Cliffs Wilderness; this is a grand backpacking trip.

the confluence with the Paria River.) The fourth trailhead is Lee's Ferry, but this is the traditional end of the hike, as it's much easier to walk downstream (especially when walking in the river). A permit and nominal fee are required (available from the US Bureau of Land Management, which administers most of the canyon). The prime months to walk are April and May, when days are long, wildflowers (including flowering cactuses) are at their peak, cottonwoods and other trees have leafed out, providing shade, freshwater springs are running, it's not too hot, and flash flood danger is relatively low. Drinking water is available from several natural springs that are marked on hiking maps; you're likely to see other small springs as well, if you look for them, especially around vegetation growing on canyon walls. This water must be treated for drinking; it's not feasible to purify river water for drinking because it's too silty. When it's hot, the general rule for hiking in arid lands is to drink a gallon of water per person per day; therefore, when you find spring water, it's a good idea to stock up. Since you're often walking in the stream or in soft sand, hiking is slow; take at least four days for this hike. Aggressive sampler day hikes include walking down Buckskin Gulch to the confluence with the Paria River and then following the river upstream to the White House Trailhead, but this is a long and tiring hike. An easier option is an out-and-back hike starting at the White House Trailhead and reaching the confluence with Buckskin Gulch. Consider wearing neoprene socks to keep your feet from getting too cold, packing lightweight dry bags to keep vital supplies safe, and using trekking poles to enhance balance and probe the silt-laden river water. Convenient commercial shuttles service hikers over the full length of the Paria River Canyon hike; park your car at Lee's Ferry and the shuttle takes you to upstream trailheads.

The Paria River Canyon is unlike any other walk described in this book; in fact, it's almost like being on another planet. This deeply entrenched red rock canyon with its unusual and lovely desert riparian habitat is filled with red rock amphitheaters, striped and streaked with sandstone layers and desert varnish, illustrated with Native American rock art panels, and punctuated with lush hanging gardens, natural springs, and stone arches, plus offers wooded terraces with shady cottonwoods tailor-made for camping. Consider walking the Paria River Canyon—it's worth getting your feet wet!

Resources

Website
Bureau of Land Management: www.blm.gov/visit/paria-canyon-vermillion-cliffs-wilderness-area

Guidebook
Kelsey, Michael, *Hiking and Exploring the Paria River* (6th edition), 2004

Map
National Geographic Trails Illustrated Map 859, *Paria Canyon, Kanab Map*, 2019

The South Downs Way offers a pleasing 100-mile walk between the coastal town of Eastbourne and historic Winchester.

South Downs Way

The English tradition of afternoon tea is lovely, but teatime combined with walking is divine! What a joy to stroll into yet another quaint English village, pleasantly fatigued and always hungry, and find a beckoning tearoom. Here we enjoyed—more than once—the refreshing and revitalizing nourishment of homemade scones, cakes, or even sandwiches (with their crusts properly removed, of course), and an invigorating pot of freshly brewed tea. The English have perfected this mini-meal to an art form, and we thoroughly appreciated the times we could share in this ritual while walking the South Downs Way. Because the route runs from town to town, we timed our daily walks with this afternoon break in mind. When a convenient tearoom wasn't available, we made do with store-bought treats carried in the packs (we recommend the coconut macaroons); the elevated route along the trail always provided us with inviting vistas out over the beautiful English countryside for these self-service teas.

When is "down" really up? When walking the South Downs Way, of course! The word "down" has its seemingly perverse origin in the Old English "dun," meaning "hill." The South Downs Way is a trail perched on the gentle ridgeline that winds its way across much of southern England.

People seem to be drawn to the high places in a landscape; perhaps this has origins in the life of early humans, when being uphill had strategic advantages. Whatever the motivation, we all like viewpoints that allow us to see and understand the landscape in ways that are difficult where the earth lacks such topographic relief. The South Downs Way offers a nearly continuous succession of viewpoints that meander gently across this beautiful section of southern England. The tops of the downs have been used throughout history and before for burial sites, fortifications, homes, signaling beacons, and farming. In the most recent iteration, paragliders and hang gliders delight in the updrafts associated with this elevated landscape. In a sometimes uneasy combination of old and new uses, one of our guidebooks suggested that standing on tumuli (ancient burial sites) affords the

LOCATION
England

LENGTH
100 miles

ACCOMMODATIONS
Commercial (e.g., Inns, B&Bs): Yes
Huts/Refuges: Some
Backpacking/Camping: Limited

BAGGAGE TRANSFER
Yes

OPTION TO WALK IN SECTIONS
All

DEGREE OF CHALLENGE
Low-Moderate

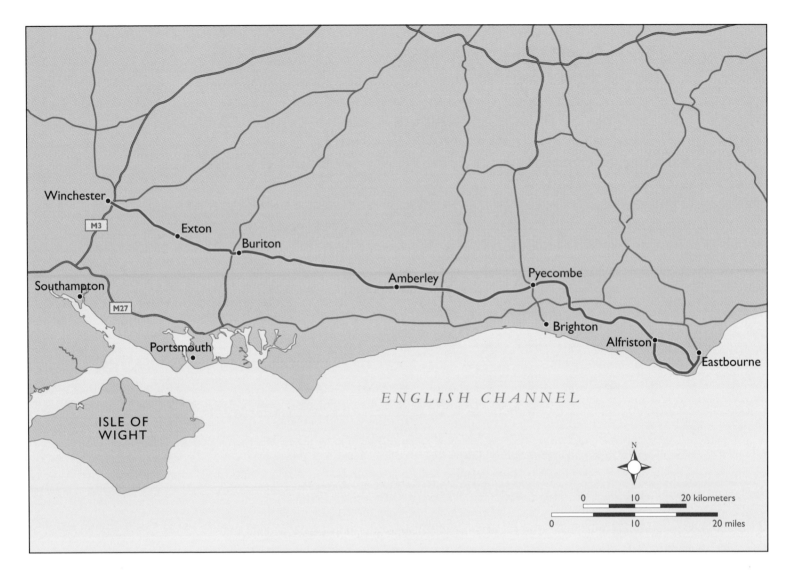

best views—and we saw folks happily picnicking on a large tumulus. The South Downs Way is a welcoming landscape that can be easily walked and appreciated for its many natural, historical, and recreational features.

Located roughly an hour's train ride south of London, the South Downs Way—one of sixteen National Trails in England and Wales—is a 100-mile walk in one of the newest national parks in

The South Downs Way celebrates England's downs, gentle hills of chalk that meet the sea and form the spectacular and famous White Cliffs of Dover.

England. This large national park and its namesake trail offer an unusual opportunity for so many Londoners and others in the country's densely populated South East. South Downs National Park, established in 2011, celebrates the downs, gentle hills of chalk that meet the sea in the spectacular and famous White Cliffs of Dover. Originally the bottom of a shallow sea, the land was formed 70 to 100 million years ago (during the Cretaceous period) from the tiny shells of marine organisms. These shells fell to the seafloor and slo-o-o-w-ly accumulated and consolidated at a rate of 1 foot every 30,000 years. Then, approximately 20 million years ago (during the Tertiary period), tectonic plates collided and the land was raised into a huge dome. Erosion has worked on the dome since this time and transformed it into gentle rolling hills and valleys with isolated patches of ancient forests. Originally 1,000 feet high, this chalk layer is still impressive, with some of the cliff faces measuring over 500 feet.

Deep chalk is underfoot at all times—and you'll see bands of flint as well; these are fossilized sea sponge skeletons. These fist-size nodules of stone are one of the primary building materials in this region, and many buildings and fences are constructed of the fossils cemented together. There are trees in some of the gentle valleys, but most of the downs are now open, having been denuded of trees in Neolithic times (roughly 5,000 years ago). Erosion has worked aggressively on this deforested land, and now the topsoil is too thin in many places to support trees. However, the topsoil does support a wonderful green turf that makes walking on much of the downs as smooth as walking on a golf course.

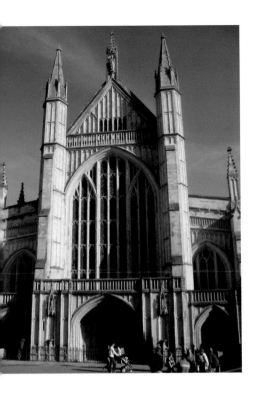

We chose to walk the South Downs Way from east to west because we thought Winchester would make a fitting finale with its tourist-friendly downtown and historic Winchester Cathedral.

We chose to walk the South Downs Way from east to west (from Eastbourne to Winchester), from the more open and exposed sections to the more wooded, because we thought Winchester would make a fitting finale—it's a lively market town full of interesting history, and very tourist friendly. But the walk can easily be done in either direction—or you might choose to do a segment or two anywhere along the trail. Eastbourne is only 75 minutes from London by train, and the trip from Winchester back to London is just over an hour. Trains run several times per hour, so it's easy to position yourself. There's even train service from one end of the trail to the other. Eastbourne is a Georgian/Victorian seaside resort town, and there are signs directing you to the South Downs Way right outside the train station.

We started the walk with a modest ascent of the Downs to Beachy Head, where we could see the first of the "Seven Sisters" (though we counted eight), a series of gentle rises with impressive white cliff faces meeting the sea. These cliffs continue to erode and slump into the English Channel, evidence of geology in action—it's best to stay back from the edge! Mostly you follow the rim of the South Downs escarpment, gaining surprisingly panoramic views from roughly 650 feet above sea level. The trail stays on top of the Downs, dropping only to cross river valleys called "wind gaps." Rivers include the Cuckmere, Ourse, Arun, Ardur, and Meon. (There's a saying that after the River Ardur, "the way gets 'arder and 'arder," but we didn't notice much difference.) You also occasionally cross or travel parallel to delightful chalk streams.

One of the driest and warmest parts of England, the South Downs are home to many wildflowers. Cowslips are the symbol of the Downs and grow on southern slopes. There is surprisingly diverse plant life in the "grass deserts" of the Downs, with up to fifty species per square yard. There are lots of butterflies in summer—you have the chance to see over twenty species. Crossing the rivers and their estuaries (on bridges) offers the best opportunity to see lots of birdlife. Our first wide water was Cuckmere Haven, where we saw tufted ducks, swans, dabchicks, cormorants, and herons. Other days we watched larks and saw many gray pheasants and partridges. We weren't fortunate enough to see hares, but there certainly are lots of their holes along the Seven Sisters. We want to believe that the cows we saw (black-and-white ones like those in our former home state of Vermont) mooed with a British accent, but we just couldn't hear it. At any rate, they provided a picturesque punctuation for the pastoral vistas.

The trail opened in 1972 (in places following trails worn by nomadic tribes) and is well maintained and marked with the white acorn symbol (used on all National Trails) on posts. The landscape is wonderfully British, a mixture of pasture, arable fields, and woodlands, and the landscape is bigger and more open than in other parts of the country. We think of it as Britain's "Big Sky Country." Towns are in the lowlands and are conveniently located about a day's walk apart.

Gently up and down you go, passing rich remnants of early human history along the way. Of course there are impressive and historic buildings in the towns, notably Saxon and Norman churches.

The trail finds its way through a number of estuaries where we enjoyed seeing tufted ducks, swans, dabchicks, cormorants, and herons.

Alfriston has a large flint church called "The Cathedral of the Downs," and this town is home of the first property—the Clergy House—adopted by the now-powerful National Trust.

But it's up on the high land that we found the most interesting history. No matter what your favorite period of history, the South Downs Way can accommodate you. Neolithic people farmed the downs and mined them for flint to use for tools. The Bronze Age saw primitive farm sites, burial barrows (places where an interment was followed by the building of a mound of soil), and hill forts (areas of earthwork-enclosed high ground used for defense). There are 400 burial barrows (sometimes called long barrows) and many tumuli (individual burial mounds) along the path's route. There are Iron Age lynchets (ancient field systems), defensive dykes, and ancient tracks. Later, Romans built trade and communication routes, now used as rights-of-way. Near Bignor Hill there's a sign at the remains of a Roman road pointing the way to *Londinium* (Latin for London) to remind walkers of the Roman period of history. This road dates from about 70 CE, and there are remains of villas nearby.

Many of the summits along the Downs have been used for coastal defense and communication. Ditchling Beacon (now part of a nature reserve) was one of a chain of bonfire sites used for centuries to send signals along the coast. Bonfires here and farther along the coast were used to warn Queen Elizabeth I of the approach of the Spanish Armada.

More recent history is represented as well. Chanctonbury Ring, a circle of beech trees planted in 1780, marks one especially beautiful hilltop. (Iron Age people also used this site, and there are remains of a Roman temple.) One of the many legends associated with this site has it that if you run around the ring of trees seven times the devil will come—we decided it was best not to test this. Several hilltop dew ponds were built about 200 years ago; these large, shallow depressions collected rainwater for sheep rearing. Once there were over 200,000 ewes and lambs in the region, and the dew ponds were necessary because there's virtually no surface water on the Downs. The two Clayton windmills (local landmarks known as Jack and Jill) date from 1866 and 1821, respectively. You walk past a (very) large white chalk horse (the figure of a horse outlined in chalk on the side of a hill) from the 1920s, but have to detour if you want to see the Long Man, which is England's largest chalk figure (and the largest representation of a human in Western Europe). General Eisenhower addressed the Allied troops prior to D-Day from Cheesefoot Hill, where the landscape forms a natural amphitheater. After the war the Downs were used for growing grain. A huge telecommunications tower is on Butser Hill, the highest point of the walk at 889 feet.

Amberley was our favorite village, an especially picturesque town with thatched roofs and the ruins of a fourteenth-century castle (now an upscale hotel where a guest had parked his private helicopter on the lawn). At the end of each day, you come off the Downs and spend the night in one of the communities dotted along the way; there you'll find B&Bs, pubs, and hostels. There aren't as many towns as in some parts of England, so you may have to walk an extra mile or two. If the distance between lodgings is greater than you want to walk, it's possible to arrange rides; baggage service is doable, too. There are only a few designated campsites, and you must ask the landowner for permission before camping elsewhere. It's important that you close all gates you pass through—and the ingenuity of some of the closures themselves is entertaining.

Of course everyone enjoys Winchester, our end to the walk. It was a clear day, and we could see the steeple of Winchester Cathedral several miles before we reached town. Once the Saxon capital of England, Winchester is now a small city with a college founded in 1382, and it has a ramparted town wall. Its impressive cathedral was started in 1079 and finished in 1404 and incorporates many different building styles from work over the ages. It's one of the longest cathedrals in Europe at 556 feet, but has a short tower. We finished our walk on a Saturday, which allowed us to attend the Sunday service the next morning; we found it to be an interesting cultural experience and especially enjoyed the boys' choir.

When the weather is dry, it's possible to walk the South Downs Way in trail running shoes; the path is sometimes on a bridleway, sometimes a footpath, sometimes a country lane—many of these travel ways having their origin in old routes and animal driveways. Be aware that you'll want some cushioning because the chalk and flint are right under the vegetation, and this can be hard on the

feet; moreover, if it's wet, the chalk can be a little slippery. On weekends we saw some equestrians and bikers, but there are also horse and bike variants to the trail in places. Lots of folks enjoy the South Downs Way—in ways as varied as training fox hunting hounds to mountain biking—so this is not the trail for someone seeking solitude.

There is little opportunity to get fresh water on the trail, so you'll have to carry some. Many of the sections are fully exposed, so this trail is more safely enjoyed when the weather is cooperative. Perhaps you'll enjoy standing on the high ground to savor the views of the sea or the attractive inland towns. Or maybe you'll like imagining people from an earlier period of history living their lives in this gentle landscape. Maybe you'll prefer studying the area's plants, or perhaps it's the animals that are of greatest interest. It doesn't matter—the South Downs Way can accommodate all these interests—and more. And be sure to take time for afternoon tea!

Resources

Websites
National Trails: www.nationaltrail.co.uk/southdowns
South Downs Way National Trails: www.southdownsway.org

Guidebooks
Fiona Barltrop, *South Downs Way*, 2011
Jim Manthorp, *South Downs Way: Winchester to Eastbourne*, 2009
Paul Millmore, *South Downs Way*, 2010
Kev Reynolds, *The South Downs Way*, 2004

Map
Harvey Maps, *South Downs Way*

(LEFT) Many of the buildings along the trail are constructed of local flint—fossilized sea sponge skeletons fused together.

(CENTER) Several towns feature historic buildings with thatched roofs.

(RIGHT) At the end of most days, walkers descend from the downs into local towns to find B&Bs and pubs.

Much of the Superior Hiking Trail winds through the Sawtooth Mountain Range overlooking Lake Superior, but it makes occasional forays to the lake's dramatic shoreline.

Superior Hiking Trail

The bull moose lifted its head from the pond where it had been grazing, vines draped across its impressive rack of antlers. The beaver stopped its work on the dam that formed the pond and followed the glide of a bald eagle overhead. Sunlight illuminated the red maple leaves, and the bright yellow leaves of the birch trees fluttered in the light breeze. That night the wolves and coyotes serenaded the shimmering northern lights. OK, so we didn't really experience all these things on our walk of the Superior Hiking Trail. But the point is that we could have. The Superior Hiking Trail offers a glimpse into the vast "North Woods," an important component of America's natural and human history. The trail remains relatively unvisited—especially among long-distance walkers—despite its accessibility and growing reputation.

≈

With a name like "Superior," it's got to be great. And it is! The 312-mile Superior Hiking Trail follows the "North Shore" of legendary Lake Superior, the largest freshwater lake in the world (as measured by surface area). Excavated by glacial action some 10,000 years ago, Lake Superior is the greatest of the Great Lakes, comprising 32,000 square miles (about the size of the state of Maine). Moreover, much of the trail is carved out of the historic 3-million-acre Superior National Forest, by far the largest national forest in the eastern United States. No wonder *Backpacker* magazine named this one of the top ten long-distance trails in America (though, paradoxically, it's not well known).

The trail is in far northern Minnesota (what the tourism marketers have dubbed the "North Coast of America"), starting well south of Duluth at Jay Cooke State Park and extending north to the Canadian border. It's exceptionally diverse in both natural and cultural history. Much of the trail winds through the Sawtooth Mountain Range overlooking the lake, with occasional forays and side trails to the lake's shore. Landscape features include mountain summits, deep gorges, streams and waterfalls carved by mighty and historic rivers such as the Cascade, Temperance, and Devil Track; extensive inland lakes, ponds and bogs; and the rocky shores of Lake Superior. Most of the land is

LOCATION
Minnesota, United States

LENGTH
312 miles

ACCOMMODATIONS
Commercial (e.g., Inns, B&Bs): Some
Huts/Refuges: No
Backpacking/Camping: Most

BAGGAGE TRANSFER
Some

OPTION TO WALK IN SECTIONS
Most

DEGREE OF CHALLENGE
Moderate–High

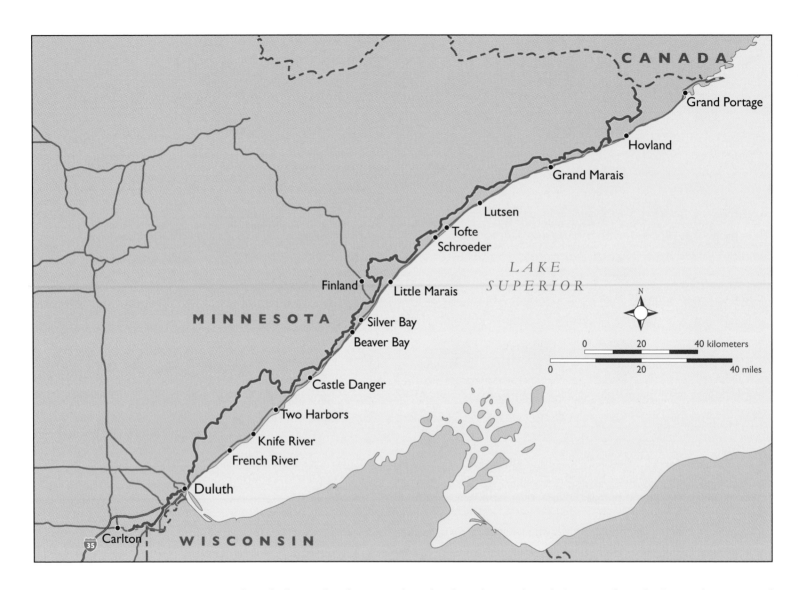

heavily forested—classic northern hardwoods (maple, oak, basswood) in the lower elevations and boreal forest (balsam, pine, spruce, cedar, and tamarack) cloaking the higher areas.

The trail is often described as having two distinct reaches: a 41-mile section (plus 2 miles of spur trails) in the south that runs north through Duluth, and a classic "North Shore" section north of Duluth that extends 255 miles (plus 14 miles of spur trails) to the Canadian border. The southern

section offers day hiking only, but the northern section has more than ninety campsites, allowing for a thru-hike. Backpackers are required to stay at designated campsites; permits/reservations are not needed. There are more than fifty trailheads that provide access to the trail.

This diverse, protected landscape supports a great variety of animal life, including black bears, moose, deer, coyotes, bobcats, mountain lions, eagles and other raptors, snowshoe hares, and marten. The area is one of the last strongholds of the gray wolf in the lower 48 states. Though hikers may not be fortunate enough to see many of these animals, it's exciting to know that you're walking through a vast wilderness that still provides home to many of America's most iconic wildlife species.

The human history of this area is equally impressive. Native Americans first settled in the North Shore region in 8,000 BCE after the glaciers retreated. Frenchmen were the first Europeans to explore the area in the early 1700s while searching for a northwest passage, and later, in spite of conflicts with the native tribes, began the fur trade. They were supplanted by the British, who continued the trade, establishing a series of trading forts, including Grand Portage. Grand Portage National Monument, a part of the National Park System, commemorates this colorful history near the northern terminus of the Superior Hiking Trail. Henry Wadsworth Longfellow's epic poem *The Song of Hiawatha* is set here on the shores of what he called "Gitchee Gummee" and tells of the love of Hiawatha and Minnehaha. Longfellow exercised substantial editorial license in this poem, but his lines conjure up the romantic North Woods mystique.

(ABOVE LEFT) The 312-mile Superior Hiking Trail follows the "North Shore" of massive Lake Superior, the largest freshwater lake in the world (as measured by surface area).

(ABOVE) Some strategically placed trail infrastructure is required to navigate this wild landscape.

Dramatic Split Rock Lighthouse on the shores of Lake Superior is the symbol of the Superior Hiking Trail.

When Americans started moving west, surveys showed rich mineral resources in this area. In 1854, Native American lands were ceded by treaty to the United States (though this remains controversial) and, after some boom and bust stages, growth began in earnest in the region in the 1880s. Fishing became a major industry. Iron mining was followed by taconite mining, and the railroad built during the mining boom allowed the lumber industry to flourish after 1890. In the early twentieth century, tourism began to grow as extractive industries declined. Large and exclusive resorts were built along the shore of the lake, and some (Lutsen Resort and Cascade Lodge, for example) are still in operation, offering meals and accommodations for those not rich and famous, including walkers on the Superior Hiking Trail.

The Superior Hiking Trail is a relatively new addition to the stock of long-distance trails in the United States. It was officially opened at a ceremonial "log-cutting" in 1987, and was built and is maintained by the Superior Hiking Trail Association, a nonprofit group founded in 1986. The trail connects seven state parks, two state forests, the vast Superior National Forest, and several stretches of private lands (where walkers must remain on the trail). The trail is highly accessible, periodically crossed by mostly small country roads, allowing for relatively easy day walks. A number of small towns and resorts are adjacent to the trail, providing resupply opportunities and motels, bed-and-breakfasts, and historic inns for those who choose not to camp. Duluth and the larger towns of Two Harbors and Grand Marais offer walkers a full range of supplies and services. Two Harbors houses the Superior Hiking Trail Association offices and store, and tourist-friendly Grand Marais includes a concentration of art galleries, shops, and restaurants. Commercial shuttle services operate along the trail, and there may be commercial lodge-to-lodge services that will arrange treks of any length along selected sections of the trail.

We enjoyed our ten-day walk on the Superior Hiking Trail (all of it north of Two Harbors), where we soaked up the rich history and culture of the North Shore and the beauty and naturalness of the off-the-beaten-track geography. Highlights were seemingly unending views over Lake Superior, including the distant outlines of Apostle Islands National Lakeshore and Isle Royale National Park, visiting the habitats of so many animals that now live only in the remote corners of the United States such as northern Minnesota, the solitude we experienced along the northern sections of trail (some days we saw no one else), and the accessibility of colorful towns and hospitable people when desired or needed. We found the trail to be well marked (blue rectangular blazes) and maintained, but the natural topography can make walking long distances challenging; hikes of more than 8 to 10 miles often seemed hard. Even though the highest point on the trail is only about 1,800 feet in elevation, most days on the trail require several steep (but short) climbs and descents; the total elevation gain over the length of the trail is nearly 38,000 feet. The trail is generally rugged, and the website for the Superior Hiking Trail Association suggests that hikers should plan on traveling at an average speed of about 1 mile per hour; we found that about right. The trail has been incorporated into the nearly 5,000-mile North Country National Scenic Trail that runs from Vermont to North Dakota, but retains its identity as the Superior Hiking Trail.

The trail is generally accessible from May through October. June through August typically offers warm days and unending shades of green (but biting insects can be a nuisance—or worse); fall features colorful foliage, and late fall provides extended views otherwise hidden by billions of leaves. Our best advice: Walk when you can and as much as you can—you'll be glad you did.

Resources

Website
Superior Hiking Trail Association: www.superiorhiking.org

Guidebooks
Annie Nelson, *Thru-Hike the Superior Hiking Trail*, 2020
Superior Hiking Trail Association, *Superior Hiking Trail Guidebook*, 2022
Superior Hiking Trail Association, *Superior Hiking Trail Data Book*, 2022

Map
Superior Hiking Trail Association, *Trail Atlas of the Superior Hiking Trail*

App
Superior Hiking Trail by Avenza Maps (recommended by the Superior Hiking Trail Association)

(ABOVE) Wild rivers and numerous cascades and waterfalls are common landscape features along the trail.

(BELOW) The trail leads along large wetlands fed by deep winter snows.

The Tahoe Rim Trail makes a 165-mile loop around lovely Lake Tahoe; the lake's depth and purity manifest themselves in the deep blue color of the open lake and sparkling turquoise along its beaches and bays.

Tahoe Rim Trail

We made a lot of new friends on the Tahoe Rim Trail—well, sort of. John Muir, the preeminent walker of the Sierra Nevada, wrote that recognizing the plants and animals he encountered on his walks was like greeting old friends. So we decided to take his advice and introduce ourselves to the impressive trees along the Tahoe Rim Trail. The Tahoe Basin's range of elevations, aspects, geology, and climate offer a special richness of trees that vary widely and impressively in form and function. Learning about these trees— telling one species from another, how they've adapted to their environment, what they tell us about the places they live—deepens our appreciation of the natural world and adds to our enjoyment of walking among them. Take, for example, ponderosa pines, stately trees that grow in open groves at lower elevations and derive their name from their "ponderous bulk." They can grow to nearly 250 feet high and 8 feet in diameter, living up to 500 years. The bark on their massive trunks is a distinctive cinnamon-brown to orange-yellow color, but their most distinguishing (and pleasing) characteristic is that they smell like vanilla when warmed by the sun. Walking through a ponderosa pine forest on a sunny day can delight many of the senses. Trees can be interesting friends indeed. They're beautiful, of course, but they also help us by controlling soil erosion, providing wildlife habitat, moderating the weather, improving air quality, conserving water, providing building materials, and helping neutralize excessive emissions of carbon dioxide that contribute to the threat of global climate change. Trees do a lot for us, but are we responding in kind? Joyce Kilmer wrote in his most famous poem:

> *I think that I shall never see*
> *A poem lovely as a tree.*

LOCATION
California and Nevada, United States

LENGTH
165 miles

ACCOMMODATIONS
Commercial (e.g., Inns, B&Bs): Most
Huts/Refuges: No
Backpacking/Camping: Yes

BAGGAGE TRANSFER
No

OPTION TO WALK IN SECTIONS
All

DEGREE OF CHALLENGE
Moderate–High

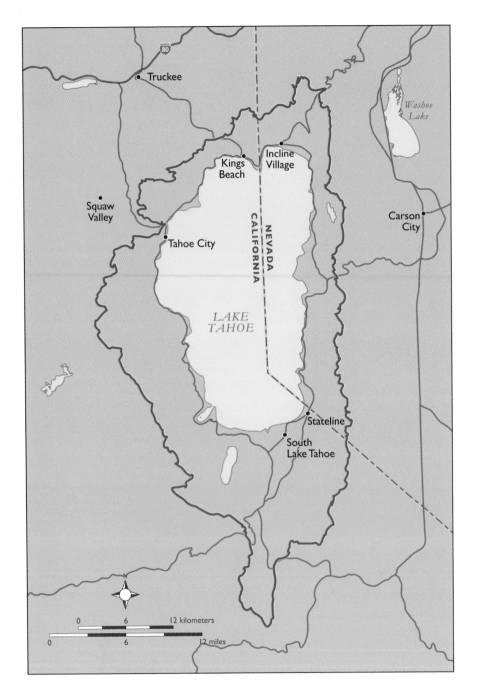

More recently, humorist Ogden Nash replied in parody:

I think that I shall never see
A billboard lovely as a tree.
Perhaps, unless the billboards fall,
I'll never see a tree at all.

———— ≈ ————

The Tahoe Rim Trail (most walkers call it the "TRT") makes a 165-mile loop around lovely Lake Tahoe, the third-largest lake in the United States (eighth-largest in the world) at roughly 12 by 22 miles, covering over 500 square miles. It straddles the California–Nevada state line, with extensive shoreline in both states. But Lake Tahoe is more than big—it's strikingly beautiful. Its depth (more than 1,600 feet) and purity (you can see objects more than 100 feet below the surface) manifest themselves in its rich, deep blue color on the open lake and sparkling turquoise along its beaches, coves, and bays. The TRT is one of the world's great long-distance trails that encircles one of the world's most lovely lakes, and the combination is extraordinary. And then, of course, the trail wanders through the world-renowned Sierra Nevada. No wonder this is one of our very favorite hikes!

Most of the TRT is set back off the shore along the ridges and slopes of the surrounding Sierra Nevada in California and Carson Range in Nevada, offering sweeping views of the lake as well as stately forests, mountain wildflowers, and peaks of more than 10,000 feet. If you choose to walk the entire trail, you have the option of

backpacking or doing a series of day hikes, as roads (mostly paved) break this loop into eight neat sections ranging from 13 to nearly 20 miles. By utilizing side trails and some more-minor Forest Service roads, you can shorten some of these sections even further. Loop trails are fun because you can see where you're going as well as where you've been. We hiked the trail using a combination of day hikes and short backpacking trips. But be forewarned that some of the pockets of strip development on Lake Tahoe's shore can shock the senses after a blissful day on the trail.

It took a lot of geologic history to make the lake and the surrounding lands, including faults, volcanoes, and glaciers. Initially, the Tahoe Basin sank along two fault lines, making a deep depression. About 2 million years ago, lava created a dam where the Truckee River now flows, and the lake reached a height of 600 feet higher than its current surface elevation of 6,200 feet. Subsequent glacial action reduced the height of the dam and shaped the surrounding landscape by scouring out the Tahoe Basin and polishing the surrounding granite.

The TRT also reflects the human history of this area, following travel routes of Native Americans (the Washoe tribe) and pioneers. Historic artifacts along the trail include remnants from the silver mines that started with discovery of the famous Comstock Lode in nearby Virginia City in 1859, as well as enormous stumps of trees cut to fuel those mines and support their underground labyrinths. Lake Tahoe became a retreat for the rich families of San Francisco, Sacramento, and Virginia City around the turn of the twentieth century, and was opened to the masses when improved roads and the prevalence of cars made travel easier after World War II. The 1960 Winter Olympics were

(ABOVE LEFT) The trail traverses three large wilderness areas, including the famous Desolation Wilderness, where a permit is required for camping.

(ABOVE) A side trail leads to world-class views of Emerald Bay, perhaps the most photographed spot in the Tahoe Basin.

The trail spends most of its miles along the ridges and slopes of the surrounding Sierra Nevada and Carson Range, but it makes occasional forays to the shore of the lake.

held in Squaw Valley (now more sensitively named Palisades Tahoe), bringing the Lake Tahoe Basin into the international spotlight.

Interesting plants and animals are found in abundance and variety in this area, as the elevations along the trail range from 6,200 feet at the surface of the lake to over 10,000 feet at the summit of Relay Peak. Bald eagles and red-tailed hawks soar, but black bear, mountain lion, bobcat, mule deer, and coyote sightings are less common. Wildflowers are abundant in the open slopes and meadows—our favorite was the distinctive yellow mule ears.

But it's the trees that stole the show for us. In addition to the ponderosa pines noted earlier, sugar pines were a favorite. This is a tree of superlatives, the tallest of all the pines and growing the longest cones, which sometimes reach over 20 inches. When you see a sugar pine cone, you'll know it! In keeping with their name, sugar pines produce a sweet resin, which John Muir liked better than maple syrup. White fir is probably the most common tree in the Tahoe Basin. They're large trees that favor moist soils; look for them near the lake. Red firs also form extensive forests in the area, but are larger than white firs and present a classic, narrow, conical, symmetrical crown, and this "magnificent" character is reflected in their scientific name, *Abies magnifica*. The name "lodgepole pine" also suggests something about its character; they grow especially straight in their customarily dense groves, and the resulting poles were used by Native Americans to support their lodges. Western white pine, whitebark pine, and western juniper are all higher-elevation trees, growing between 10,000 and 12,000 feet. Western white pine is a large tree—sometimes massive; we measured one by the side of the trail with a circumference of 24 feet! Whitebark pine tends to grow in exposed locations; its crown is often distorted by the wind, with most of its substantive branches clinging to the leeward side of the trunk. Western juniper can live as long as 1,000 years; it prefers dry, rocky areas that are often exposed, and it can take on a twisted, gnarly appearance. The principal deciduous tree in the Tahoe Basin is quaking aspen. It's readily recognized by its white (sometimes pale yellow-green) bark, its toothed, egg-shaped leaves with flat stems that "quake" in the breeze, and its yellow, gold, and occasionally orange fall colors. It prefers wet areas, and its presence suggests that surface or groundwater is nearby. The seeds of aspen are so small (it takes 2 million to make a pound!) they are easily and widely distributed by the wind.

The TRT is located primarily on national forest lands and passes through three wilderness areas—Mount Rose, Granite Chief, and Desolation. The 35-mile stretch through the Desolation Wilderness may be the most dramatic—a quintessential Sierra Nevada landscape with exposed

The trail passes lush meadows well-stocked with wildflowers; lupines and paintbrush are common.

A highlight of hiking the TRT was following the advice of John Muir and introducing ourselves to the region's diverse and impressive trees.

granite peaks, high mountain passes, and more than a hundred lakes to swim in or just admire. Look closely at the granite outcrops and see the glacial polish and the grooves and chatter marks where the glaciers advanced and retreated. A side trail leads to world-class views of Emerald Bay, the most photographed spot in the Tahoe Basin. From Meiss Meadows to Twin Peaks (on the western shore) the trail coincides with about 50 miles of the Pacific Crest National Scenic Trail, which runs from Mexico to Canada—we enjoyed talking with the extraordinary PCT thru-hikers we encountered.

The Tahoe Rim Trail is a relatively new addition to the world of long-distance walking, officially opening in 2001. Over 10,000 volunteers toiled to make this trail happen. The TRT is a multiuse trail, with just over half the trail open to mountain bikers and all of it open to equestrians. The rules state that hikers yield to horses and bikers yield to hikers and horses, and for the most part, it works pretty well.

Lake Tahoe is roughly 200 miles northeast of San Francisco, 100 miles east of Sacramento, and 60 miles southwest of Reno, so access to the area is fairly easy—and you'll want to spend a little time in the basin to acclimate to the elevation. The trail is open year-round to allow for cross-country skiing and snowshoeing, but the hiking season is July through September. Water is an issue. Although many streams drain into Lake Tahoe, most of these are seasonal, so it's important to check locally

Deep snows have left this forest with its unusually shaped trees.

about both water and any remaining snowfields—you want to avoid walking through challenging wet spring snowfields, locally called "Sierra cement." Dispersed camping is allowed along most of the trail, although you need a permit for the Desolation Wilderness (you need a permit to hike there, too), and you're restricted to three primitive campsites while walking through Lake Tahoe Nevada State Park.

If you want to experience some of the most outstanding portions of a truly sensational trail, we recommend the three days from Echo Lake to Barker Pass in the Desolation Wilderness, showcasing a dozen or more alpine lakes and open meadows with lush displays of wildflowers. If you're into long-distance views, the best are from the top of Mount Rose and Relay Peak, where you can look into the Sierra Nevada, the Carson Range, out over the lake, and north to Mounts Lassen and Shasta. Another highlight is Christopher's Loop (probably the most photographed section of the trail).

The trail is managed by the Tahoe Rim Trail Association (TRTA), and their helpful website conveniently divides the trail into fourteen-day hikes. TRTA even conducts some guided hikes. The TRT is well maintained, and wayfinding was easy. Backpackers should use bear canisters to keep food away from the area's black bears and other wildlife. There is substantial elevation change over most sections (the trail ranges from 6,300 to 10,338 feet), but the trail was designed to maintain a modest grade. The two large towns of Tahoe City and South Lake Tahoe offer full-service resupply centers, plus there are several post offices near the trail. Neither a front-country trail nor a true wilderness experience, the Tahoe Rim Trail is challenging in places, but the rewards are great.

It would probably be irresponsible not to mention the issue of wildfires that are plaguing much of California and the American West more generally. Check the TRTA website and contact their office for the status of fires and the trail, and be especially careful with fire while hiking the trail. A California Campfire Permit is required to use a camp stove anywhere on the trail (permits are available for free online); no campfires are allowed on the TRT.

You'll see lots of our tree friends along the trail, living together in some of the most impressive forests in North America. Take time to meet them and say thanks for all they do for us. And tell them we sent you.

Resources

Website
Tahoe Rim Trail Association: www.tahoerimtrail.org

Guidebook
Tim Hauserman, *The Tahoe Rim Trail: The Official Guide for Hikers, Mountain Bikers and Equestrians*, 2018

Maps
Eric Asorman, *Tahoe Rim Trail Pocket Atlas*, 2021
National Geographic Trails Illustrated Map 1013, *Tahoe Rim Trail*, 2018
Tom Harrison, *Lake Tahoe and Tahoe Rim Trails*, 2018

App
Tahoe Rim Trail by FarOut (official map of the TRT)

Washington, DC, is one the great cities of the world and was designed to be appreciated on foot.

The World's Great Cities (e.g., Washington, DC)

We were enjoying walking through the large National World War II Memorial that honors the more than 16 million soldiers who served the nation during this war, including the more than 400,000 Americans killed during the conflict. The memorial includes a graceful fountain, granite pillars, bronze panels illustrating scenes from the war, and even a couple of representations of the famous "Kilroy Was Here" drawings left by American servicemen everywhere they fought. It's a moving memorial in its own right, but to our delight, in marched a high school band that proceeded to play a stirring series of patriotic songs, the perfect democratic exclamation point to our walk through the great cultural landscape of the US capital.

———— ≈ ————

It's obvious from this book that much of our walking has been focused on the world's great landscapes: places like the lovely Coast to Coast Walk across England, the dramatic Tour du Mont Blanc around the Mont Blanc Massif, the John Muir Trail's roller-coaster journey through the incomparable High Sierra, the Great Ocean Walk along the wild coast of Australia, and the trek across the arctic tundra of Sweden's Kungsleden.

But lately we've been adding the world's great *cultural* landscapes to our hiking agenda. And we've learned that walking in cities has a rich history. Charles Dickens walked up to 20 miles a day in his native London, giving him welcome respite from his writing desk and enriching his stories with firsthand observations of urban life. Phyllis Pearsall obsessively walked the 3,000 miles of the 23,000 streets of London in 1930s. But it was in Paris that the art of urban walking may have reached its zenith. Nineteenth-century intellectual Walter Benjamin richly described the life of the *flaneur*, or bohemian, who famously explored the city's nooks and crannies on foot and who went "botanizing on the asphalt." Benjamin wrote:

LOCATION
The World's Great Cities (e.g., Washington, DC)

LENGTH
Variable

ACCOMMODATIONS
Commercial (e.g., Inns, B&Bs): Yes
Huts/Refuges: Some
Backpacking/Camping: No

BAGGAGE TRANSFER
No

OPTION TO WALK IN SECTIONS
Yes

DEGREE OF CHALLENGE
Low

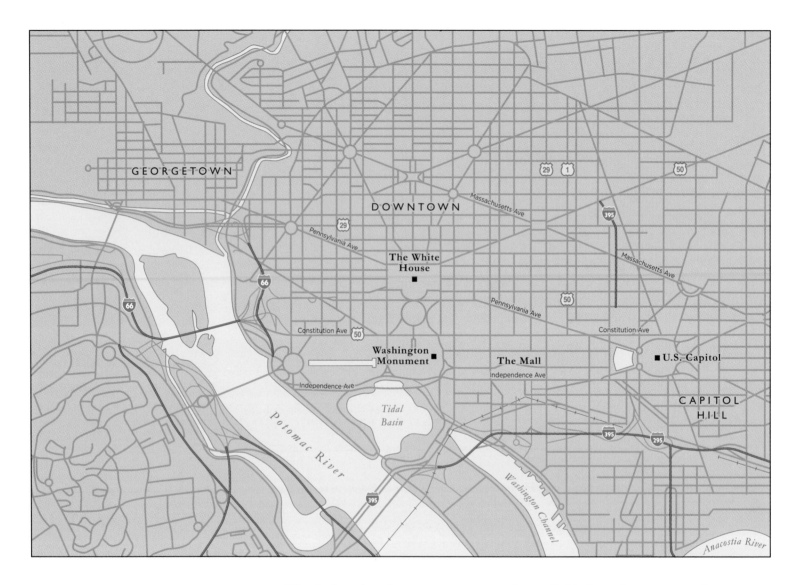

The signboards and street names, passers-by, roofs, kiosks, or bars must speak to the wanderer like a crackling twig under his feet, like the startling call of a bittern in the distance, like the sudden stillness of a clearing with the lily standing erect at its center. Paris taught me this art of straying.

Much of the National Mall is designed as a grand promenade.

The Smithsonian Institution Building, nicknamed "The Castle" for obvious reasons, serves as a visitor information center.

We walk the countryside to appreciate its natural history, but Rebecca Solnit writes in her brilliant history of walking, *Wanderlust*, that there is an analogy with urban walking: "The streets are repositories of history, walking a way to read that history." Another theme is the surprising way in which some writers have likened the city to a different type of wilderness—a mysterious and adventurous place that must be experienced on foot. We would only add that the beauty of the human creations that are our great cities can be appealing as well, even complementing their natural settings.

Intrigued, we decided to pursue long-distance walking—walks of a week or two—in several of the world's great cities, and we described several of these walks in our book *Walks of a Lifetime: Extraordinary Hikes from Around the World*. Our approach was to think of city sidewalks as vast trail networks suggesting nearly unlimited walking adventures, and to incorporate the more conventional urban parks, trails, and open spaces in our walks. Our long-distance urban walks have taken us to and through some of the world's great cities, including New York City, San Francisco, Paris, London, and Sydney. More recently, we walked for a week in Washington, DC, and that's what we describe here.

Washington's history as our nation's capital started in 1780 when Congress authorized President Washington to choose a site. He acted quickly, selecting a large site (10 square miles) on the Potomac River, much of it swampy wetlands; the site incorporated land from both Maryland and Virginia. Choice of this site was a deliberate attempt to satisfy the competing interests of both the North and South (though it might have also been influenced by the location of Washington's home at nearby Mount Vernon). The relative newness of the United States and its largely undeveloped character

The Washington Monument is an icon of the National Mall and offers sweeping views from the top.

account for the unusual choice to site the capital in such a deliberate fashion, rather than allowing its location to evolve in a more organic manner as is the case in most older countries, particularly in Europe. Moreover, here was a rare opportunity to design the capital city from scratch. Just a year later, Pierre Charles L'Enfant devised a masterplan for the city. Influenced by the European style of urban planning and the design of the grounds of the Palace of Versailles, L'Enfant emphasized marble and granite monuments and buildings and incorporated a grand esplanade designed for walking. Evidence of this plan is still enjoyed today, especially by those who choose to walk the city.

Core elements of the plan are evident in the triangle created by the Capitol Building, the White House, and the large National Mall; grand avenues radiating from many plazas; and the four quarters of the city with the Capitol at the center. (In the late 1700s, a "mall" was a tree-lined green space where people walked and socialized.) L'Enfant chose a rise called Jenkins Hill for the Capitol (he described the site as a "pedestal waiting for a superstructure") and sited the White House on a lower terrace with a view of the Potomac. Construction of the White House was begun in 1792, followed by the start of the Capitol Building the following year. Pennsylvania Avenue runs between these buildings, emblematic of the separate but connected branches of government (executive and legislative, respectively). The third branch of government (judicial), represented by the Supreme Court, wasn't housed in its own building until 1932.

The National Mall (and associated memorials) is the appropriate place to start walking tours of the city. It's generally accepted that this is the large area of open space, with its significant buildings and monuments, that lies on an east–west axis between the Capitol Building on the west and the Lincoln Memorial and Potomac River on the east. (The more technically correct definition of the Mall is the grounds of the Capitol on the east to the Washington Monument on the west.) The distance from the Capitol to the Lincoln Memorial is about 2 miles, and the Mall has an estimated 26 miles of walkways; you're ensured a good workout by the end of each day, as most visitors will walk extensively through and around many of the area's buildings and monuments and even to surrounding neighborhoods and attractions. The Mall is what most people consider the core of the city, and management of the area was entrusted to the National Park Service beginning in 1933; look for NPS rangers in their recognizable "Smokey Bear" hats throughout the Mall—they're knowledgeable and helpful sources of information (and directions!). The National Mall, with its monuments, museums, and public spaces, is the place that helps define the history and character of the nation, and this has been the traditional location of public gatherings such as the 1963 March on Washington for Jobs and Freedom at which Dr. Martin Luther King Jr. gave his inspiring "I Have a Dream" speech from the steps of the Lincoln Memorial.

The list of significant places included in the Mall is long and diverse and would take more than even a full week of walking to appreciate, so choose wisely. However, have confidence that the long vistas over the Mall and surrounding areas are as important and meaningful as visiting each individual site (look east from the steps of the Lincoln Memorial at sunrise, if you need convincing!). Walt Whitman called these "democratic vistas." However, there are a number of places that would be on just about everyone's "must-see" list: the quintessential markers of democracy as manifested in the Capitol Building and White House, the National Mall's most iconic monuments and memorials (e.g., Washington Monument, Lincoln Memorial, World War II Memorial, Vietnam Veterans Memorial, Martin Luther King Jr. Memorial), and at least one of the Smithsonian Institution museums (e.g., National Museum of American History, National Museum of Natural History, National Gallery of Art [East and West Buildings], National Air and Space Museum, National Museum of the American Indian, and National Museum of African American History and Culture). In keeping with the democratic character of the nation, entrance to all of these places and buildings is free. Visits to the Capitol can be arranged at the Capitol Visitor Center; tours of the White House must be arranged through your congressional representatives well in advance, though the White House Visitor Center, with its interpretive panels, archival footage, and historic artifacts, is a good substitute.

Not all the important places in Washington are monumental. Smaller monuments, historic homes, and lovely gardens often go unnoticed, especially by those who are not traveling at the leisurely pace of 2 to 3 miles an hour. A few of our favorite "discoveries" were Ford's Theatre, the National Archives, Belmont-Paul Women's Equality National Monument, a walk on the Chesapeake & Ohio Canal National Historical Park in Georgetown (see the chapter on the Chesapeake and Ohio [C&O] Canal Towpath earlier in this book), Union Station, and Eastern Market (the latter two are great places for lunch).

The core area of the city also includes substantial parkland and open space; much of the National Mall itself is green space with grass and trees and makes for great walking (and picnics and playing). Located on the banks of the Potomac River, West Potomac Park and East Potomac Park offer extensive open space and a network of trails, many of them along the banks of the Potomac, that are surprisingly natural-seeming. Farther afield, walk through the parkland of Theodore Roosevelt Island

The appropriately monumental Martin Luther King Jr. Memorial is carved from a single block of granite and resonates forcefully with many visitors to the National Mall.

(ABOVE) The Vietnam Veterans Memorial is a powerful tribute to those who lost their lives in this traumatic conflict.

(ABOVE RIGHT) The National Mall and its memorials are part of the National Park System, and rangers can be seen around the area offering information and directions.

in the Potomac River (and visit his namesake memorial with appropriately larger-than-life statue), visit Arlington National Cemetery (across the Potomac River; watch the meaningful Changing of the Guard at the Tomb of the Unknown Soldier), take a stroll along Pennsylvania Avenue National Historic Site, enjoy the streets of trendy Georgetown with its upscale stores and restaurants, and walk through leafy Rock Creek Park, where Theodore Roosevelt went birding. You may wish to use public transportation to reach some of these areas to spare your legs; the city's modern subway system is the Metro, Metrobus is the local bus system, there are lots of taxis, and you may want to consider using the local "hop-on, hop-off" buses and trolleys.

Like any long walk, you'll be more successful if you plan ahead. We recommend good sources of information in the "Resources" section below. Washington can be walked just about any time of the year, though spring and fall are the best; winter brings occasional snow, and summer can be hot, humid, and busy. Cherry trees grace many locations in the city, though they are concentrated in the Tidal Basin area. Originally, they were a gift of friendship from Japan in 1912 and have become a defining attraction; the showy National Cherry Blossom Festival takes places in late March to early April.

Experience Washington on foot, the way L'Enfant and others designed it, with the grand promenade that is the National Mall, the great avenues that extend out in all directions, and the area's prominent parks and open spaces. Walking allows you to use all your senses to more fully appreciate this great city, to admire its size and scale, to understand the interrelationships among its monuments and buildings, and to discover for yourself the very best vantage points and the hidden gardens, sculptures, and other prizes that await those on foot. Consider walking some of the other great cities of the world as well.

Resources

Websites
National Park Service: www.nps.gov/nama
Destination DC: https://washington.org

Guidebook
National Geographic, *Walking Washington, DC* (2nd edition), 2021

Maps
Michelin, *Streetwise Washington, DC*, 2018
National Geographic City Destination Map, *Washington, DC*, 2018

The Tour du Mont Blanc (translated as "around Mount Blanc") is one of the most historical and popular walks in all of Europe, perhaps even the world.

Tour du Mont Blanc

We were walking the three-day Swiss section of the Tour du Mont Blanc through the farming region of appropriately named Bovine. It was midafternoon, and we'd been serenaded on and off all day by the bells of the local cows grazing in the high pastures. Now, the sounds were growing louder. As we rounded the next bend in the trail, we understood why—one of the local farmers had converted part of his barn into a small outdoor restaurant for walkers, and his herd of milk cows was there to greet us. In fact, the large cows had congregated on the trail and were a little intimidating; fortunately the cows were used to walkers and it was easy to sweet-talk enough of them off the trail so we could reach the barn, where we enjoyed our afternoon snack of fresh-baked bread and local creamy cheese. Other walkers were enjoying a late lunch of soup, sandwiches, and wine, and we were all enjoying the lovely views of the valley below and preparing ourselves for the last leg of the day's climb.

~

The Tour du Mont Blanc (TMB) is one of the most historical and popular walks in all of Europe, perhaps even the world. Translated as "around Mont Blanc," this is a circular journey around Mont Blanc, affectionately known as the "Monarch of the Alps," the highest mountain in Western Europe. More properly, the trail encircles the Mont Blanc Massif, a complex of many summits and the dramatic glaciers that flow off them in all directions. The trail wanders about 105 miles (depending on a range of alternative routes or "variants" chosen) through three countries: France, Italy, and Switzerland. Many walking days start in one of the major valleys that radiate from the mountain, climb a high pass, and descend into the next valley, each with its own character, and each seeming more dramatic and beautiful than the last. Some days the route stays high, and nights are spent in cozy mountain huts/refuges.

Walkers have been trekking around Mont Blanc since the late eighteenth century, though its popularity began in earnest during the Victorian Age, when the area began attracting the English gentry. Now, thousands of walkers take to the trail each year, and for good reason, as this is a walk worthy

LOCATION
France, Italy, and Switzerland

LENGTH
105 miles

ACCOMMODATIONS
Commercial (e.g., Inns, B&Bs):
Most
Huts/Refuges: Yes
Backpacking/Camping:
Limited

BAGGAGE TRANSFER
Most

OPTION TO WALK IN SECTIONS
Most

DEGREE OF CHALLENGE
Moderate–High

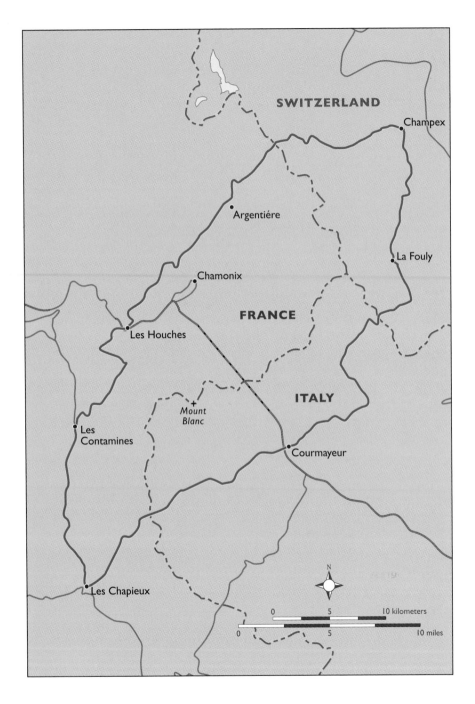

of its reputation. The classic TMB walk is conducted in eleven days, but this leaves no time for rest days or, more importantly, for exploring the famous mountaineering centers of Chamonix, France, and Cormayeur, Italy, along the way. We highly recommend two weeks for this walk.

The classic walk is done in an "anticlockwise" direction, as the European guidebooks say, and the traditional starting point is the village of Les Houches, just a few miles from Chamonix (though, of course, the hike can be done in either direction and can be started at any of the many accessible towns and villages along the route). Starting in Les Houches leaves the especially scenic Col de la Forclaz-to-Argentiére portion of the hike for the end—the route's grand finale. We suggest a day in Chamonix at the beginning or end of the hike (or both!) to soak up the mountaineering history of this area and generally enjoy this tourist-friendly town.

After a few days in France, walkers enter Italy and the historic Italian village of Dolonne, then cross a glacier-fed river to Courmayeur. Sometimes called the "Italian Chamonix" (which Italians probably don't appreciate), Courmayeur is a relatively large town with its own history of mountain culture and a thriving tourism infrastructure. A layover day here is a good idea, not just to rest the legs, but to have an adventure on Mont Blanc itself. A short ride from Courmayeur on the public bus takes you to Palud, the base of a network of cable cars that traverse Mont Blanc and ultimately descend (dramatically!) into Chamonix. The engineering of these cable cars is a marvel, and views are truly stunning, including the surrounding Alps in all directions, glacial crevasses, and groups of climbers roped together as they move to and from the summit area. A return trip to Courmayeur at the end of the day is easy by local bus through the 16-mile Mont Blanc Tunnel.

(ABOVE LEFT) Plan for an extra day or two in Chamonix before or after the hike to soak up the rich mountaineering history of this tourist-friendly town.

(ABOVE) The TMB leads walkers through gentle valleys and into the surrounding mountains.

The next day of walking climbs steeply to gain the long, open ridgeline of Mont de la Saxe, and, if the weather is fine, this day is stunning. The whole eastern profile of the Mont Blanc Massif is presented for close inspection, and the grassy meadows along the ridge offer suitable viewing platforms and lunch spots. Listen carefully for distant avalanches and rockfalls if you need any convincing that this is a dynamic landscape, a masterpiece of nature still in the making.

In a few more days on the trail, you reach the cultural landscape that is Switzerland, and you know it. The following few days are distinctly Swiss, with traditional wooden chalets, flower-filled window boxes, meadows filled with cows, and the melodies of cow bells that seem to "yodel" through the hills. Views of Mont Blanc have receded, as the trail is now a considerable distance north of the Massif. However, there are fine views of the impressive Grand Combin mountain complex (which can be inspected more closely on the Walker's Haute Route, described in a later chapter; in fact, these two famous walks through the Alps share about two days of hiking).

Upon reentering France, the trail ascends a series of ladders and handrails to the Grand Balcon Sud, where it traverses the slopes and ridges on the Aigulles Rouges and looks across Chamonix to the impressive western face of the Mont Blanc Massif. Be sure to look for chamois and ibex (wild goats) through this section of the trail, and you'll undoubtedly be impressed by the avalanche barriers, wooden structures erected at right angles to the steep slopes to minimize avalanche danger. Mountain huts/refuges offer simple accommodations with five-star views, or you can descend by one of the several cable cars to the creature comforts of Chamonix, returning to the trail the next

(ABOVE) At the higher elevations along the trail, hikers stay in cozy huts with five-star views.

(BELOW) To reach the small outdoor restaurant in appropriately named Bovine, we had to carefully navigate a small herd of large cows.

morning. The last stage of the hike is a gentle descent back to the village of Les Houches, where you began your journey some two weeks earlier.

A complete list of highlights for this walk would be unwieldy. The natural environment encompasses high peaks, glaciers, rivers and lakes, alpine meadows full of flowers, and some surprising wildlife. The remarkable cultural overlay includes charming towns, well-adapted architecture, historic buildings, Roman roads, local foods and wine, and the distinctive history of mountain climbing, skiing, and hiking linked to this place. We particularly enjoyed the views of Mont Blanc and its glaciers, and it was very satisfying to know we had walked all the way around "The Monarch." We also delighted in being outdoors in areas of great beauty by day and indoors in great comfort by night. This trail is one that energizes its walkers—remember, the uphills are always followed by complementing downhills!

The TMB is generally rated as difficult, though much of it is only moderately so. While Mont Blanc is an impressive 15,770 feet, the trail does not go over the mountain, as that would require technical climbing. Elevations along the trail generally range from about 4,000 feet to just under 9,000 feet. The total elevation gain along the trail is nearly 33,000 feet; local guides enjoy noting that this is substantially more than climbing Mount Everest (from sea level!). But most sections are well graded and maintained, and the trail is clearly marked, though the markings vary by country. There is some exposure to steep drop-offs in a few isolated spots, but fixed chains, ladders, and metal handrails are in place to compensate where needed, and there are a number of alternative routes ("variants") that can be taken to avoid steep climbs and bad weather. Occasional ski lifts and good local bus and train service offer convenient options to shorten the hike or walk the trail in sections. Luggage transfer service is generally available, but not at huts/refuges. Just be warned that if you do only a few sections or a "best of" hike, you'll want to come back for more.

Because of its elevation, the walking season on the TMB is short—mid-June through the middle of September. Depending on snowfall, several of the higher passes may be snow-covered in June, requiring gaiters and even an ice axe. Mountain huts/refuges begin closing as fall snowstorms approach in the latter half of September. August is the traditional European holiday period, and reservations for accommodations during this time are advised. The trail is well-served by an especially diverse range of accommodations, including huts/refuges in the higher elevations, small hotels and B&Bs in valley villages, and even (if you wish) five-star hotels in Chamonix and Courmayeur. There are few camping options. Walkers should take maximum advantage of the fine-quality local foods of the region, with special emphasis on cheese, bread, and (possibly) wine carried in the pack for lunch. For example, we particularly enjoyed the Beaufort d'Alpage, a cow's milk cheese from the tiny village of Les Chapieux; this cheese has been made in the region since Roman times. These foods complement the scenery by offering other sensory perceptions of the region's distinctive landscape as manifested in its "terroir."

Despite the multinational nature of this walk, French is the unofficial language of the TMB. English can be spotty, so brush up on your French or carry a simple phrase book. There is also the issue of multiple currencies, though the Euro is generally accepted. Some huts/refuges do not accept credit cards, so carry some cash; there are cash machines in several of the largest towns along the trail.

This is more than a fine walk—the TMB is a unanimous choice on lists of "the world's greatest hikes." The landscape is overwhelming with its soaring height, its massive scale, its active and powerful glaciers, its flower-filled meadows, and its gentle, sculpted valleys. The cultural overlay complements the landscape with its French, Italian, and Swiss adaptations of lifestyle, language, architecture, food, and mythology. Be sure to put a checkmark on your life list next to the Tour du Mont Blanc.

Resources

Guidebooks

Jim Manthorpe, *Tour du Mont Blanc*, 2008
Andrew McCluggage, *Tour du Mont Blanc*, 2019
Gareth McCormack, *Explore the Tour of Mont* Blanc, 2005
Kev Reynolds, *Tour of Mont Blanc: Complete Two-way Trekking Guide*, 2020

The sleepy village of Two Harbors near the west end of the trail offers services to hikers and return ferry trips to the mainland.

Trans-Catalina Trail

Many of us baby boomers are familiar with the song "Twenty-six Miles" by the pop band The Four Preps. Perhaps the lyrics of the first bar will bring it back to you:

Twenty-six miles across the sea
Santa Catalina is a-waitin' for me,
Santa Catalina, the island of romance,
romance, romance, romance.

It's a catchy tune, but that's the problem; it's one of those songs that gets stuck in your head. We walked for four days across Santa Catalina Island, enjoying the wildness of this big, mostly undeveloped island, finding ourselves silently singing "Twenty-six Miles." So our advice is to just not think about this song (if possible!).

———————≈———————

Want a peek at the California of a few hundred years ago, before it was "discovered" by European-Americans? Then explore the wild side of Catalina Island on the adventurous multi-day trail that traverses it. Catalina is one of the eight dramatic Channel Islands that lie off the coast of Southern California, just an hour or so boat ride from the megalopolis of Los Angeles. The name "Channel Islands" is derived from the deep ocean troughs that separate the islands from the mainland. Though humans have occupied Catalina Island for thousands of years, the land remains mostly undeveloped, suggesting the character of what much of coastal California originally looked like. Moreover, the islands are alive with an unusually diverse collection of plants and animals, at least partially due to the range of elevations and associated habitats.

The Channel Islands emerged from the sea millions of years ago as a result of plate tectonics, volcanism, and sea levels that changed as a function of the rise and fall of ice ages. During the ice ages, ocean levels fell and several of the islands were joined, but when the polar caps began to melt,

LOCATION
California, United States

LENGTH
38+ miles

ACCOMMODATIONS
Commercial (e.g., Inns, B&Bs): Some
Huts/Refuges: No
Backpacking/Camping: Yes

BAGGAGE TRANSFER
Some

OPTION TO WALK IN SECTIONS
Some

DEGREE OF CHALLENGE
Moderate–High

(ABOVE) Five campgrounds are scattered across the island to help support TCT thru-hikers.

(ABOVE RIGHT) Much of the TCT follows the ridgeline of the island's mountains, offering hikers 360-degree views out over the ocean and to the mainland.

even a casino. However, the town is limited in size to 1 square mile. The small, sleepy town of Two Harbors lies near the other end of the island.

The Trans-Catalina Trail (TCT) joins a network of island trails and gravel roads into a continuous trail of 38.5 miles that traverses the island in an east–west orientation. (Fact check: To walk the full length of the trail and return to Two Harbors for the ferry requires walking another 10 miles or so.) We found this a challenging thru-hike with lots of elevation gain (estimated at nearly 10,000 feet in total) and some steep climbs and descents (consider trekking poles); the island's interior is often described as "rugged." However, the walk is strikingly beautiful, with 360-degree views extending out over the ocean all the way to the mainland and to neighboring islands. Other highlights included dropping down into the island's more biologically rich valleys and secluded ocean beaches and other attractions that provide lovely camping spots. We spotted lots of wildlife, including bison, the miniature island foxes, many species of birds, and some marine mammals. However, be prepared for lots of signs of human presence—power lines, firebreaks, reservoirs, gravel roads, ranches, and even the island's Airport in the Sky; most of these are artifacts of prior farming, ranching, stone quarrying, and tourism. In this sense, the island isn't a wilderness, as many hikers might hope, but the area is returning to its more natural state thanks to management by the Catalina Island Conservancy. We hiked the trail in four days, but another day or two might have been more comfortable; the trail was well marked, including mileage markers, and we saw few other hikers along the trail.

Like most thru-hikes, there are some logistics to attend to, probably more so because this is an isolated island. There's ferry service from the mainland to both Avalon and Two Harbors. You can fly to and from the island, but not many people do (besides, the ferry ride is a pleasure). Start your

The TCT is a challenging hike as it makes its way across Catalina's rugged terrain.

hike in Avalon at the Catalina Island Conservancy Trailhead Visitor Center, where you can pick up your hiking permit, and end your hike at Two Harbors (after reaching the ocean at Parson's Landing and returning to Two Harbors on the loop at the west end of the island), where you can take the ferry back to the mainland. You must reserve campsites from the conservancy well in advance; brace yourself, because they're expensive (it costs a lot to staff and maintain these isolated facilities). There are five campgrounds, so you have a choice of how you divide up the hike; all but one has water (and water can be provided for a fee at the other). The night sky is fabulous, though fog can be an issue. The island's Wildlands Express Shuttle can help with rides where needed, and there's even a commercial service that will haul your gear between campsites. Bikes are allowed only on short sections of the trail. Be aware that there's relatively little shade along the trail and summers can be hot (sun protection is a necessity); we hiked in the spring and it was delightful. The island gets most of its annual precipitation in the winter. Bring plenty of water with you, as there's little available along the way (except at campgrounds and the towns of Avalon and Two Harbors). The conservancy has maps for distribution to hikers for a nominal fee. With a little creativity and a couple of long days on the trail, you can "slackpack" the trail by using commercial accommodations in Avalon and Two Harbors and arranging for a ride or two to connect all the trail sections.

The Trans-Catalina Trail offers walkers an unusual opportunity to look into the distant past of the California landscape, long before it became the modern mega-state. Moreover, the sparsely developed landscape of Catalina Island is a stark and welcome contrast to metropolitan Los Angeles—a mere 26 miles away!

Resources

Website
Catalina Island Conservancy: www.catalinaconservancy.org

Guidebook
Sam Ward, *Plan and Go/Trans-Catalina and Backbone Trails*, 2017

The distinctive towers of San Gimignano reflect the town's wealth and power and contributed to the village's defenses.

Via Francigena

We were checking in to our hotel in magnificent Siena when we saw a brochure advertising "Italian Opera in Siena." We were tired from our walk, but the performance sounded intriguing, so we asked the hotel clerk to arrange tickets for that night. After a short phone call, he told us we had just purchased the last two seats for the evening's performance. Yes! The seats were in the back row, but the performance space in a converted twelfth-century church wasn't huge. That evening, we were treated to a concert of famous arias and duets written by Puccini, Verdi, and Mozart, a perfect musical manifestation of the cultural heritage of Siena and Italy's Via Francigena.

———— ≈ ————

Pilgrimages emerged more than a thousand years ago as a ritual of penance, a source of healing, a means of seeking grace, and a way of meeting religious obligations. The oldest and largest pilgrimage is the Hajj, the calling of all Muslims to Mecca, Saudi Arabia, at least once in a lifetime. And there are several other pilgrimages as well, the most famous of which are to Jerusalem, Santiago, and Rome. (The Camino de Santiago [Camino Francés] is described in an earlier chapter, and the Camino Portugués and Kumano Kodo are described in our book *Walks of a Lifetime: Extraordinary Hikes from Around the World*.) The Via Francigena leads to Rome (the "Eternal City") from Canterbury, England, a distance of 1,180 miles, though most pilgrims join the walk somewhere along the route that travels through England, France, Switzerland, and Italy. We walked the last 260 miles of the route, from Lucca to Rome, in three weeks. The popularity of this pilgrimage has begun to rise in recent years, though the walk's still not well known, and use is light compared to the much more widely known and popular Camino de Santiago (Camino Francés).

The Via Francigena had its birth in the fourth century with the Edict of Milan in 313 CE, which proclaimed Christianity as the official religion of the Roman Empire. Many Christians began to make their way to Rome by following the vast network of Roman roads. A few of the earliest journeys are documented in written form, including that of the English monk Gildas the Wise in 530,

LOCATION
England, France, Switzerland, and Italy

LENGTH
1,180 miles

ACCOMMODATIONS
Commercial (e.g., Inns, B&Bs): Yes
Huts/Refuges: Some
Backpacking/Camping: No

BAGGAGE TRANSFER
Some

OPTION TO WALK IN SECTIONS
Yes

DEGREE OF CHALLENGE
Moderate

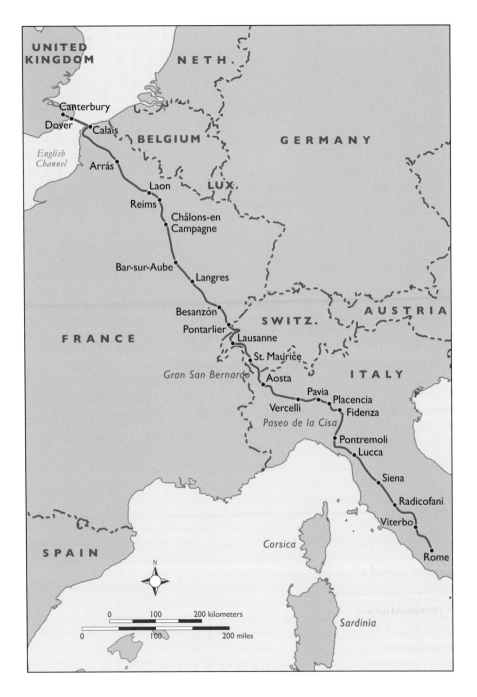

and the two pilgrimages of Saint Wilford in 666 and 673. However, the first "guidebook" to the pilgrimage was made at the instigation of Sigeric, Archbishop of Canterbury, who walked to Rome and instructed his secretary to record the route of the return journey. This description became known as the "Sigeric route," which serves as the basis of the modern-day Via Francigena and was instrumental in guiding more pilgrims to Rome. Generally, the modern-day route begins in Canterbury, crosses the English Channel by ferry from Dover to Calais, traverses much of France, climbs up and over Switzerland's Great St. Bernard Pass, and runs south and east through Italy to Rome.

As would be expected from such a long route, the path is exceptionally diverse, crossing many varieties of terrain and passing through some large cities, but it's mostly rural; the path is generally along quiet trails and minor roads (there are even a few stretches of original Roman roads), and through small towns and hamlets that are highly historical in nature and offer basic services to pilgrims, including accommodations, shops, and restaurants.

Our journey of three weeks began in the lovely walled city of Lucca, a tourist-friendly town that makes a good place to rest up from travel and do some low-key sightseeing. Lucca dates from Roman times and is sometimes called "the city of one hundred churches," though it has far fewer now; it was also an important stop for pilgrims in the Middle Ages, offering many *ospidales* (accommodations designed to house and care for pilgrims). The old town is enclosed by a 2.8-mile wall that was constructed in the sixteenth and seventeenth centuries, and a walk along the top of the wall offers an interesting perspective on this medieval town (and is a warm-up for the long walk ahead). See the relief sculpture of a labyrinth, the symbol of pilgrimage, in the Duomo di San Martino.

A few days of walking offered open views of the dramatic Tuscan landscape, including the world-famous Chianti vineyards, groves of olive trees, and copses of oak and chestnut trees, and brought us to San Gimignano, another visitor-friendly walled hilltop town that's distinguished by its medieval architecture and numerous high towers. At one time, there were more than seventy towers that were manifestations of the residents' great power and wealth, and were useful for defensive purposes as well, but now there are only fourteen. Nevertheless, the towers give the town a prominent character and contributed to its designation as a UNESCO World Heritage Site.

Two more days of walking brought us to the large and important city of Siena, sited on three hills, and one of Italy's finest, also designated as a UNESCO World Heritage Site. For centuries, Siena and Florence were rivals for

(ABOVE) Early-morning fog fills the valleys of the rolling hills of Tuscany.

(BELOW) The resort town of Bolsena is located on the shores of Lago di Bolsena and features a promenade and graceful pine trees.

political power and wealth, and this has left Siena with a city center that's rich in architecture and culture. Most pilgrims will want to visit the important Duomo di Siena and splurge on dinner at one of the many restaurants that line the Piazza del Campo. Consider taking an extra day in Siena to do this great city justice. (And don't forget to go to the opera that we describe in the introduction to this chapter.)

On we walked through lovely Tuscany, up and down its flowing hills with great views out into the countryside, along tree-lined rural roads, on farm tracks and hiking trails, and beside the occasional busy paved roads. This landscape is part of the famous Val d'Orcia (Valley of the Orcia River), renowned for what some observers have called a utopian "perfect landscape," a place of true harmony between humans and nature. We enjoyed a night in Buonconvento, a small walled medieval town with narrow, winding streets, and the next day, as we approached the town of Castiglione d'Orcin, we decided to spend the night at a small *agritourisma*, an accommodation that features the agricultural heritage of the region. We rented accommodations in the large farmhouse and ordered our meal to be served in our spacious room, enjoying the locally produced meats, cheeses, bread, and wine. It was a lovely way to appreciate the foods that are so synonymous with Tuscany.

Our second week of walking offered more of the history and beauty of Tuscany and the transition into the region of Lazio. The walking was only moderate in difficulty, up and down the hills,

(LEFT) We enjoyed the pattern of the traditional tile roofs of Radicofani as seen from the town's *rocca* (defensive tower).

(CENTER) The Via Francigena ends at Vatican City and St. Peter's Basilica in Rome.

(RIGHT) The Tuscan countryside features iconic olive groves and vineyards.

around countless olive groves and vineyards, through the occasional patches of forest, along lakeshores, and to the doorstep of so many historic towns. We especially liked Radicofani, where we rented a small apartment and walked steeply uphill to climb the *rocca* (defensive tower) of the Castle di Tacco. Bolsena is a resort town on the shores of Lago di Bolsena; visit Castello Rocca Monaldeschi for striking views out over the lake. The medieval town of Viterbo served as a safe haven for popes doing the Middle Ages, when Rome was experiencing political strife; the architecture is lovely, and the Piazza San Lorenzo is great for lunch or dinner. Vetralla features the lovely gardens of Villa Lante.

Our thoughts over the last several days of walking were turning to Rome and the impending crescendo of the journey. But there was still the pleasing landscape to admire, including extensive hazelnut orchards, and a string of small, historic towns to enjoy along the way, such as Capranica with its steep, winding streets and Sutri with its impressive Roman amphitheater. But signs of Rome were becoming more obvious. Our last day on the Via Francigena was a long walk into Rome, through the inevitable suburbs with busy streets and heavy commuter traffic. Fortunately, the walking route veers sharply away from the roads into extensive parklands that offer the peace and quiet we'd grown accustomed to on the walk. Monte Mario presented extended views over the city and featured St. Peter's Basilica and the graceful Tiber River.

We made our way to Vatican City and enjoyed experiencing the square that is seen so often in the media. The streets were busy, but the atmosphere was calm. After soaking in the iconic sights, we found our way to the Vatican's Pilgrim Office, where we presented our credentials/pilgrim passports that we had gotten stamped at many locations along the walk, and each of us received our *Testimonium* certifying that we had completed our pilgrimage.

It's only natural to compare the Via Francigena and the Camino de Santiago (Camino Francés), the two major Christian pilgrimages. The former is much like the latter was perhaps thirty to forty years ago; the Via Francigena has far fewer walkers, and the pilgrimage "infrastructure" (e.g., accommodations, special "pilgrim meals") is largely underdeveloped. It's unusual to meet other pilgrims on the Via Francigena, but interaction with local residents is more common and genuine. And the Via Francigena is a longer and more challenging walk. But both offer rewarding walks through their respective cultural landscapes and are rich experiences that promote a strong sense of introspection, simplicity, gratitude, and spirituality. And as is true with most such intentional walks, both end and means are vital to their success.

The logistics of walking the Via Francigena are relatively straightforward, at least for the section of the trail we walked. Though it's a long walk, there are enough towns along the way to accommodate pilgrims without having to walk too far each day. And, of course, most of these towns are attractions in and of themselves. Walking is of only modest difficulty, though the Tuscan hills are appropriately described as "rolling." Walks can be conducted in spring through fall, though summers are frequently hot. The Via Francigena is only now starting to be popular, but there are good guidebooks to help with planning, and though the route is relatively well marked, there is an app for the trail that we found especially helpful. There are two organizations associated with the Via Francigena (European Association of Via Francigena and Confraternity of Pilgrims to Rome), and their websites offer lots of useful information. The walking company CaminoWays specializes in booking services for this walk, as well as for other European pilgrimages.

Resources

Websites
Confraternity of Pilgrims to Rome: https://pilgrimstorome.org.uk/the-via-francigena
Via Francigena: www.viefrancigene.org/en

Guidebooks
Sandy Brown, *Walking the Via Francigena Pilgrim Route: Part 3—Lucca to Rome*, 2021
Paul Chin and Babette Gallard, *The Lightfoot Guide to the Via Francigena—Canterbury to the Great Saint Bernard Pass* (8th edition), 2022
Paul Chin and Babette Gallard, *The Lightfoot Guide to the Via Francigena—Great Saint Bernard Pass to Saint Peter's Square, Rome* (8th edition), 2022

App
Via Francigena—Official App (European Association of the Via Francigena)

Like most medieval towns, the streets of Buonconvento are narrow and winding.

The Walker's Haute Route offers a series of dramatically sited huts that provide hikers a bed, shower (usually), dinner, breakfast, and the company of potential new friends from all over the world.

Walker's Haute Route

Everyone knows about glaciers—rivers of ice that "flow" downhill, advancing and retreating, sculpting the landscape. But for most people, all this is learned in textbooks and can sound very abstract. The Walker's Haute Route brought it all to life for us in one special day. There, right before us, was a river of ice flowing off the mountain we were traversing. Our route led us directly across the surface of the glacier, where we saw the fissures (crevasses) in the ice as it turned downhill more sharply, and we walked carefully among the rocks and other debris the glacier had excavated from the mountain. We climbed and walked atop long, linear deposits of rock and gravel—lateral glacial moraines, just like the textbooks describe. We climbed a large (and rough) terminal moraine and skirted some glacial erratics (large rocks carried and eventually dropped by the flowing ice far from their origin). And we walked around a series of tarns—small ponds formed from glacial meltwater. Never again will we be confused about glaciers and their signature impacts on the land. The Walker's Haute Route should be a required field trip for all students of geology and glacial action—and it's a delightful walk as well!

Mont Blanc and the Matterhorn are the two most famous Alps: Mont Blanc is the highest mountain in Western Europe, and the Matterhorn may be the world's most recognizable mountain with its distinctive pyramidal shape. And Chamonix, France, and Zermatt, Switzerland, two of the greatest mountaineering centers in the world, sit at their respective bases. The Walker's Haute Route is a glorious 132-mile (or thereabouts) hike that connects these two world-class centers of outdoor activity, and it's one of the most iconic treks in Europe. Winding through the largest collection of high peaks in Western Europe, the route crosses eleven passes that approach 10,000 feet. Although challenging in difficulty, the Walker's Haute Route's combination of scenery, cultural experience, and availability of creature comforts makes it well worth the effort—in fact, it's such a wonderful walk that the effort required is overshadowed by the rewards of the experience.

LOCATION
France and Switzerland

LENGTH
132 miles

ACCOMMODATIONS
Commercial (e.g., Inns, B&Bs): Most
Huts/Refuges: Yes
Backpacking/Camping: Limited

BAGGAGE TRANSFER
Some

OPTION TO WALK IN SECTIONS
Most

DEGREE OF CHALLENGE
High

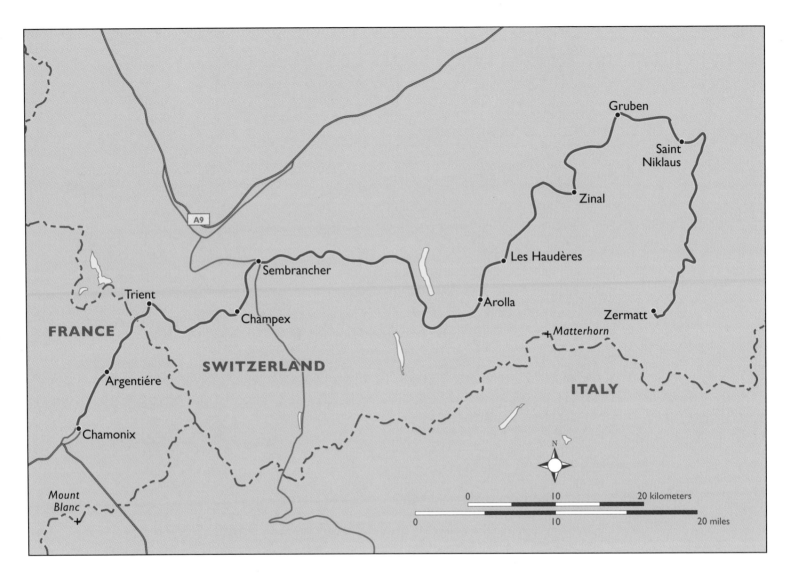

In the 1860s, a route was developed between Chamonix and Zermatt, but this could only be done as a mountaineering expedition. In the early twentieth century, the towns were linked by a ski touring route popular in the spring, and later a hiking route was established that evolved into today's Walker's Haute Route. Climbing an accumulated 46,000 feet, the trail crosses the grain of the landscape. Typically, each day involves climbing over a high mountain pass and dropping through forests

and high pastures to the next valley town to rest and refresh for the following day's walk. The towns offer varying (sometimes quite luxurious, if you're interested) types of accommodations as well as places to eat and (usually) to resupply. On the few occasions where staying overnight at the higher elevations is best, there are mountain refuges offering a bed, shower, dinner, breakfast, and the company of walkers from all over the world; walkers can choose to stay in huts/refuges exclusively, but the villages along the route have charms of their own.

It's best to allow two weeks for this hike, as progress can be slow over some stretches and you want to allow adequate time to appreciate the landscape and the towns of Chamonix and Zermatt at the two ends of the trail. One appealing aspect of the Walker's Haute Route is that there are many "variants" available if the weather deteriorates or the legs need a break (the route is really a network of trails). We suggest a variant from Cabane de Prafleuri to Arolla, the alternative route via Cabane des Dix. Cabane des Dix has an especially dramatic setting and offers lunch on the deck (we warmed ourselves with delicious homemade soup and bread). If you choose to spend the night at Cabane des Dix, be forewarned that the water (from the glacier just up the hill) for the outdoor shower is solar heated and has a long recovery time; be early in line! All the villages along the trail are accessible by

(ABOVE) The Walker's Haute Route is an open book of glacial geology; here, walkers skirt a series of tarns— small ponds formed from glacial meltwater.

(ABOVE RIGHT) With its distinctive pyramidal shape, the Matterhorn may be the world's most recognizable mountain.

local buses or train, so walking the trail in sections (or skipping some sections if needed) is easily done. Access is complemented by the occasional chairlift as well, if desired.

Expect some of the best weather in all of Switzerland, with warm days, sunshine, and relatively little precipitation. Nights are cold—good for sleeping. June is the earliest the trail is open and September is best, with clear bright days. Marmots, chamois, and ibex may be seen—in this order of likelihood. You'll definitely see the wonderful Hérens cows with their melodious bells. Descended from ancient aurochs raised to fight in the ring, these placid-seeming giants and the milk cows of Switzerland add a "Heidi-like" quality to an already achingly beautiful walk. If that weren't enough, the route passes through the richest flora in all of Switzerland. There are meadows filled with wild-flowers and lots of edelweiss, the unofficial national flower.

The latter stages of the Walker's Haute Route pass from French-speaking to German-speaking Switzerland—and there are some subtle changes in building forms. For the most part, though, you're looking at chalets, more chalets, and even more chalets, each seemingly competing with its neighbors in floral display. Of particular interest are the Valasian buildings. Built of local larch trees (which blacken after centuries) and roofed with heavy stone slabs up to several inches thick, these buildings are further distinguished by rounded stone plates that separate the wooden pillars that elevate the building from the upper part of the building itself. These stones protect the building's contents from rodents, although the technique means that nothing is binding a Valasian building to the ground—each structure represents a strong faith in the forces of gravity!

Other highlights of the walk were dining on the terrace of Cabane du Mont Fort (one of the mountain refuges) and watching the sunset, the Grand Hotel La Sage with its conservatory (complete with billiard table) and gourmet meals, and tourist-friendly Zermatt, where automobiles are not allowed. And, of course, let's not forget the Alps themselves, with their massive (though retreating) glaciers.

No special equipment is needed for the Walker's Haute Route, although trekking poles are helpful with the descents and for a little extra security on the few exposed areas (there are fixed chains in a couple of spots). Of course you should be prepared for rain and/or snow whenever you hike at altitude.

The Walker's Haute Route has a reputation as one of the more challenging hikes in the Alps (the Tour du Mont Blanc—described in a previous chapter—is similar, but a little less demanding; these two trails are co-located between Chamonix and Champex, Switzerland, so you may want to consider starting your hike in Champex if you've already walked the TMB). But the Walker's Haute Route richly rewards the walker in terms of truly awe-inspiring scenery, rich cultural experiences, and the ease with which civilization can be gracefully blended with the natural world.

The classic route is to walk from Chamonix to Zermatt, which allows hikers more time in the shade to climb the trail's higher passes. It's easiest to fly to Geneva and use public transportation to get to Chamonix. Don't overlook the possibility of taking the Mont Blanc Express train partway, as it's an engineering marvel and a good introduction to the Alps. Zermatt is served by the Glacier Express, proud of its reputation as "the world's slowest express train," which is a good first step when returning to Geneva and home. Remember, this is Switzerland, and public transportation is clean, efficient, and on time—to the minute! The contrast between the wild beauty of the Alps and the civilized lifestyle makes this an unforgettable experience. And in the future, you'll truly understand glaciers.

Resources

Guidebooks
Andrew McCluggage, *Walker's Haute Route: Chamonix to Zermatt*, 2019
Kev Reynolds, *Chamonix—Zermatt: The Walker's Haute Route*, 2019

Map
National Geographic Trails Illustrated Map 4001, *Haute Route Map*, 2022

(ABOVE) Original routes through this region of the Alps were established for mountaineers and then ski tourers; more recently, a network of trails has been developed for walkers.

(BELOW) Shop owners in this region of the Swiss Alps seem to compete for the most bountiful displays of flowers.

The West Coast Trail is cut from the lush temperate rain forests that cover the Pacific Rim National Park Reserve, but there are many opportunities to drop down and walk along the area's expansive and pristine beaches.

West Coast Trail

It was the second day of our backpacking trip along Vancouver Island's West Coast Trail, and the weather was good. More importantly, the weather forecast was good—little or no chance of Pacific storms—and that meant we were in an equally good mood (more about the weather later). It was late in the day when we approached Camper Creek, the first of four rivers along the trail that the guidebook said must be crossed by cable car. We were intrigued, but a little anxious as well—how does one go about using such a personal conveyance? We smiled as we reached the river to find a shiny, two-person cable car strung across the river on steel cables and pulleys—sort of like a carnival ride in the middle of the wilderness. But the car was resting above the midpoint of the river, hanging in the slack of the cables. We mounted the wooden platform at the side of the creek and read the directions. Accordingly, we both pulled on one of the cables and moved the car slowly toward us. When it reached the platform, one of us hopped in and stored both our packs. Then the other got in and we let go of the platform. Wheee! Using gravity, we were racing (it seemed) across the river—until we were just beyond the halfway point and gravity began to work against us. From this point, we pulled on the appropriate cable, hauling ourselves toward the platform on the other side of the river, which became increasingly difficult as we approached the platform. It was with great satisfaction that we successfully completed our journey across the river, unloaded our packs and ourselves, and continued along the trail, looking forward to our next cable car ride.

———— ≈ ————

Pacific Rim National Park Reserve is a 197-square-mile gem in the outstanding system of parks managed by Parks Canada. As the name suggests, this park hugs the Pacific coast and is located in the southwest part of Vancouver Island, British Columbia. Following the Pacific coast for 47 miles, the West Coast Trail has been described as "the best the west coast has to offer," "the definitive hike of

LOCATION
British Columbia, Canada

LENGTH
47 miles

ACCOMMODATIONS
Commercial (e.g., Inns, B&Bs): No
Huts/Refuges: No
Backpacking/Camping: Yes

BAGGAGE TRANSFER
No

OPTION TO WALK IN SECTIONS
Limited

DEGREE OF CHALLENGE
High

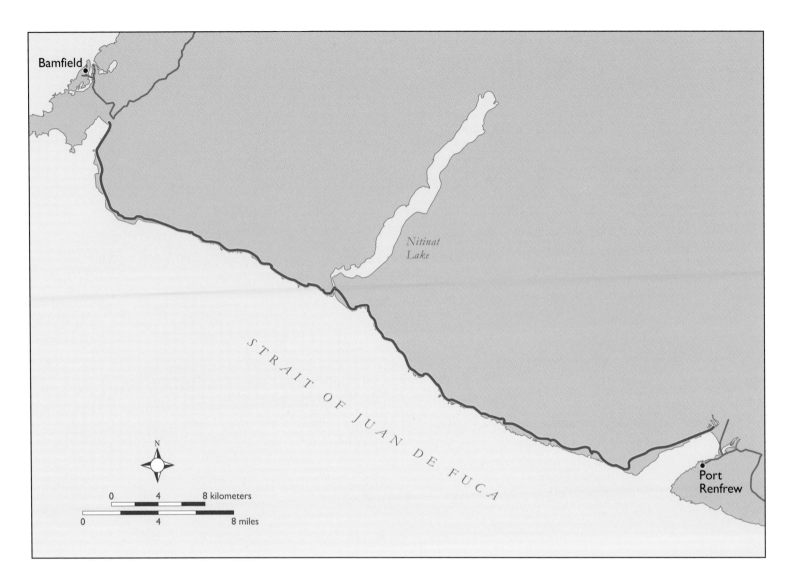

the temperate rain forests on the west coast of North America," and "among the best beach hikes in the world." And it delivers. The trail is cut from the lush temperate rain forests that cover the park's steep headlands, but there are plenty of opportunities to drop down and walk along the area's expansive and pristine beaches—and we recommend taking advantage of these opportunities when possible. When walking the beaches, search out the more firmly packed sand at the edge of the high

Several rivers are too wide to bridge and too deep to wade, so self-service cable cars carry walkers over them.

(BELOW) Many river valleys and ravines are so steep, they require a system of ladders to climb down and back up.

water mark, where walking is easier, and look for old fishing buoys that are tied to trees marking the points where walkers should return to higher ground.

The contemporary version of the trail was opened in 1980, but it has a much longer history. In fact, it has many histories, beginning as a gathering and trading route for people of the First Nations. In the latter half of the nineteenth century, it provided a route for a telegraph system connecting the city of Victoria in the south to the frontier town of Bamfield in the north. Walkers will see occasional poles and wires along the trail from this era. Later, the trail was used primarily as a lifesaving route in response to the more than sixty shipwrecks along this section of the coast, known as "The Graveyard of the Pacific." The sinking of the *Valencia* in 1906 was especially tragic, as many survivors were able to swim ashore but ultimately perished due the difficulty of reaching civilization. Today, the trail has been upgraded and serves as one of the world's great coastal walks.

It's hard to decide which of the trail's environments is the most compelling—the shoreline or the headlands; trail miles are about equally divided between the two. The beaches are frequent and expansive, and with tides and waves constantly washing the slate clean, each walker gets the sense that he or she is the first to traverse this area. Waves crash, broad tidal shelves extend into the sea, sea stacks and caves add drama, tidal pools teem with sealife, beds of kelp and rock outcrops demand closer inspection, and marine mammals—gray whales and orcas, harbor seals, dolphins, and porpoises—swim just off shore. Beaches are littered in places with massive piles of driftwood and offer many lifetimes of beachcombing.

The headlands offer a rare and intimate experience with the continent's majestic and cathedral-like old-growth rain forests of Douglas fir, western hemlock, western red cedar, and Sitka spruce, some of the tallest trees in the world, with a rich understory of ferns, trilliums, and bunchberries.

The trail includes historic lighthouses, including the last original wooden light tower on the west coast of Canada.

Animals of this forest include black bears, mountain lions, and wolves, clear manifestations of the remote and wild character of this area. The forests and sea together support diverse birdlife, including eagles, herring gulls, Steller's jays, cormorants, and red-beaked oystercatchers.

Every mile of this trail is an adventure. Walkers often have their choice of beach or headland trail, but this decision has to be made wisely. Some portions of beach are flooded at high tide right up to the steep cliffs they adjoin, and walkers must carry a tide table (and be able to read it—it's not difficult) to avoid the danger of entrapment and exposure to the sea. Headland soils are wet and boggy (after all, these are rain forests) and can make for slow going. Miles of boardwalk have been constructed to keep walkers up and off these fragile environments, and they are a convenience to walkers as well. While there is only moderate elevation to be gained along the trail (the high point is only 600 feet above sea level), the land is steeply cut by many rivers emptying into the sea. Many ravines are so steep that they're virtually impassable without the extensive system of dozens of tall wooden ladders that lead walkers up and down. The longest ladder is 70 feet, but often many ladders are joined together; there are more than one hundred ladders in all. Four of the rivers are too wide to bridge, and these are crossed on self-service cable cars. Two of the rivers are broader still and must be crossed by ferry (operated by local people).

Other distinctive features of the trail are more cultural and include reserves for three tribes of First Nations people: Pacheedaht, Didadaht, and Huu-Ay-Aht. These groups have inhabited this area for over 4,000 years, and the First Nations village of Clo-oose is thought to be one of the oldest on the west coast of all of North America. "Guardians" from these tribes help maintain the trail and provide ferry service across the two largest rivers. Walkers must stay on the trail when passing through these reserves (clearly marked on trail maps), and no camping is allowed in these areas. The trail also passes two historic lighthouses—Carmanah Point Lighthouse, constructed in 1891, and Pachena Point Lighthouse, the last original wooden light tower on the west coast of Canada. And when you're walking on the beach, watch for remains of the many shipwrecks that are periodically exposed by tides and storms.

The striking beauty of the West Coast Trail must be weighed against the challenges it presents. Parks Canada calls it "one of the most grueling hikes in North America." The most common danger is the weather, which can sometimes legitimately be called horrendous. Periodic storms blow in from the Pacific Ocean with high winds and days of rain. The trail should not be attempted when the weather report is bad. Even when the forecast is good, be prepared for the unexpected and take warm clothes, serious (breathable) rain gear, a good tent (with fly), a lightweight stove, and extra food. The extensive boardwalks and system of ladders make walking easier, but they are often coated with slippery moss and are sometimes in disrepair. Muddy bogs try to suck your boots off. Gaiters are highly recommended for the upland portions of the trail. Rock shelves sometimes extend into the sea and can be walked at low tide, but be careful of "surge channels" where water flows quickly out to the sea and can be very dangerous. Use the cable cars and ferries when crossing the larger rivers; don't be tempted to try to wade or swim across cold and dangerous waters, especially when they're flooded by recent rains. This is a remote area that must be backpacked, where there are no resupply points, and where rescue is difficult and time-consuming. In the amusingly understated language of Parks Canada: "This is not necessarily the most convenient location for the injured hiker." Nevertheless, dozens of hikers must be evacuated each year. Be prepared, and enjoy this hike on its own terms.

The trail is only open from May 1 to September 30 (caution: May and June have a reputation for being rainy) and a permit is required; make reservations early and be prepared to pay a considerable fee (the highest we've experienced!). A Parks Canada information station is located at each end of the trail, and walkers must watch an information and safety video prior to being issued a permit. Most walkers complete the trail in six to eight days; walking is slow and there are many attractions to enjoy. Camping is allowed in most locations (except the First Nations reserves noted above), and we recommend planning your trip to camp at least one night on the beach at Tsusiat Falls, where the river drops directly onto the beach, providing a convenient (but cold!) shower. The villages of Port Renfrew (Gordon River Trailhead) in the south and Bamfield (Pachena Bay Trailhead) in the north reflect their timber and fishing heritage and offer limited services to walkers. Access to the trail is also possible at Nitinaht Village (Nitinaht Village Trailhead), about the midpoint of the walk. Commercial shuttle bus service from both ends of the trail is provided and connects to the beautiful and tourist-friendly city of Victoria.

The West Coast Trail asks a lot of walkers, but it gives back even more. Carefully prepare yourself for this walk and you'll be richly rewarded, as we certainly were.

Resources

Websites
Pacific Rim National Park Reserve: https://parks.canada.ca/pn-np/bc/pacificrim
Reservation website: https://reservation.pc.gc.ca

Guidebooks
Tim Leadem, *Hiking the West Coast of Vancouver Island*, 2015
Tim Leadem, *Hiking the West Coast Trail: A Pocket Guide*, 2006

Map
Parks Canada, *West Coast Trail Map*

(ABOVE) Rock shelves sometimes extend into the sea and can be walked at low tide, but be careful of "surge channels" where water flows quickly out to sea, as these can be very dangerous.

(BELOW) Beaches are littered with massive piles of driftwood, offering many lifetimes of beachcombing.

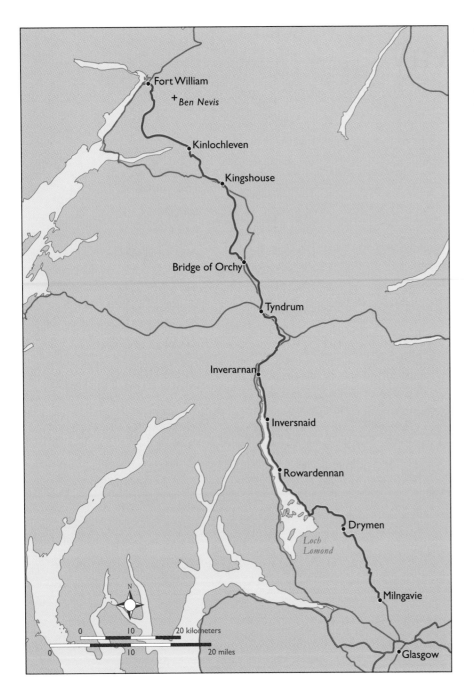

woods, and other romantic landforms). Don't overlook the appeal of the human mark on the land. Whether this anthropological history is represented by Bronze Age stones at Dumgoyach Hill, early Christian sites on wooded islands on Loch Lomond, a cave and prison used by Rob Roy (Scotland's real-life version of Robin Hood), or by more modern-day farms and forests, the cultural record of tensions, conflict, trade, and traffic greatly enrich the walking experience, and this trek is a wonderful combination of the "civilized" with the "wild."

Offering surprising variety, the West Highland Way follows historic routes from the lowlands around Glasgow into the Scottish Highlands. You'll walk on ancient footpaths and drove roads used to get cattle and sheep to market, on old military roads built by troops in the 1700s to help control the uprising of Jacobite clansmen, and on former coach roads and even abandoned railway rights-of-way. Some stretches were always open to walkers, but designation of the official route was formalized into a coherent entity in 1980, and a portion runs through the country's first national park. This route is definitely greater than the sum of its parts and, while day-hiking sections is easy because of the availability of public transit, we recommend you walk the entire trail. In fact, we suggest you consider adding on the Great Glen Way, one of Scotland's newest long-distance trails (see the description of this trail in our book *Walks of a Lifetime: Extraordinary Hikes from Around the World*), to make a total walk of 170 miles from Glasgow to Fort William and then across the country to Inverness.

Although hardy souls walk the West Highland Way in every season, our advice is to skip the unpredictable winter weather (and the risks associated with potential hypothermia in a desolate spot) and enjoy this walk either from April through August or, our favorite time to

walk in Britain, September to early October. The West Highland Way has a reputation for rain, and there's just no reasonable hope of walking in dry weather the whole way. Waterproof boots, jacket, pants, gloves, and hat, as well as a plastic bag lining your pack will prove invaluable. This is Scotland—it's supposed to be wet! And the rains do encourage the lush vegetation with its many shades of green. The eastern shore of Loch Lomond supports one-quarter of all known British flowering plants and ferns, and the forests are spectacular. The heathers and heaths on the moor are particularly lovely—and you'll enjoy them more if you've tucked some extra cold-weather clothing in your pack.

Milngavie, the trail's southern terminus, is a 7-mile train ride from Glasgow, the best staging point. The hike can be divided into seven or eight moderate stages, and each night offers a bed-and-breakfast or hotel. Pubs (including the Clachan in Drymen, the oldest pub in the country), cafes, and hotels are available for most lunches, though we generally packed our own. In most cases you'll be spending the night in a quintessential Scottish village—with the exception of an overnight in the Kingshouse (sometimes "Kings House") Hotel a couple of days from the end. This lodging dates from the seventeenth century, when the building was used as a barracks for George III's soldiers. While somewhat funky, we appreciated the enormous bathtub attached to our room—and the Kingshouse is the only place to stay unless you leave the trail for a town 11 miles away. Kinlochleven, the next stop, has an old electrical generating plant that has been turned into a climbing center complete with an indoor ice climbing room, a fun, and unexpected, diversion. Should you choose to

(ABOVE LEFT) We particularly enjoyed the expanses of heathers and heaths as we crossed the vast moors of the West Highland Way.

(ABOVE) Sheep are a traditional part of the Scottish landscape and seen in large numbers along the West Highland Way.

(ABOVE) Walkers along the West Highland Way will encounter many small creeks, or "burns," as they're locally known.

(ABOVE RIGHT) The West Highland Way follows historic routes from the lowlands around Glasgow into the Scottish Highlands.

break your journey at atypical junctions, area B&Bs often will provide rides. We recommend making reservations, given the popularity of this route.

Most folks walk south to north, working their way from the more pastoral to the "savage" (by UK standards). The West Highland Way is well signed with the thistle and hexagon motif, and the route can be supplemented (if one is a "peakbagger") by climbing some of the nearby mountains. We were quite happy without those additions, though it's important to respect the munro-collecting tradition. (A "munro" is a mountain over 3,000 feet, named for the man who cataloged—and climbed—all 284 of them.) It's helpful to recognize some of the local idioms: "glen" for valley, "loch" for lake, "moor" for heather slope, "burn for creek, "fell" for hill, for example. It's also best to learn the correct pronunciation of local names, as they are often, shall we say, surprising.

In terms of fauna, you'll mostly see domestic animals (particularly sheep) at the beginning of the walk. Later, you'll encounter some Highland cattle—large-horned, furry beasts. On the moors you might see red deer and, if lucky, wild goats. Golden eagles may soar overhead. But the fauna you're most likely to encounter and remember are the midges, wee mosquito-like insects that can be most irritating. Bring insect repellent and a head net. Hiking either early or late in the season greatly diminishes the likelihood of these critters, and we only had a few brief encounters, none deemed worthy of net or repellent.

Geologically speaking, the West Highland Way is rich. Glacial action scoured the valleys, and there are obvious fault lines as well. For example, as you view Loch Lomond's 22-mile length from

the top of Conic Hill, a highlight of the second day, note the islands that mark the Highland Boundary Fault, which divides the two distinct environments of Scotland's lowlands and highlands.

We found the Scottish people warm and welcoming. They're not known for their culinary efforts, but we found the hearty pub meals to be tasty and regenerative. We fondly remember the piping hot french fries ("chips") served with everything, though they are perhaps best when accompanied by fish and "mushy" peas. Of course there is lots of beer for the thirsty walker—and single malt liquor is a specialty in Fort William, where a toast to completing the West Highland Way is a rich tradition.

The West Highland Way traverses 96 miles of lovely Scottish countryside.

Resources

Website
West Highland Way: www.west-highland-way.co.uk

Guidebooks
Bob Aitken and Roger Smith, *The West Highland Way: Official Guide*, 2018
Charlie Loram and Joel Newton, *West Highland Way*, 2019
Andrew McCluggage, *Trekking the West Highland Way: Two-Way Trekking Guide*, 2022
Jacquetta Megarry, *The West Highland Way*, 2020

Maps
Terry Marsh, *West Highland Way Map Booklet*, 2016
Vertebrae Publishing, *West Highland Way*, 2020

About the Authors

Bob Manning is professor emeritus at the University of Vermont, where he taught the history, philosophy, and management of national parks and conducted a long-term program of research for the US National Park Service. **Martha Manning** is an artist whose work has been featured in national journals and shows. They've walked dozens of multi-day trails around the world, including all the trails described in this book.

The authors in one of the perched medieval villages along their walk through the Maritime Alps of France.